Napoleon's Stolen Army

How the Royal Navy Rescued a Spanish Army in the Baltic

John Marsden

Helion & Company

I dedicate this work to my wife for her help and forbearance throughout the duration of the project.

Helion & Company Limited
Unit 8 Amherst Business Centre
Budbrooke Road
Warwick
CV34 5WE
England
Tel. 01926 499619
Email: info@helion.co.uk
Website: www.helion.co.uk
Twitter: @helionbooks
Visit our blog at http://blog.helion.co.uk/

Published by Helion & Company 2021
Designed and typeset by Mach 3 Solutions Ltd (www.mach3solutions.co.uk)
Cover designed by Paul Hewitt, Battlefield Design (www.battlefield-design.co.uk)

Text © John Marsden 2021
Illustrations © as individually credited
Maps drawn by George Anderson © Helion & Company 2021

Cover: Prince of Pontecorvo's Guard of Honour formed by men belonging to the regiment of Zamora, with a Catalan officer, 1807. (NYPL Vinkhuijzen Collection)

Every reasonable effort has been made to trace copyright holders and to obtain their permission for the use of copyright material. The author and publisher apologise for any errors or omissions in this work, and would be grateful if notified of any corrections that should be incorporated in future reprints or editions of this book.

ISBN 978-1-913118-98-3

British Library Cataloguing-in-Publication Data.
A catalogue record for this book is available from the British Library.

All rights reserved. No part of this publication may be reproduced, stored in a retrieval system, or transmitted, in any form, or by any means, electronic, mechanical, photocopying, recording or otherwise, without the express written consent of Helion & Company Limited.

For details of other military history titles published by Helion & Company Limited, contact the above address, or visit our website: http://www.helion.co.uk

We always welcome receiving book proposals from prospective authors.

Contents

Acknowledgements and Sources   iv
Introduction   vi

1   Napoleon Demands the Assistance of Spanish troops in the Baltic Region   11
2   The Story of Brother James Robertson, British agent   42
3   The Revolt of La Romana's Army in the Baltic   49
4   The British Naval Operation to Rescue La Romana's Army   84
5   The Men Left Behind in Denmark   118
6   The Transportation of La Romana's Troops to Spain and the Battle of Espinosa   124
7   La Romana and Sir John Moore, November 1808 to January 1809   130
8   La Romana in the Wilderness, January 1809 to January 1811   139
9   Formation of the Régiment Joseph–Napoleon   151
10   Notes on the Russian Campaign by Manuel López and Rafael de Llanza   163

Bibliography   191

Acknowledgements and Sources

I formed the idea of writing this story after reading of the Royal Navy's presence in the Baltic during the Napoleonic wars. Various sources make mention of the operation to rescue the Marqués de La Romana's army from Denmark at the outbreak of the Peninsular War, but most of the works I looked at touched only lightly upon the story, and where there was a more comprehensive coverage of the subject the writer, understandably, usually focused their attention on the related documentation available from what were mainly British sources. There was, I felt, a lot to be brought to an English readership with regard to the Spanish perspective of this interesting and somewhat romantic story, and so began my quest to seek it out.

The first of the modern Spanish sources I turned to was Andrés Cassinello's biography of La Romana, and it is in chapters four and five of his work that he covers the marqués's Denmark expedition, making reference to a fascinating collection of primary source material held at the *Archivo General Militar de Madrid*. It was to that source that I turned when compiling the chapters of this story which cover the events in the Baltic during July, August and September 1808. It comprises a number of statements written by Spanish officers who were with La Romana in Denmark during that period, the various contents of which have enabled me to provide the reader with what I hope is a fair and factual treatment of the Spanish contribution to the success of the Baltic affair. So, I would like to thank Andrés Cassinello for producing such an interesting and comprehensive life of Romana, without which I might never have learned of the work of the *Comisión de Jefes*, which sat in Madrid during 1818 with the aim of investigating the marqués's Denmark expedition, and was responsible for commissioning the statements just referred to.

Many people take up an interest in a topic after being inspired by a connection to a leader in a particular field, be they a writer, teacher or academic. My interest in the Peninsular War was first stimulated by reading Charles Oman's history of the conflict, and as I widened my field of research I continued to be inspired by current authorities on the subject, such as Professor Charles Esdaile, Rory Muir, Dr Arsenio García Fuertes and other associates of the Wellington Congress, not forgetting Andrés Cassinello.

ACKNOWLEDGEMENTS AND SOURCES

Of course, once I had discovered the existence of the primary source material referred to above, I could not resist the urge to visit the Archivo General Militar de Madrid (AGMM) Madrid, where they are held. Whilst in contact with people at the AGMM, and when I later visited them, I received a lot of help from the archivists working there. The documents I mention were available only in paper form at the time of my visit, and the volume of material that I hoped to copy and take back to England was such that I would not have had time to gather all that I required without making further visits to Madrid. Luckily, the archivists were at that time engaged in a project to digitise their collections and suggested to me that it might be an opportune moment for them to make electronic copies of the material I so dearly sought, thus allowing me to access them on line from England. So, I would like to thank Agustín Pacheco Fernández and Laura Mantecón Alonso for their help, their patience, and for the work they did in providing me with the means to produce what I hope is an interesting account of Spanish endeavours in the Baltic. Whilst talking of archivists, I think it would be appropriate to mention the unsung heroes at The National Archives in Kew; I have always found them polite and helpful and I would like them to know that their work is much appreciated, if not always given the recognition it deserves.

No acknowledgement would be complete without mention of family and friends, and in my own case I would firstly like to thank my wife, Carmen Fernández–Marsden. It was whilst reading Oman's history that I discovered what I suppose I could call a somewhat tenuous family connection to the conflict. It was from his story that I learned that Sir John Moore's army passed through the village of Congosto, León whilst on their celebrated retreat to La Coruña in December of 1808. Congosto, as you may already have guessed, is the village where my wife was born and brought up. Since the day of that chance discovery my interest in the Peninsular War has continued to grow, so I suppose that is one thing, amongst many others, of course, that I have to thank her for!

For the onerous task of proof reading my translations from various French sources, I turned to a long–standing friend, Michel Labit of Toulouse who, I am pleased to say, was a willing hand, and I would like to express my thanks to him also. Needless to say, my wife, a lexicographer and lecturer in Spanish, cast a careful eye over my translations of the Spanish texts I made reference to. Finally, I think I should mention Mark Thompson, another Wellington Congress associate and writer of books on the Peninsular War. Should my story ever come to print I will have Mark to thank for his encouragement and help.

John Marsden, December 2020

Introduction

Many readers will be familiar with Goya's famous painting, *El Tres de Mayo*, which depicts the execution by firing squad of a number of Spanish civilians in Madrid on 3 May 1808. The soldiers in the portrait belong to the French Army and the crime of their victims was that, on the previous day, they had taken part in the disturbances which occurred on the streets of the Spanish capital as *Maréchal* Murat's men attempted to remove the Queen of Etruria and her brother, Francisco, from the Palacio Real. The siblings were children of the Spanish Bourbon King, Carlos IV and his consort queen, Maria Louisa de Parma, both of whom, together with their eldest son and heir Fernando, had recently been detained at the French city of Bayonne. Napoleon had intrigued to entice the royals to France with the ultimate intention of securing the presence of every member of the Spanish Bourbons on French soil, as a prelude to his usurpation of the Spanish crown.

French forces had entered Spain as allies in October of the previous year, under the specious pretext of enforcing Napoleon's Continental System, his strategy for denying Britain commercial access to her markets in mainland Europe. The plan was to mount a joint Franco–Spanish invasion of Portugal whose ports, despite French threats, had remained open to British trade. Initially the French were welcomed into Spain as trusted friends, but even after Portugal was subjugated imperial forces continued to cross the Pyrenees, their presence on Spanish soil becoming ever more imposing until, by the spring of 1808, it had become a de facto occupation.

The forceful removal of the young royals to Bayonne on 2 May 1808, was the defining act which sparked a popular uprising amongst the *Madrileños* against the French. Much blood was to be spilt on both sides during the disturbances that followed, albeit with a significant surplus amongst the Spanish civilians. As the crowds gathered at the gates of the Palacio Real on that fateful day, an attempt was made to prevent the young royals from being driven away. In the face of such resistance a battalion of French troops was summoned to restore order, bringing with it two pieces of artillery with which the soldiers opened fire on the people swarming around the palace entrance. The noise of the canon and the cries of the protesters served only to bring more townsfolk onto the streets to seek vengeance against their erstwhile allies, and add to the growing tumult.

INTRODUCTION

There is much dispute about the number of casualties sustained by each side on that day, a day that has gone down in the annals of Spanish history, but what is not in doubt is that those executed on 3 May 1808 at la Montaña del Príncipe Pio, the scene depicted in Goya's painting, numbered 43, and it is claimed that there were other sites of execution around the city. The mortal remains of the victims represented by the artist now lie in the Cementerio de la Florida in Madrid, and their common grave is a lasting monument to the incident which marked the beginning of what the Spanish came to call, *La Guerra de la Independencia.*

How could it be that, at the very moment of Spain's ultimate rejection of French hegemony on the streets of its capital city, the Marqués de La Romana, a respected military figure, was in command of a Spanish army of some 15,000 troops then stationed on the northern fringes of the French Empire? The truth is that Romana's men were in Denmark in support of Napoleon's campaign against Sweden and Britain. They had already taken part in French operations against the Swedes in Pomerania during August 1807, and were helping to ensure the security of Napoleon's northern flank, guarding it against the possibility of amphibious operations by the British.

This story attempts to explain how La Romana came to find himself in such a compromising situation and how, against all the odds, and with the dogged support of the Royal Navy, he brought away the larger part of his force; returning with it to Spain to help in the struggle against the French occupation of his beloved homeland. Ultimately, about one third of his men failed in their bid to escape from the Baltic region, with the result that they were subsequently taken into captivity by the French. In the course of our story, we will give an account of what became of them from the time of their capture in 1808, through the intervening years to 1815, when Napoleon, finally defeated by an alliance of European powers, was forced to abdicate as Emperor of France.

Many students of the Peninsular War, along with readers of the Napoleonic Wars in general, will be familiar with the Royal Navy's operation to rescue Romana's army from Denmark's Baltic territories during the summer of 1808. However, in many cases their understanding of why and how it came about will have been gleaned from texts providing a mainly Anglocentric perspective of events. Only those possessing a working knowledge of Spanish and French will have benefitted from a wider viewpoint, by having at their disposal the historiography of Franco–Spanish politics during the years 1807-1808. It is only via an acquired understanding of the interplay between French ambitions and the Spanish reaction to them, that one can gain an insight into the reasons for Romana's northern expedition and its eventual denouement.

There is indeed a rich Spanish perspective to this romantic story, and an appreciation of it will add much to one's understanding of its ramifications, the effects of which led to the establishment of a strong Anglo–Spanish alliance against Napoleon; a relationship which was to prove both durable and effective in helping to bring about the eventual collapse of the French Empire. It was for this reason that the author decided to translate into English some of the more relevant Spanish sources on the subject, the content of which may otherwise have remained inaccessible to an English readership. A similar treatment has been given to a more limited selection of French sources, each of them relating to the events in the Baltic and their resulting aftermath. One of them is the personal story of Manuel López, who did not make it aboard the ships of the Royal Navy in August 1808, and as a result was taken into captivity on the isle of Zealand before being sent to France as a prisoner of war. López's experiences are mirrored by those of Rafael de Llanza, and both men were later recruited into the *Grande Armée* as members of the Régiment Joseph-Napoleon, an almost exclusively Spanish unit created with the original intention that it should fight in Spain against Wellington's Anglo-Portuguese army and the mixture of regular and irregular forces which formed the backbone of Spanish resistance after 1809. Napoleon, having gained an understanding Spanish attitudes towards his ambitions, later came to the conclusion that such a deployment would be unwise; deciding instead to employ the Spaniards in eastern Europe. As a result, each of the two soldiers mentioned was able to leave us an incredible account of their experiences during the emperor's ill-fated Russian campaign of 1812, and of the divergent paths their lives were to follow after the surrenders of France in 1814 and 1815.

After examining the military events in Denmark, this story will attempt to follow the fate of the Baltic escapees as the war progressed in Spain. Their Peninsular campaign began almost from the moment they were repatriated to Spain at Santander in October 1808, soon to be marched into the battles then raging in the province of Biscay as the Spanish armies, under the likes of Blake, Castaños, and Cuesta, struggled desperately to stem a renewed French advance into Spain. Much chastened after their defeat by Castaños's army at Bailén in July 1808 and their subsequent retreat to the line of the Ebro, the French were to be newly invigorated by the reappearance of Napoleon on Spanish soil in October of that year, determined, finally, to crush all resistance to the installation of his brother upon the Spanish throne. La Romana, given notice to prepare himself to take up a political position with the *Junta* in Madrid almost as soon as he had stepped ashore at La Coruña on his return from Denmark, would not be with his men in their early efforts to stem the French onslaught. Eventually, after a series of heavy defeats, Blake was relieved of his command of Spain's Army of the Left; ever more depleted, demoralised and dispersed as it fell back towards León where La Romana, newly released from his prospective duties in Madrid, was waiting to take up the responsibilities of command once more.

This is an interesting and important story, but it is one which is often overlooked. The events in the Baltic during the summer of 1808 enabled Britain to form an alliance with a country hitherto inimical to her interests, an alliance which was to provide an extended theatre of operations in which Wellington's army could challenge the French. Before the Spanish took up arms against Bonaparte, Wellington had mused upon the possibilities of defending Portugal should she ever be threatened with invasion via her frontier with Spain. Unfortunately, a joint Franco–Spanish force under the command of the French general, Junot, occupied Britain's Iberian ally in November 1807, before Wellesley had had an opportunity to put such a strategy to the test, but

INTRODUCTION

his time would come. It was only after the events in Madrid on 2 May 1808, that a sustainable British presence in Portugal became a viable possibility. That an opportunity of cementing a new relationship with Spain so readily presented itself in the Baltic during the summer of that year, was nothing less than a godsend to the British.

With the notable exception of Charles Esdaile, many British historians have tended to view the contribution made by the Spanish during the course of the Peninsular War as something of a sideshow. However, to the people of Spain the Peninsular War never existed, they speak only of their War of Independence, and they are as ignorant of the British efforts against the French on the Iberian Peninsula as we are of theirs. In fact, of those few Spaniards who nowadays are even aware that the British army fought on their side for some six years during the conflict, the author once heard one claim that, the only thing the British did on the Peninsula was win all the big battles! That might sound like a silly thing to say, but the war in Spain – apart from the big battles – was a continuous and savage affair fought, to a great extent, by Spanish irregulars against the French invaders between 1809, by which time many of the Spanish regular forces had been defeated in battle and dispersed to the periphery of the country's land mass, and 1813. Quarter was rarely asked or given by either side in that quasi–guerrilla struggle, and the toll in human life was heavy indeed. It is the hope of the author that English and Spanish readers of the war will one day each come to appreciate fully the efforts of their ally's warriors in the struggle to keep Europe free from French domination in the early nineteenth century.

1

Napoleon Demands the Assistance of Spanish troops in the Baltic Region

The Treaty of San Ildefonso, June 1796

Between 1793 and 1795, France and Spain were enemies in what came to be known as the War of the Pyrenees. After two years of fighting the conflict was concluded by the Peace of Basel, agreed on 22 July 1795, and almost one year later the Treaty of San Ildefonso was signed by the two nations, negotiations on the Spanish side having been conducted by Manuel de Godoy, then prime minister to King Carlos IV. Godoy's prominent role in the talks was to earn him the appellation of The Prince of Peace, a title used with increasing sarcasm during subsequent years as suspicion about his ambitions and his loyalty to Spain began to surface. Woven into the Franco–Spanish treaty was a clause which stated that, in the event of either nation being subjected to an external threat, it could call upon the other to place at its disposal a substantial military force which could be sent into action should the need arise. It was a clause which Napoleon would later invoke.

In December 1805, Napoleon inflicted a crushing defeat upon the empires of Austria and Russia at the Battle of Austerlitz, pacifying, for a while at least, his enemies in the east. In the west he was still concerned about the threat offered by Britain, the dominant sea power of the time, and her allies, Sweden and Portugal, who might at some time provide the British with *points d'appui* should they attempt an incursion onto the European mainland by landing troops in either of those countries. To forestall any such plans the emperor decided to strengthen his ability quickly to launch opposing forces against the British, if ever they appeared upon his western or northern flank. His strategy was to create a number of strongpoints on the French mainland at Boulogne, Pas de Calais, St Lô in Normandy and Pontivy in Brittany to cover the Channel coast. To guard against seaborne landings at places along the Baltic coast, similar strongholds would be located in Denmark and Northern Germany. To the east, he would deter the Austrians by raising several new army corps in Switzerland, Holland and the German Confederation. Such precautions would, of course, require a significant commitment of manpower. Spain, his southern ally and bound by the Treaty of San Ildefonso, would be expected to furnish him with an army corps consisting of a strong division from within her borders, which would be augmented by reinforcements from the forces she then had stationed in her Italian territory of Etruria. The Spanish troops earmarked for this role were destined to provide garrisons in the far north, at locations on the southern Baltic shore and on the Danish Baltic islands; remote and inhospitable destinations for any soldiers, more so, perhaps, for men accustomed to the warmer climes of southern Europe. Napoleon's plans for the Spanish contingent were put into motion when he wrote to Talleyrand in March 1807:

> Send a letter to Spain asking that 3,000 cavalry be directed immediately to Antwerp, and that the division which is at Livorno marches upon Augsburg, whence I will direct it to Hamburg to oppose any landings by the English. I will pay [the costs] for both corps. I think it is something that has already been agreed with Spain. The blockade of Hamburg will be worth the restitution of her colonies once peace is made. Do not engage in any complications regarding this matter. If it is to be done it is necessary that within twenty-four hours of making the demand, the division located in Tuscany should be on the march; that is, 3,000 cavalry. If, to 3,000 horse, they wish to add 6,000 infantry we will have to accept them. For Beauharnais it will be easy to make the Spanish cabinet understand that, as well as the advantage of contributing to the peace and of obtaining the restitution of her possessions, they will be able to harden and discipline their troops.[1] With regard to everything else, it will be enough to be clear in one's mind about the issues. If they do not wish to do it then all is finished. I have a dual interest in having the Spanish division removed from Tuscany.[2]

The 'dual interest' mentioned by Napoleon was, primarily, almost certainly that of removing from Tuscany the Spanish forces earlier introduced by the Queen of Etruria, Maria Louisa (daughter of the queen consort to Carlos IV of Spain who went by the same name). This, he calculated, would reduce the chances of armed resistance if ever he decided to carry out his plans to dethrone the Bourbons of Italy. His secondary aim was that of bringing Spanish forces into direct confrontation with the British in the Baltic region, thus reducing the chances of an Anglo–Spanish pact should his future plans for Spain go awry.

One can perhaps discern an underlying threat implied by the words, 'then all is finished' in his letter to Talleyrand. Napoleon was probably half-hoping that Madrid would refuse to accede to his demands, thus providing him with

---

1 Francois Beauharnais: French ambassador to Spain and brother of Josephine Bonaparte's first husband, Alexandre de Beauharnais.
2 Napoleon to Talleyrand (Prince de Bénévent) 25 March 1807, Napoleon Bonaparte, *Correspondance de Napoleon Ier*, (Paris: Plon and Dumaine, 1864) no.12169, t. XIV, pp.528–529.

NAPOLEON DEMANDS SPANISH ASSISTANCE

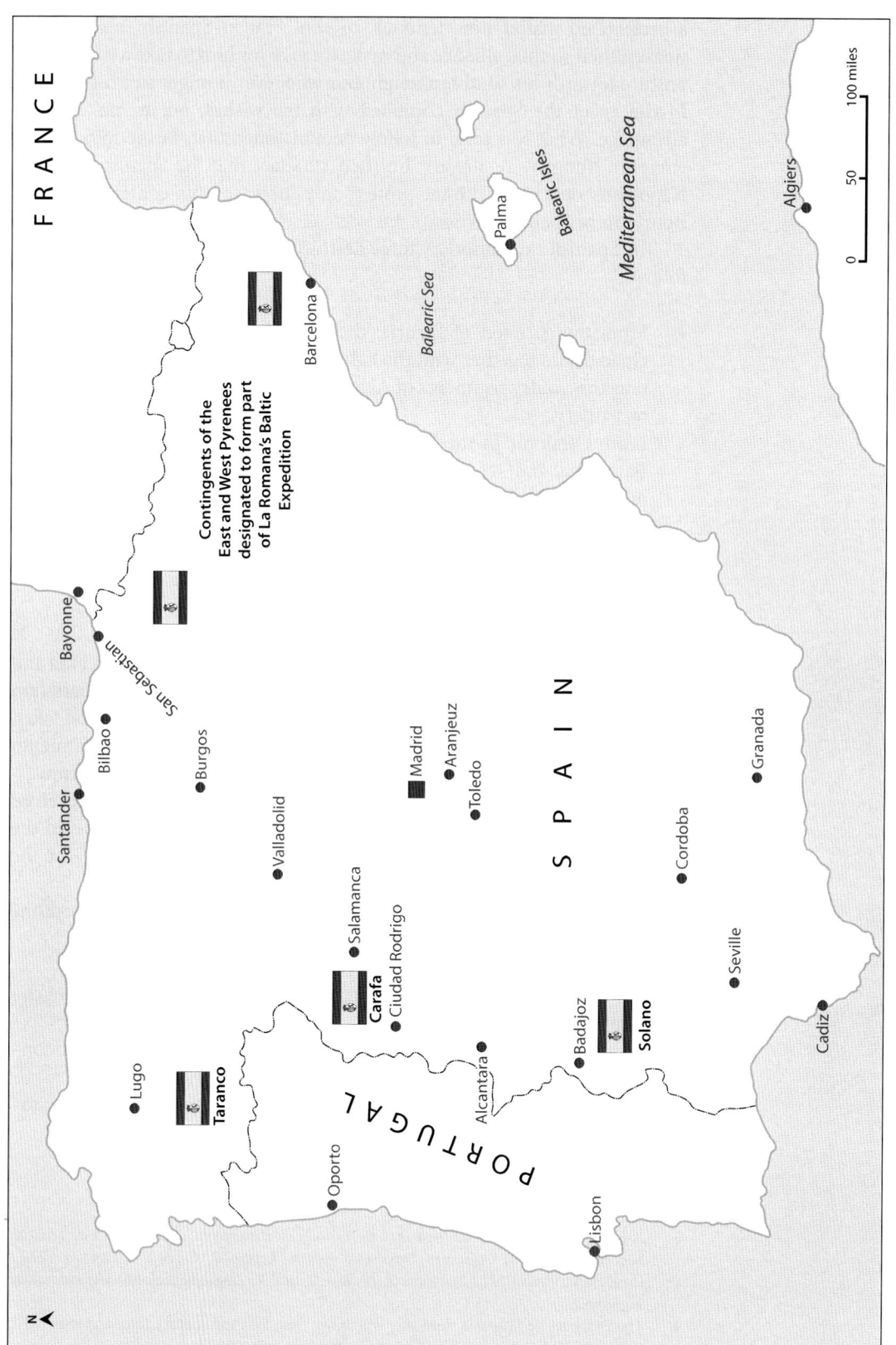

Major concentrations of the Spanish Army, Spring 1807.

a pretext, no matter how tenuous, to cool Franco–Spanish relationships, weaken their mutual alliance and make it easier for him to take a threatening posture towards his southern neighbour whenever it might suit his designs. In the event the Spanish complied with his wishes, but to no eventual advantage. What was soon to follow demonstrated that, in the mind of the emperor, things were already 'finished'; the fact that the Spanish accepted Napoleon's demands without protest only increased his contempt for the Bourbons of Spain.

The Spanish expeditionary force destined for the Baltic was assembled as follows.[3]

- From the garrison of Etruria: the infantry regiments of Zamora and Guadalajara together with the light infantry battalion, 1er de Catalunya, plus the cavalry regiments of Algarve and Villaviciosa, and one company of artillery.
- From Catalonia in the Eastern Pyrenees: the infantry battalion, 1er de Barcelona, and 3er de Princesa, plus two regiments of dragoons, those of Almansa and Lusitania, one company of artillery and one company of Zapadores (sappers).[4]
- From Navarra in the Western Pyrenees: the infantry regiment of Asturias together with the battalions, 1er and 2o de Princesa, plus the cavalry regiments of El Rey and El Infante.

At this point it may be worth noting that the regiments, 1er de Barcelona and 1er de Catalunya (1st Barcelona and 1st Catalunya) were single-battalion light infantry regiments, which means that '1er de Barcelona' may be taken to be the '1er Regimiento de Barcelona' or the '1er batallón del Regimiento de Barcelona', which are synonymous. The same goes for '1er de Catalunya'.

On 22 April 1807, the Etrurian contingent led by *Brigadier* Salcedo received their marching orders; two weeks later, on 8 May 1807, Godoy ordered the *Capitán General* of Catalonia to invoke the march of the contingent from the Eastern Pyrenees.

The Spaniards were to march in three separate columns and the outline itinerary for each is given below.

- For the force from the W. Pyrenees: Irun–Bayonne–Dijon–Kreuznach–Mainz.
- For the force from the E. Pyrenees: La Junquera–Perpignan–Besancon–Espira–Mainz.
- For the force from Etruria, N. Italy: Florence–Bologna–Mantua–Trento–Brenner–Innsbruck–Nuremberg–Mainz.

---

3   *Archivo General Militar de Madrid (aka Instituto de Historia y Cultura Militar de Madrid; henceforth AGMM) Colección Duque de Bailén, Legajo 2, Carpeta 4, Asunto 7272.2* (henceforth, *Bailén 7272.2*) *Memoria de José Agustín de Llano* (henceforth, *Memoria de Llano*) p.2.
4   The Dragones de Lusitania were later withdrawn from the expeditionary force and returned to Spain. *AGMM, Bailén 7272.2, Memoria de Llano,* p.2, *nota 1ª*.

NAPOLEON DEMANDS SPANISH ASSISTANCE

Once united at Mainz on 16 July 1807 the army came under the command of *Teniente-General* Don Pedro Caro y Sureda, Marqués de La Romana, his second in command was Mariscal de Campo Don Juan Kindelán.

The detailed composition of the Spanish force, which in total consisted of some 15,000 men, was as follows:[5]

Estado Mayor (GHQ):
- General in Command: *General Marqués de La Romana.*
- Second in Command: *Mariscal de Campo* D. Juan Kindelán.

Ayudantes de General Romana:
- *Coroneles*: *Marqués* de Crevecoeur, D. Juan Caro (brother of *Romana*), D. Luis Moreno Godoy and D. Pedro de Ríos.
- *Capitánes*: D. Agustín de Llano, D. Francisco Javier Riera and D. Julio O'Neill.

Ayudantes de General Kindelán:
- *Teniente* Don José Kindelán

Jefe del Estado Mayor:
- *Brigadier*: D. José Montes Salazar.

Primeros Ayudantes del Estado Mayor:
- *Coroneles*: D. Ignacio Martínez Vallejo, D. Mariano Rengel, and D. Juan Antonio Caballero.

Segundos Ayudantes del Estado Mayor:
- *Comandante*: D. José O'Donnell
- *Capitánes*: D. Juan de la Vera and D. Pedro Guerrero
- *Secretarios*: Los *Capitánes* D. Estanislao Salvador and D. Juan Ricaud.

Secretario de Romana:
- D. Nicolás Cachapero

Auditor General:
- D. Juan Miguel de la Cadena.

---

5   *AGMM, Bailén 7272.2, Memoria de de Llano*, pp.41–43.

Table 1 Army units leaving from Spain for northern Germany.

	Unit	Commander	Strength
Infantry	*Regimiento de la Princesa* (3 bns).	*Coronel* Conde de San Román.	2,282
	Regimiento de Asturias (3 bns).	*Coronel* D. Luís Dellevielleuze.	2,332
	Regimiento de Guadalajara (3rd bn only).	*Comandante* Antonio Falqués.*	778
Light Infantry	*Voluntarios de Barcelona* (2nd bn only).	*Comandante* D. José Borrellas.	1,240
Cavalry	*Regimiento del Rey.*	*Coronel* Lastres.	540
	Regimiento del Infante.	*Coronel*	540
Dragoons	*Regimiento de Almansa.*	*Coronel* D. Juan Antonio Caballero.	540
Artillery (Foot, Horse & Train)	*Artilleria de a Pie.*	*Capitán* Pola.	270
	Artilleria de a Caballo.	n/k.	89
	Tren de Artilleria.	n/k.	68
Sappers	*Zapadores* (1 company).	*Capitán* Aspiroz.	100 (approx.)
Total			8,779

* Falqués was deputising for Coronel Matorell who was with the 1er and 2o batallones.

Table 2 Army units leaving from Etruria for northern Germany

	Unit	Commander	Strength
Infantry	*Regimiento de Zamora* (3 bns).	*Coronel* D'Acourt.	2,256
	Regimiento de Guadalajara (1st & 2nd bns).	*Coronel* D. Vicente Matorell.	1,504
Light Infantry	*Voluntarios de Catalunya* (1st bn only).	*Comandante* Don Francisco Dionisio Vives.*	1,200
Cavalry	*Regimiento del Algarve.*	*Coronel* D. José de Yebra.	540
Dragoons	*Regimiento de Villaviciosa.*	*Coronel* Barón de Armendáriz.	540
Artillery	*Artilleria* (1 company).	*Capitán* D. José López	100
Total			6,140

*Incorrectly given in source as Don Juan Francisco Vives

Regarded as auxiliaries of the French Empire, the troops coming from the Western Pyrenees were to receive the same pay and rations as French soldiers from the moment they arrived at Bayonne. Those coming from the Eastern Pyrenees received their improved pay and conditions once they arrived at La Junquera; that is: five francs per day for colonels, falling to five cents per day for soldiers of the rank and file. Those from Etruria were similarly compensated from the date of their arrival in Bavaria.[6]

---

6   Andrés Cassinello, *El Capitán General Marqués de La Romana* (Aranjuez: Doce Calles, 2012), p.59.

NAPOLEON DEMANDS SPANISH ASSISTANCE

Grenadiers of the regiment of Guadalajara. (From the Suhr brothers series *Abbildung der Uniformen aller in Hamburg seit den Jahren 1806 bis 1815 einquartirt gewesenen Truppen*; collection of Markus Stein)

Musketeers of the regiments of Asturias, Princessa, and Guadalajara. (From the Suhr brothers series *Abbildung der Uniformen aller in Hamburg seit den Jahren 1806 bis 1815 einquartirt gewesenen* Truppen; collection of Markus Stein)

The Arrival of La Romana's army on the Elbe

The first Spanish troops to arrive on the Elbe were those belonging to the infantry regiments of Guadalajara and Catalunya together with the Dragones de Villaviciosa, all of which left Etruria on 22 April and made rendezvous with their French allies in the north of Germany on 10 June.

The Hansiatic towns in the coastal regions of the North and Baltic seas were of great importance to Napoleon's Continental System, but they were often visited by British merchants willing to ply a risky, blockade-running trade with mainland Europe. It was in an effort to prevent this that Napoleon appointed *Maréchal* Bernadotte, Prince de Pontecorvo, as governor general of all the coastal and market towns of the province. Upon taking up his post Bernadotte set about the task of creating an army corps of occupation in the region, and La Romana's men were directed upon Hamburg to join the newly formed force. By 14 July 1807, the division commanded by the French *Général de Division* Molitor, contained the regiments of Guadalajara, Zamora, Catalunya, Algarve (cavalry) Villaviciosa (dragoons) and a small unit of the Spanish Artillería which had been sent to the north with the expeditionary force. In total these formations represented a force of some 3,417 men ready to take its place amongst the Corps d'Observation de la Grande Armée.[7]

Once incorporated with Molitor's division, then part of *Maréchal* Brune's corps, these Spanish formations took part in the siege of Stralsund, a fortified port located on the southern shore of the Baltic and at that time garrisoned by Swedish forces, allies of the British in the war against France. The siege ended on 20 August 1807 when the Swedish king, Gustav IV, ordered the evacuation of the town and the nearby island of Rügen, at the time occupied by a force which included the King's German Legion, a Hanoverian unit which would later provide distinguished service to Wellington in Spain and Portugal. The Hanoverians had been loyal allies of the British since the signing of the Convention of the Elbe in July 1803, in which the French demanded the dissolution of the Electorate of Hanover and the disbandment of its army.

By most accounts the Spanish troops performed well during their first action in support of the French, sustaining only a small number of casualties, one of whom was the commander of a squadron of Catalan cavalry, *Brigadier* Terra–Veglia, who died of a heart attack after the fighting. Molitor afterwards reported on the conduct of the Spaniards in a letter to Brune:

> Monsieur le Maréchal,
> Your Excellency has asked for details regarding the conduct of the allied troops under my orders during the recent campaign.
>
> I can only praise the honourable spirit, the enthusiasm and the valour that animated the Spanish troops. Every officer and every soldier appeared to understand the sentiments of loyalty and attachment which unite their Catholic Majesty with our august Emperor.

---

7   Paul Boppe, *Les Espagnols A La Grande Armée* (Paris: Berger–Levrault, 1899), pp.20–21.

NAPOLEON DEMANDS SPANISH ASSISTANCE

Barón Armendáriz, colonel of the Dragones de Villaviciosa, played a particularly distinguished part in the action of 6 August, his proud bearing at the head of his troops [providing an inspiration to all].

On the same day, *Brigadier* Terra–Veglia, commander of the Catalan Chasseurs, led the charge of his men up to the palisade [of the enemy position]; his courage greatly admired by all [who witnessed it]. This brave officer, at the age of 75 the same man who was so moved by the welcome he received from Your Excellency when he visited your quarters on the occasion of the recent celebration held in honour of the Emperor, sadly died on the day following the action.

Brigadier Salcedo, commander of the regiment of Zamora, and *Coronel* Matorell, commander of the regiment of Guadalajara, each managed their troops in distinguished fashion, the two regiments executing their movements perfectly well …[8]

Whilst La Romana's men were in the Baltic cutting their teeth in their new role as soldiers of the French Empire, Napoleon's gaze had begun to focus upon the Iberian Peninsula. On 30 July 1807 the Spanish ambassador in Paris, the Principe de Masserano, sent a secret message to the government in Madrid informing it that Napoleon was planning a joint invasion of Portugal by French and Spanish troops. On 7 August Prime Minister Godoy issued orders to his army commanders in Spain, instructing them to prepare the Spanish units he had already earmarked to participate in the French-led adventure.

Meanwhile, in the Baltic the Swedes were not readily cowed into submission after their recent defeat. Despite the loss to the French of Stralsund and Rügen they were determined to remain detached from the French Continental System and to preserve their trading links with Britain. However, in an attempt to ensure that British traders were unable to make full use of a Scandinavian gateway into Europe, Napoleon, after dissolving the corps of *Maréchal* Brune on 27 October 1807, decided to re–organise the Grande Armée by dividing it into six separate commands, each responsible for a designated area of the southern Baltic coast. The second of these districts, under *Maréchal* Soult, would include Swedish Pomerania and the fifth, under Bernadotte, would constitute a centre of government for the Hansiatic towns. On that same day the Treaty of Fontainebleau was signed, one of the articles of which outlined a plan to carve up a conquered Portugal into three separate regions in order to provide a kingdom each for the Spanish 'facilitator', Godoy, and two other as yet unnamed 'associates' of Napoleon.

La Romana's Spanish corps eventually took up its winter cantonments in and around Hamburg, and by 15 November the marqués had become all too aware of the isolated situation of his host; it was far from home, the seas were dominated by the British and he was fully reliant upon the French for communication with Madrid. Here we will leave the Spaniards for the present, as they prepare to experience the rigours of their first northern winter, and examine the evolving situation in Portugal and Spain as Napoleon put his

---

8 Molitor to Brune, Ketenhagen 11 September 1807, *Archives Administratives du Ministere de la Guerre* (henceforth, *AAMG*) as cited in Boppe, *Les Espagnols*, p.22.

plan for dethroning the Spanish Bourbons into motion, but before we do so it might be of interest to see what their French comrades in the Baltic had so far made of them. Here are some words by the French historian, Thiers:

> The Spanish were grand soldiers. Of brown complexion, with their sharp limbs shivering in the cold air of the sad, freezing coastlines of the northern ocean, they provided a singular contrast with our Germanic allies, thus reminding us of the strange diversity of peoples submitted to the yoke of Ancient Rome during its time of greatness. [Wherever they went] they were accompanied by a swarm of women and children mixed with horses, mules and asses loaded with luggage. They were always poorly dressed, but in a somewhat original manner, always lively, animated and noisy, and knowing no language other than their own. In fact, they tended to stay together and ventured little to explore their surroundings, instead preferring to entertain themselves by dancing to the sounds of the guitar with the women who followed them. Unsurprisingly, they attracted much astonished attention from the dour inhabitants of Hamburg, whose newspapers carried accounts of these extraordinary scenes to an astounded Europe.[9]

The French invasion of Portugal, 1807, and the subsequent nullification of Spanish fortresses south of the Pyrenees

Before continuing with the story of La Romana's army, we shall firstly examine the course of events which led to its remarkable and sudden change of status from that of a force allied to the armies of its northern neighbour, France, to that of an enemy contingent in the Baltic, trapped amongst hostile elements of the French empire.

The evolution from the former to the latter status began when Napoleon concluded the Treaty of Tilsit with Tsar Alexander of Russia in July 1807. With Russia thus pacified Bonaparte turned his attention to Spain, of whose reliability as an ally he was never fully convinced, and decided to settle the 'Spanish question' once and for all by occupying her territory, usurping her throne and placing the Spanish crown upon the head his brother, Joseph.

The new and secret treaty with Russia provided Bonaparte with the perfect opportunity to move his troops into Spain. Portugal had long been flouting the rules of his Continental System by continuing to trade with Britain and he was now free to use force to bring her to heel. At the same time, Prime Minister Manuel de Godoy was secretly colluding with Napoleon in order to allow the French to march an army across Spain and invade her western neighbour. His generosity went even further in that he promised the Emperor of France the assistance of three strong Spanish army corps to help get the job done, his *quid pro quo* being a personal fiefdom in southern Portugal and the title of Prince of the Algarves. Shortly after *Général de Division* Junot crossed the Spanish frontier on his way to Lisbon in October 1807, Godoy took his

---

9 Adolphe Thiers, *Histoire du Consulat et de l'Empire* (Paris: Paulin, 1849) t. VIII, livre XXVIII, pp.14–15.

connivance, not to say treachery, a step further by being instrumental in the drafting and signing of the Franco–Spanish Treaty of Fontainebleau, thus formalising the anticipated dismemberment of Portugal.

On 30 November 1807, Junot led an exhausted column of 1,500 French grenadiers into Lisbon; these constituted the vanguard of his army, which had suffered greatly during the final weeks of its march across Spain due to the appalling roads by which it travelled and the heavy autumnal rains. It was said that Junot's grenadiers had hardly a dry cartridge between them by the time they reached the Portuguese capital. However, news of their approach was enough to force the Portuguese Royal Family, together with a retinue of some 8,000 hangers-on, to flee to South America with the active assistance of the Royal Navy.[10]

In the same month, whilst the gaze of Madrid was fixed firmly upon operations in Portugal, Bonaparte began to feed strong forces through the Pyrenean passes from France into Spain, using Article 6 of an annexe to the newly signed treaty of Fontainebleau as a pretext. In essence, the annexe outlined proposals for a number of necessary actions to be taken to prevent any external interference in the Franco–Spanish operation against Portugal, citing possible landings by the British at Cadiz as an example, and Napoleon would insist that his troops were simply heading to the south of Spain to discourage any such adventurism by London. As the long columns trudged deeper into Spain, they were at first welcomed by a populace who naively saw them as liberators arriving to rid them of the hated Godoy. It would not be long before they were disabused of their fantasies.

As the corps of Dupont, Moncey, Bessières, and Duhesme streamed south-west and south-east across the northern part of Spain, the mask began to slip. Soon they had overwhelmed and taken control of Spanish strongholds in the border region with France, such as Pamplona, Barcelona, Montjuich, San Sebastian and Pancorbo, with hardly a shot being fired as the Spanish monarchy and its government froze in disbelief of what was happening. Ironically it was Godoy, seeing his dreams of royalty melt away as he sensed betrayal on the part of Napoleon, who was the first to react. He sent couriers to Portugal to seek out generals Taranco, Solano and Carrafa, each in command of one of the three Spanish columns which had assisted Junot in his invasion of Portugal, and pass on his orders that they withdraw their troops into Spain. Taranco was to bring his men out of northern Portugal into Galicia, and the corps of Solano and Carrafa were to cross into Extremadura and seek to control the road south into Andalucia, as well as the easterly route to Madrid.

On 16 February 1808, with Madrid surrounded by some 40,000 French troops to the north, east and west, Godoy decided to remove himself, the Spanish royals: King Carlos IV, his wife Maria Louisa and his son Fernando, together with the garrison troops of the capital, to Aranjuez, where he intended to make a stand against his erstwhile friends and allies.[11]

---

10 Gomez de Arteche, *Guerra de la Independencia, Historia Militar de España*, (henceforth, Arteche, *Guerra de la Independencia*) (Madrid: Credito Comercial, 1868–1903), Vol. I, pp.177–180.
11 Arteche, *Guerra de la Independencia*, Vol. I, pp.219–259.

Despite the almost total acquisition of Spain's defensive infrastructure immediately south of the Pyrenees, there was one extremely valuable asset which did not fall into the hands of Napoleon; something he really longed to acquire. If France was to have any chance of establishing a realistic threat to the Royal Navy in the Mediterranean then possession of the Spanish fleet was essential, and although much of Spain's maritime resources had been destroyed or reduced by the Royal Navy at the battles of Cape St Vincent and Trafalgar, there was still a sizable squadron of intact warships sitting in the harbour at Cartagena. On 10 February, and with the agreement of the Spanish government, an act of defiance was finally made; *Jefe de Escuadra, Teniente-General (Armada)* Don Cayetano Valdés sailed from the Mediterranean port with the *Reina Luisa, San Pablo, San Francisco de Paula, Guerrero, San Román* and *Asia* to the port of Mahon on Menorca. On arrival he was relieved by *Teniente-General (Armada)* José Salcedo, who had been sent orders to ensure that the ships remained in the Balearics, out of French reach.[12]

The Spanish uprising of May 1808

The movement of the Spanish royals to Aranjuez, situated some 35 miles south of Madrid, was soon noticed by a public well aware of the presence of the French army on the outskirts of the capital. Convinced that the court was about to abandon them and sail to the Americas the people focussed their anger upon Godoy, sensing that he was in league with Napoleon. Soon they were on the march to Aranjuez where they surrounded the Royal Palace, and it was there that their mood began to swing violently between expressions of support for the king and queen, and cries for Fernando to be given the crown. By this time Godoy, sensing that his life was in danger, was in hiding at the private residence he owned within the city, but he was soon discovered and was lucky to be rescued by men of the Royal Guards who then escorted him to the palace. By that time King Carlos and Maria Louisa were in open conflict with their son Fernando, and the competing factions within the royal court had attached themselves to their preferred cause. As the bickering went on the growing allegiance of the mob to Fernando became apparent and, fearful of the consequences should its desire to see the enthronement of the young prince not be granted, the king and queen were advised to abdicate in favour of their son. Suddenly, on 19 March, King Carlos called together all of the ministers and dignitaries of the Court then present at the palace and announced to them his abdication, nominating Fernando as king.[13]

Whilst chaos was engulfing the Spanish royal family at Aranjuez, the Grand Duc de Berg, Joachim Murat, husband of Napoleon's youngest sister Caroline, Marshal of the Empire and Lieutenant of the Emperor, arrived at the gates of Madrid. Upon Murat's entering the city, the populace saw his arrival as further evidence that their great ally, France, was in tune with their

---

12 Arteche, *Guerra de la Independencia*, Vol. I, pp.224–226.
13 Arteche, *Guerra de la Independencia*, Vol. I, pp.266–290.

NAPOLEON DEMANDS SPANISH ASSISTANCE

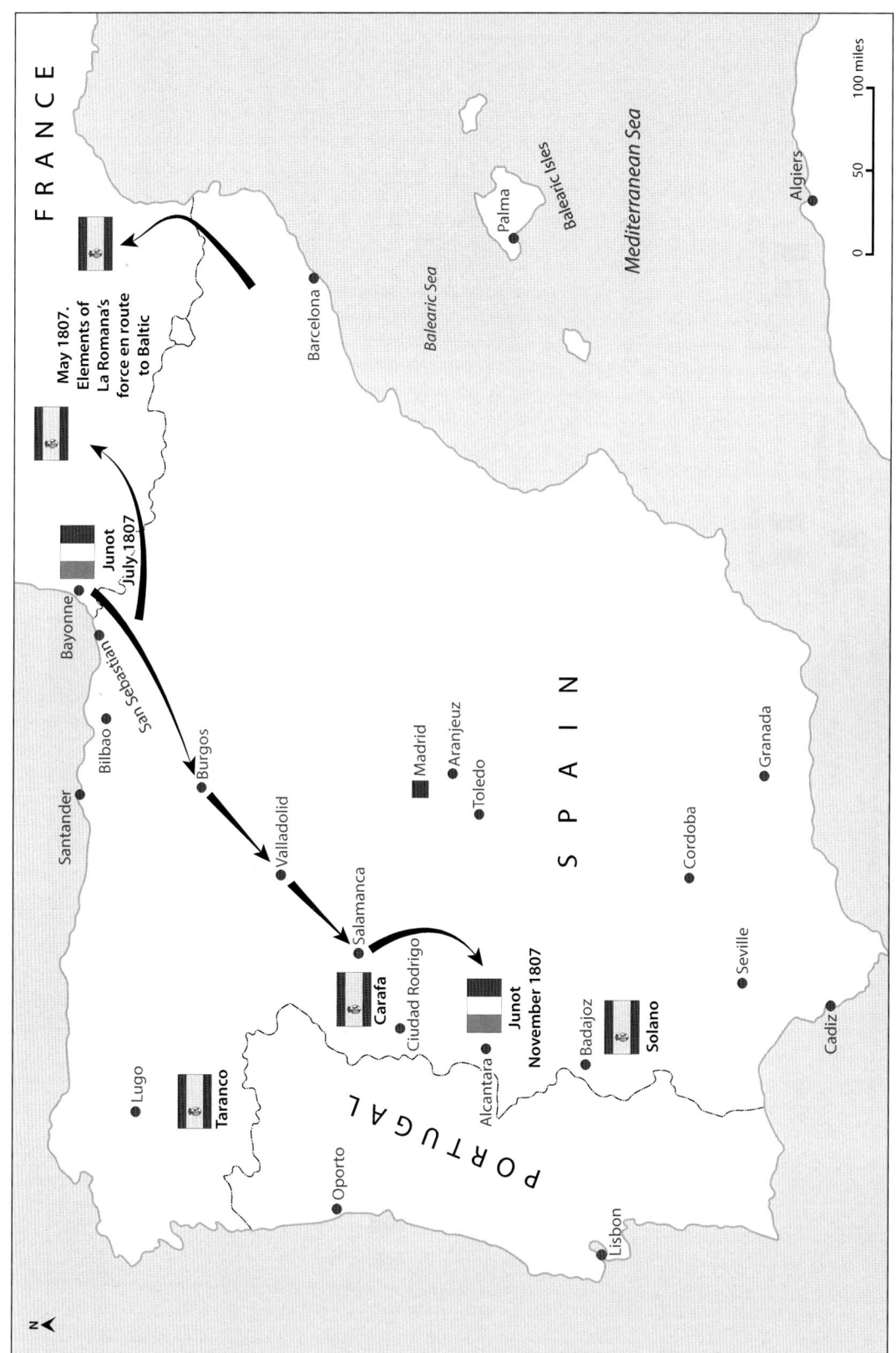

Elements of La Romana's force en-route to Baltic, spring 1807, and the route taken by Junot to the Portuguese frontier in autumn 1807.

NAPOLEON'S STOLEN ARMY

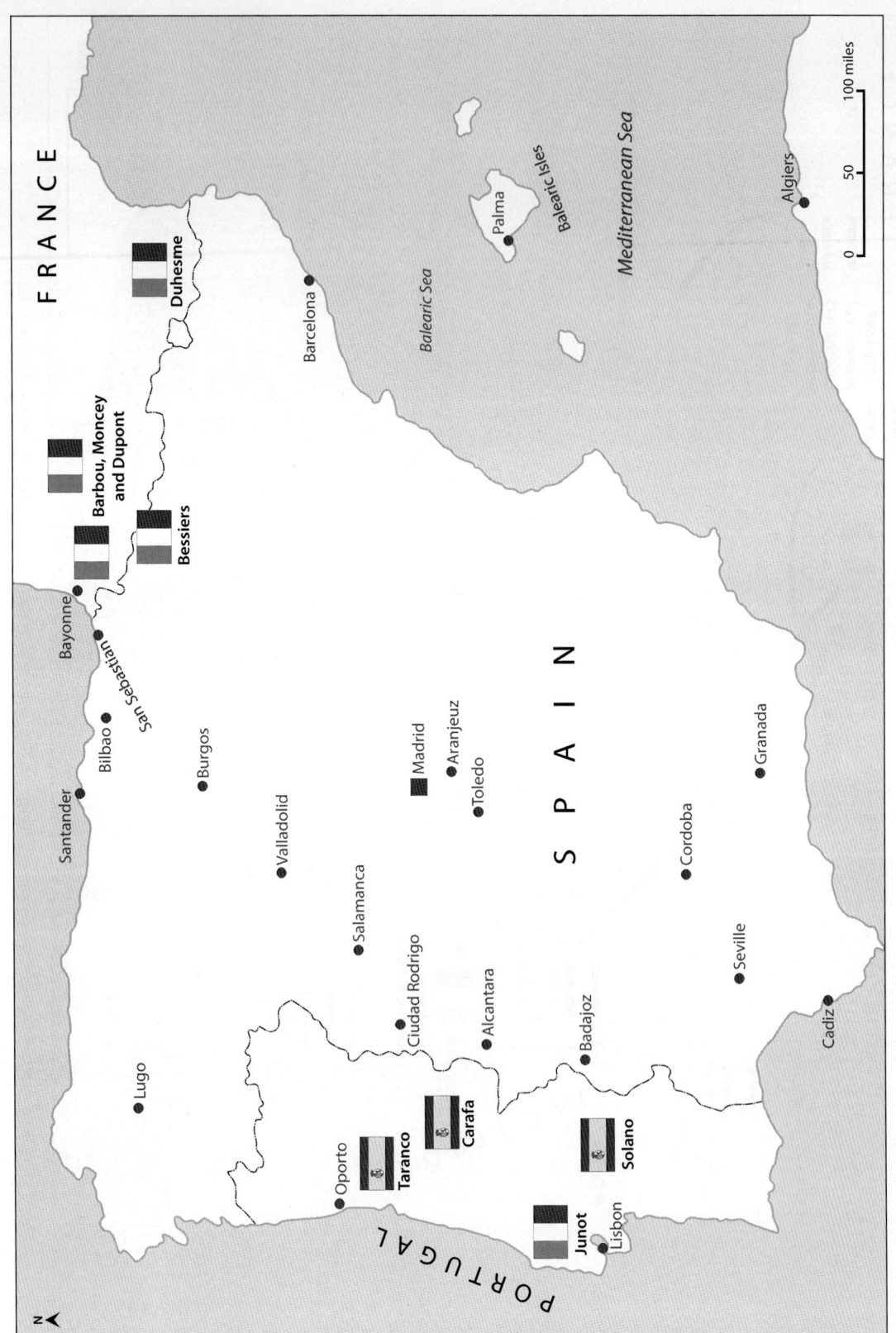

Franco-Spanish forces occupying Portugal, whilst French forces are poised to invade Spain, late November 1807.

NAPOLEON DEMANDS SPANISH ASSISTANCE

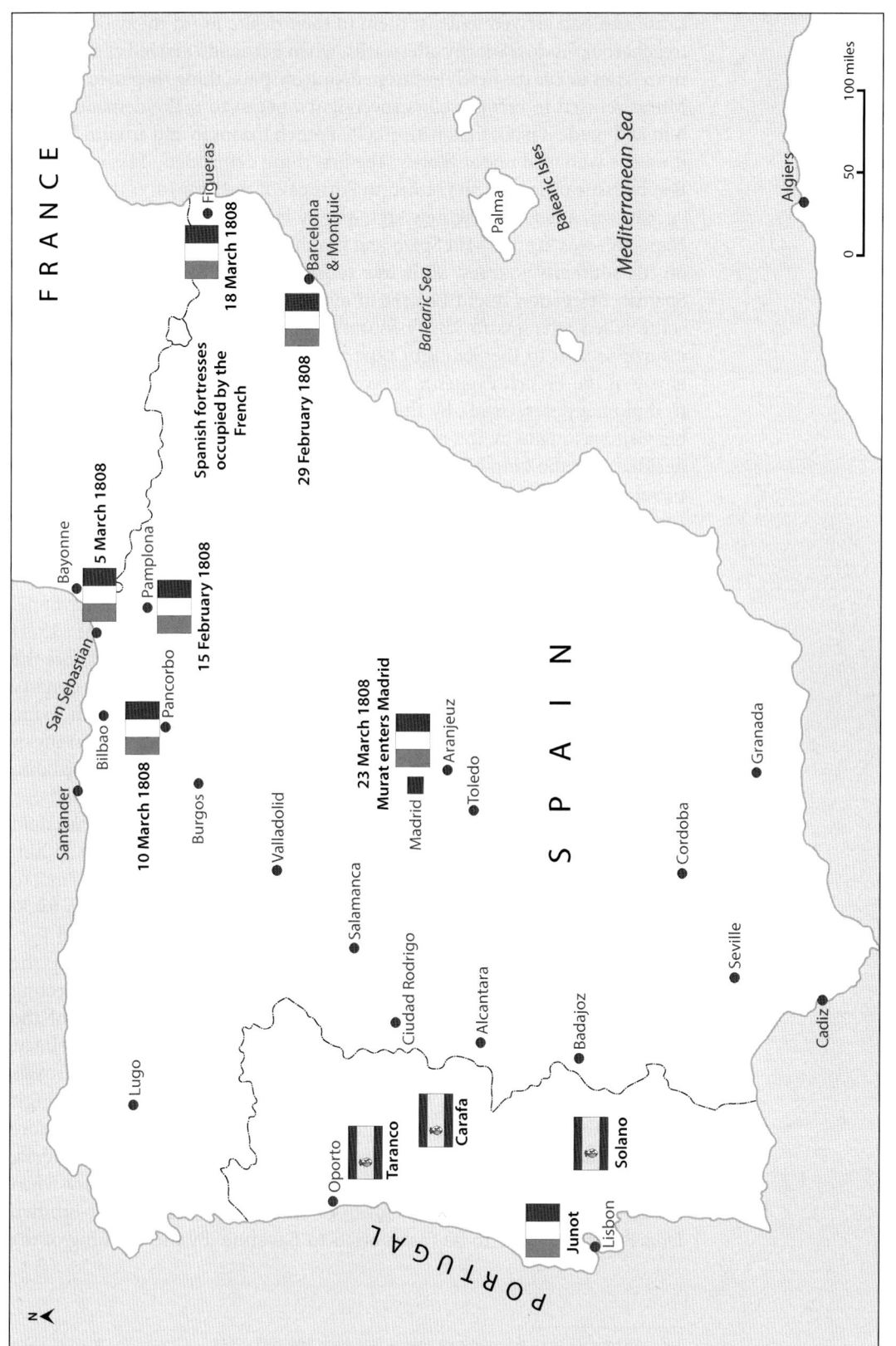

French occupation of Spanish fortresses in northern Spain and Madrid in the centre, February & March 1808.

cause and had arrived to assist them in their desire to rid themselves of the treacherous Godoy. Shortly afterwards, when Fernando arrived at the capital from Aranjuez as the newly enthroned king of Spain, things began to go awry. Murat refused to recognise his sovereignty, began to make demands upon him and made it plain that, with 40,000 French troops in and around the city, it was he who held real authority. The first thing demanded of Fernando was that he issue orders for the return to Portugal of the Spanish troops recently withdrawn, a demand the new king quietly ignored. Later, he was told that Napoleon was keen to visit Spain and that he had already set out from Paris on his southerly journey, so it was subsequently suggested to him that a Spanish delegation might be sent to await his arrival at the frontier. After some failed attempts to satisfy Murat's desires in this respect, there came a surprise visit to the Spanish Court by the Duc de Rovigo, M. de Savary, envoy of the French Emperor. It would seem that some oblique references to diplomacy were made by the French diplomat, and after an analysis of his visit was made by the members of the Spanish Court it was eventually decided that the king himself should agree to leave for Burgos, or perhaps travel as far as Vitoria, to meet with the emperor. Under significant pressure, Fernando set off on 10 April 1808 with an entourage of dignitaries, including de Savary, but when they arrived at Vitoria on the 14th to find no sign of Napoleon they decided to go no further. The envoy, obviously part of the French plot to lure them on, then convinced them to continue to Bayonne. The monarch crossed the frontier on the 20th and arrived at Bayonne a short time later. It was exactly the outcome Napoleon had wished for. Before the day was out, de Savary would have told Fernando that the Bourbon dynasty had ceased to exist. The emperor wanted one of his brothers to reign in Spain, and in exchange for their compliance they were offered the virtual throne of Etruria, recently taken from another of the Bourbons and incorporated into the French Empire.

Once Murat was assured that Fernando was at Bayonne, he felt he could then safely pack off the rest of the elder royals from Madrid to keep him company whilst Napoleon, in negotiations with Fernando, dutifully attempted to find solutions to the questions of state with his southern neighbour. By 30 April Carlos IV, his queen Maria Louisa and their sons, Fernando and Don Carlos, together with the Prince of Peace, were all present at Bayonne. As the Spanish royals settled into their comfortable surroundings, each expecting the master of Europe to decide in their favour on the question of the Spanish monarchy, Murat sprang the next phase of the French conspiracy, demanding that, apart from Don Antonio, all remaining Spanish royals should travel from Madrid to Bayonne.[14] This set nerves jangling amongst the members of the temporary ruling *Junta* set up by Fernando just before he left, and the nervousness seems to have spread to the citizens of Madrid, *los Madrileños*. Thus far and no further, seems to have been the cry when the crowd discovered that the Queen of Etruria and her younger brother, Don Francisco, were to be transported to Bayonne. By the morning of the

---

14 Arteche, *Guerra de la Independencia*, Vol. I, pp.294–307.

following day, the unforgettable *Dos de Mayo*, a huge crowd had gathered at the gates of Madrid's Palacio Real. And when the royal footstool was brought out and placed by the side of the coach in which Don Francisco was about to set off, the cry of, '*Nos lo llevan!*' (*They are taking him away from us!*) was heard. It was the spark that lit the flames of resistance to Napoleon. The noise of the resultant gunfire and the cries of the crowd calling out for vengeance brought more and more people onto the streets of Madrid as the unrest spread throughout the city. The first shots had been fired in Spain's *Guerra de la Independencia*.[15]

Meanwhile at Bayonne, Napoleon began to exert immense moral pressure upon Fernando to hand the crown back to his father, but Fernando stood firm in his refusal to comply until Napoleon, walking towards him said, 'Prince, it is necessary to opt between cession and death.' Fernando could take no more; he unconditionally renounced the throne on the following morning and his father briefly became king once more, abdicating within hours. By this act the crown of Spain was ceded to the family of her enemy: without the consent of her people, without the acquiescence of its legitimate successors and without the necessary formalities as stipulated by the laws of the land.

Setting the Scene: British naval activity in the Baltic between 1805 and 1808

Britain's Baltic trade was an important element in helping her to maintain the fleet of the Royal Navy. The source of naval stores such as timber, masts, pitch, and hemp, it was important to keep the Baltic commerce alive if the navy was to remain as the most potent weapon in Britain's armoury. But the shifting politics and alliances of the early nineteenth century were always going to impinge upon the openness of the northern trading routes and the availability of strategic materials. This being the case, it was vital that Britain establish a strong naval presence in the Baltic, even if at times it led to inevitable conflict with some of those nations having coastal access to its waters.

After Napoleon's defeat of the Austrians at Ulm in October 1805, Britain, Russia and Sweden decided to seek the safety of a new triple alliance against France. Prussia's participation was requested but she eventually aligned herself to the French cause after Napoleon had granted her possession of Hanover. Sweden's price for helping the British would be their acquiescence in handing over a sizable portion of the taxes they collected from the continuation of their Baltic trade, only then would King Gustav IV agree to send occupying forces to Stralsund and Rügen on the Baltic coast of modern–day Germany, where they would be joined by Russian forces.

Britain's lingering hopes that the Prussians might yet be persuaded to join the triple alliance were finally extinguished in January 1806, after Napoleon's victory over the combined armies of Austria and Russia at Austerlitz in

---

15   Arteche, *Guerra de la Independencia*, Vol. I, pp.328–364.

early December 1805. She reacted to the new situation by bringing home her expeditionary force then based in Hanover under Lieutenant-General Cathcart, thus leaving the Russians and Swedes unsupported in their stronghold of Stralsund on the southern Baltic coast.

When the Swedes then somewhat irrationally decided to blockade Prussia's Baltic ports, thus threatening Britain's trade, protests from London were not long in the making, causing her ally quickly to change her policy. However, it would not be long before Prussia was at war with France, finally making her a *de facto* member of the alliance and allowing the Baltic trade to continue untrammelled by the restrictions of Napoleon's Continental System, formalised under the Berlin Decree of 21 November 1806. By August of that year France and Russia were again at war, but after Napoleon's victories at Jena and Auerstadt, Prussia was out of the fight and the French were on the southern shores of the Baltic with the Swedes still clinging to their possessions of Stralsund and Rügen.

Britain's prospects for maintaining its trading links in the Baltic suffered a further blow in July 1807, when Tsar Alexander and Napoleon signed the Treaty of Tilsit. This meant that Russia's sizable Baltic fleet would now be available to help enforce the Continental System, if and when the Russians finally decided to throw their full weight behind the French. With the Russians having a foot in the enemy camp it left Britain's only remaining ally in the region, Sweden, to await the inevitable onslaught against Stralsund, from which they were ejected on 20 August 1807 by French forces which included some units of La Romana's Spanish army, as mentioned earlier.

Until this time Denmark had studiously avoided committing itself to either side of the warring factions in the Baltic, but it was obvious to all that she could not maintain her neutrality for long. With the help of Sweden the Royal Navy was able to maintain a strong presence in the Baltic, and with French forces now on their land border the Danes found themselves in a rather uncomfortable position. Somewhat belatedly, having lost Prussian and Russian support, London took the view that something had to be done to keep the French at bay, and on 8 July 1807 Britain sent a large task force to the Baltic, landing a spearhead of some 8,000 men of the King's German Legion (KGL) on the island of Rügen, then held by the Swedes. By mid-July British eyes were focussed upon the powerful Danish fleet based at Copenhagen, and the decision was taken to capture or destroy the bulk of it to prevent it from falling into enemy hands. Admiral Gambier soon set sail from England with a powerful fleet and a plan to land troops on the island of Zealand, these would capture the Danish capital whilst his warships provided support from the waters of the Baltic Sound, the narrow stretch of water which separates Denmark from Sweden. The 8,000 men of the KGL on Rügen were also earmarked to assist in the land operation. When all was in place London made strenuous diplomatic efforts to avoid hostilities, offering to host the Danish fleet in British waters until the war against France was concluded and throwing in the promise of a strong British expedition to Denmark to help her fend off any aggression from the French. All entreaties were refused and on 14 August 1807 British troops were placed ashore. Soon Copenhagen was surrounded but when the Danes refused to surrender, British forces bombarded the city with the unhappy result that many of its inhabitants became casualties before the inevitable capitulation took place. Much booty was taken, mainly in the form of some 20,000 tons of naval stores, but the main prizes comprised 18 battleships, 10 frigates, 17 smaller ships and 26 gunboats. Naval vessels found in the dockyards, under repair or construction, were set ablaze before Gambier withdrew his forces. Unsurprisingly, all of this resulted in Demark allying itself to the French cause, almost certainly ignorant of the fact that on 2 August Napoleon had issued orders to *Maréchal* Bernadotte, commander of French forces at Hamburg, to invade the country should its government refuse to declare war on Britain.[16]

Vice Admiral Saumarez's fleet sails for Gothenburg with Sir John Moore's Force

In December 1807 Tsar Alexander did what London had been fearing for some time: he declared war upon Britain, and soon his fleet would be menacing Britain's maritime dominance in the Baltic. Things were now at a parlous state with Sweden offering the only friendly haven on the Baltic shores and risking an attack from nearby French and Danish forces for its trouble. Britain had to go to her assistance, and a third Baltic expedition was put in motion under Sir John Moore, who was asked to take command of a force of some 11,000 men and establish a base of operations in that theatre for both the army and the fleet, which would sail under the command of Sir James Saumarez in his flagship, HMS *Victory*. The admiral's force contained two squadrons commanded by Rear Admirals Hood and Keats, and the latter would eventually play a significant role in the rescue of La Romana's army, but Saumarez's main objective was that of providing protection for Britain's remaining Baltic trade. Having been given a brief to make the whole of the Baltic Sea the area of his operations, his fleet arrived off Gothenburg on 7 May 1808, with Moore's troopships anchoring at Wingo five days later.[17]

Things did not go well for Sir John. Unsure how he could or should put his force to best use, he decided to take himself to Stockholm for an interview with the somewhat eccentric Swedish king, Gustav IV. The meeting did not go well; King Gustav seemingly taking such a disliking to Moore that he ordered him to be imprisoned. Aware of his predicament, one of Moore's men smuggled in a suit of women's clothes, which the British general was convinced to put on in order to make his escape. Unfortunately, his embarrassment was only exacerbated when he arrived back onboard *Victory* whilst Saumarez's ball for the women of Gothenburg was in full swing. It was all too much for Moore, who called it a day and took his troops back to England, leaving the Baltic on 3 July 1808.[18]

---

16   John D. Grainger, *The British Navy in the Baltic* (Woodbridge: Boydell Press, 2014), pp.158-173.
17   Grainger, *The British Navy in the Baltic*, p.178.
18   Roger Knight, *Britain Against Napoleon*, (London: Allen Lane, 2013), p.239.

Without the distraction of Moore, his men and their transports, Saumarez began slowly to assert a strong influence in the Baltic despite the fact that his ships were continually assailed by Danish gunboat attacks. Then, when he was on the point of seeking battle with the Russian fleet, he received a message from London. It contained a request that he assist in the evacuation of the Spanish contingent of Bernadotte's army then in Denmark, the message was intended for Moore, but in his absence Saumarez opened it, and having read its contents he decided to take up the mission originally meant for the British general.

The dispersal of La Romana's army around the Danish Baltic Territories

We may now return to the situation of the Spanish army in the spring of 1808, as it began to emerge from its winter cantonments around the city of Hamburg to ready itself for the new campaigning season. Ordinarily, attempting to capture the details of the ensuing travails of the Spaniards in the Baltic would present a daunting task to an historian, due to the usual scarcity of primary source material relating to such events; not to say the difficulties of discovering the resting place of what does exist and having the means to seek it out. However, in the case of the Spanish expedition to Denmark we have been doubly blessed. In 1818 the Spanish government decided to hold an inquiry into the events relating to La Romana's Baltic expedition of 1807/08, by setting up a *Comisión de Jefes* which called for statements from several of the surviving members of La Romana's headquarters staff, who had been with him during the Denmark campaign. In fact, they employed one of the survivors, Don Francisco Dionisio Vives, to collect the statements from his fellow veterans. As a *teniente-coronel*, Vives had been the commander of the 1er de Catalunya during its time in Denmark and had risen to the rank of *Mariscal de Campo* by 1818. The officers listed below are those who answered the call and submitted statements to the commission, and their testimonies provide a rich source of information upon which to draw to provide the English language reader with what has been, until now, the missing picture of the Spanish contribution to the remarkable success which took place in the Baltic during the summer of 1808. Today, all are held at the Spanish archives in Madrid.

Spanish officers who submitted statements to the *Comisión de Jefes* in 1818.[19]

Coronel Barón de Armendáriz of the Dragones de Villaviciosa.
Teniente-Coronel José O'Donnell, ayudante del Marqués de La Romana.
Teniente-Coronel Joachin Astrandi of the Caballaría Ligera del Infante.

---

19 The associated ranks are those held by the officers in 1808.

Capitán Fernando Mijares of the Ingenieros.
Capitán José Agustín de Llano, ayudante del Marqués de La Romana.
Capitán Estanislao Salvador, ayudante del Marqués de La Romana.
Teniente Santiago Miquel of the Regimiento de Asturias.
Naval officer, *Teniente* Rafael de Lobo.[20]

Teniente Antonio Fabregues, who figured strongly in the Spanish attempts to open communication with the British Baltic Fleet, was another of those asked to provide a statement, but his submission consisted merely of a collection of testimonies confirming his contribution to the success in Denmark. They were all written by one or other of his senior officers but none of them contains much useful information, which is a great pity. However, Fabregues did dictate a statement to either Captain MacNamara of HMS *Edgar* or to Rear Admiral Keats whilst aboard HMS *Superb*, a translation of which is provided in Chapter 4.

José O'Donnell was perhaps the adjutant closest to La Romana during his Denmark expedition, and we may now begin our story of the Spanish experiences in the Baltic by turning to his statement, in an attempt to obtain a picture of the movements made by La Romana's troops during the spring of 1808.[21] He begins his testimony by saying that he would have been able to submit a more accurate account of events in Denmark had he not lost his baggage and diary during the 1809 campaign in Biscay, in which he participated after his return to Spain from the Baltic. However, he goes on to state that, by chance, his wife had saved all of the letters she had received from him whilst he was in Denmark, and that by referring to them he could at least be more confident in the accuracy of the dates and events referred to in his testimony. This is what he had to say about the Spanish deployments in early 1808, as they moved out of their cantonments in the area around Hamburg:

> In December 1807 the French newspapers were announcing the friendly occupation of Spain and Portugal, but the personal letters we were still receiving from home on a fairly punctual basis, all with signs of having been previously opened, informed us of the suspicions of our fellow countrymen, and gave rise to some bitter complaints. …
>
> Between the 8 and 16 March [1808] all of the Spanish troops were in movement towards the Baltic … The Marqués de La Romana crossed the Little Belt between Kolding and Middelfart with the two light battalions,[22] the Regimiento de Villaviciosa and the Artillería, establishing himself at Odense, capital of the island of Funen, whilst leaving the Regimiento de Asturias at Middelfart and the rest of the division widely cantoned along the Baltic shore in the provinces of

---

20   Rafael Lobo was not one of La Romana's officers, he was an officer of the Spanish *Armada* sent to the Baltic by the Spanish government to help establish communication between the Royal Navy and La Romana's army.
21   *AGMM, Bailén 7272.2, Memoria de José O'Donnell* (henceforth, *Memoria de O'Donnell*) pp.3–4.
22   1er de Catalunya and 1er de Barcelona.

NAPOLEON'S STOLEN ARMY

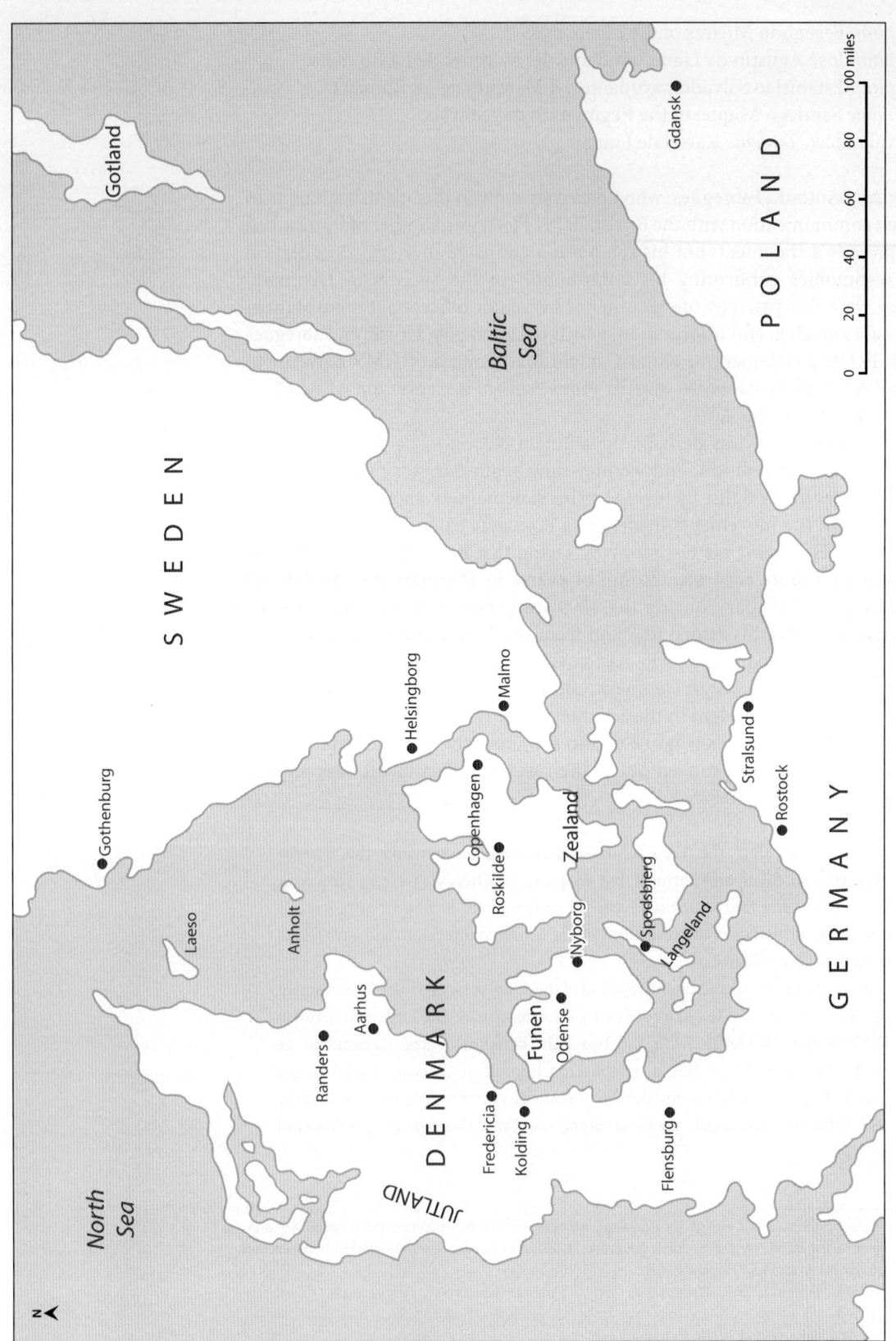

Danish & Western regions of the Baltic Sea.

Jutland and Schleswig. The general then advanced his headquarters to Nyborg on the coast of the Great Belt, whilst his second in command, *Mariscal de Campo* Kindelán, remained on Jutland at the head of the units which had not crossed to the [Baltic] islands.

O'Donnell goes on to speculate about the reason for the general movement which, he says, included the greater part of the French army, and suggests that the purported plan was to invade Sweden by pushing forces across the narrow Baltic Sound which separates it from the Danish island of Zealand, hoping that its waters would still be frozen after the winter and that the ice would be strong enough to avoid the need for shipping. He was convinced, however, that it was all merely a threatening gesture towards the Swedes, and at the same time a friendly occupation of Danish territory, opportunely carried out in the wake of the death of the Danish king.

The French impose censorship on Spanish correspondence between the Baltic and Spain

Many of the Spanish soldiers who submitted statements to the *Comisión de Jefes* make mention of French interference with their correspondence from Spain, as alluded to earlier by O'Donnell, and he reiterates his assertion a little later in his statement:

> On or about 8 April we were able to read stories in the French newspapers relating to events at Aranjuez and the abdication of our king, Carlos IV, in favour of his son Fernando. We celebrated this news, seeing it as the fall of a hated individual and his replacement by a new and beloved king. It was at about this time that we began to notice that we were receiving less and less correspondence from Spain, but the handful of letters which did get through brought hints of the violence that was taking place at home, increasing our suspicions and worries. These concerns were not confined to the officers, they also spread throughout the ordinary ranks whose public conversations aroused such discontent that there were clashes between French and Spanish soldiers, some of which resulted in the death of the participants.[23]

Fernando Mijares, a captain with the Ingenieros (Engineers) and based at Spanish headquarters, Nyborg, claimed:

> We were on Funen when we heard about the abdication of Carlos IV and the events at Aranjuez, and it was at about that time that we noticed a reduction in our correspondence from Spain, especially that of the personal mail of our chiefs and officers. It is also a fact that those letters which did arrive had clearly been opened. The mail of the ordinary soldiers was not so heavily scrutinised, but it

---

23   *AGMM, Bailén 7272.2, Memoria de O'Donnell*, p.5.

was from this, and the things we were able to read in the French newspapers, that we were able to form in idea of what was happening at home.[24]

Agustín de Llano, an adjutant of La Romana at Nyborg, says of this period:

> In March 1808, the Danes were nervous about the approach of strong columns of French and Dutch troops, but because the king of Sweden was obstinately continuing his war with France, both the direction of the march of the army and the orders it was under, allowed us to discern that it was preparing to strike a strong blow against his subjects ...
>
> But what must our general-in-chief have been thinking at that time? With his spirit and profound penetration he foresaw, and not without reason, that the increased movements of French troops [simultaneously taking place in the south of Europe] were directed towards Spain, and a mysterious silence in the official correspondence, in particular that from Godoy [based in Madrid as supreme commander of the Spanish army] caused him to agonise about the interests of our country. He could sense the moment arriving when his army would be employed, and indeed sacrificed, in the conquest of Sweden ...
>
> With his mind filled with such thoughts, on 8 March he despatched two of his *aides-de-camp*, Don Luis Moreno and Don Agustín de Llano, to Madrid with papers for Godoy; de Llano setting off with further secret instructions to monitor carefully the political and military situation in Spain and to return to the Baltic as soon as he could.[25]

De Llano would arrive in Madrid on 25 April 1808, thus allowing him to witness the insurrection of 2 May. In the meantime, there were to be some final adjustments made to the whereabouts of the Spanish units in Denmark during late spring and early summer. O'Donnell explains that:

> During the months of April, May, June and July there were changes in the disposition of the Spanish units. Bernadotte had determined that some of these, along with a company of the Artillería, should cross the Great Belt to take up cantonments on Zealand. However, there were always two British frigates anchored off Nyborg which would have made any attempt at crossing very dangerous, it being of a distance of some eight leagues.[26] But by making several night crossings in small boats we were able to avoid the British ships, and by the end of June the regiments of Asturias and Guadalajara were safely ashore on Zealand. However, the eight pieces of artillery which should have gone with them remained aboard ship at Nyborg; the transports being too big to avoid detection once at sea.
>
> By the end of July all of our units were at their required destinations. All seemed well, the troops were still in good condition and maintaining their discipline and

---

24 *AGMM, Bailén 7272.2, Memoria de Fernando Mijares* (henceforth, *Memoria de Mijares*) p.5.
25 *AGMM, Bailén 7272.2, Memoria de de Llano*, p.5.
26 One league, or *una legua* in Spanish, is the rough equivalent of 3.5 miles. This would suggest that O'Donnell's 8 leagues (28 miles) was a bit of an overestimate if he was talking about the distance between Nyborg and Korsoer, the main crossing point between Funen and Zealand.

drill. They received their pay punctually through our treasury and the country provided generous rations of bread and meat.[27]

The final Spanish deployment is detailed below together with the distance of each unit from Spanish headquarters at Nyborg. All units were under the supreme command of *Maréchal* Bernadotte, Prince de Pontecorvo, and were expected to assist with the observation of Saumarez's Baltic Fleet.

Table 3 Deployment of Spanish units in Denmark and the distance of each from La Romana's Headquarters at Nyborg

Location of Unit	Name of Unit	Distance from Nyborg in miles
Jutland Peninsula		
	Regimiento de infantería de línea de Zamora: 3 bnes at Fredericia	50
	Regimiento de Caballería de línea del Rey: at Aarhus	110
	Regimiento de Caballería de línea del Infante: at Randers	125
	Regimiento de Caballería de línea del Algarve: at Horsens	80
	Note: distances from Nyborg are all via the crossing of the Little Belt at Middelfart	
Isle of Zealand		
	Regimiento de infantería de línea de Asturias: 3 bnes near Roskilde	60
	Regimiento de infantería de línea de Guadalajara: 3 bnes near Roskilde	60
	Note: distances are via the crossing of the Great Belt, Korsoer–Nyborg.	
Isle of Funen		
	Cuartel General (GHQ): at Nyborg	n/a
	Regimiento de infantería de línea de Princesa, 1er bn: at Nyborg	n/a
	Regimiento de infantería de línea de Princesa, 2o bn: at Kerteminde	13
	Regimiento de infantería de línea de Princesa, 3er bn: at Middelfart	45
	Regimiento de infantería ligera de Barcelona, 1er bn: at Svendborg	22
	Dragones de Almansa: at Odense	22
	Dragones de Villaviciosa: at Faaborg and Assens	37 miles each
	Artillería: eight guns at Nyborg	n/a
	Artillería: four guns at Svenborg	22
	Artillería: six guns embarked at Nyborg	n/a
	Zapadores (Sappers) 1 compañía: at Nyborg	n/a
Isle of Langeland		
	Regimiento de infantería ligera de Catalunya, 1er bn: at Rudkobing	40
	Note: This distance is via the crossing of the channel which separates Funen from Tassing, between Svendborg and Vindeby, and that which separates Tassing from Langeland, between Bjerreby–Rudkobing	

---

27 *AGMM, Bailén 7272.2, Memoria de O'Donnell*, p.5.

NAPOLEON'S STOLEN ARMY

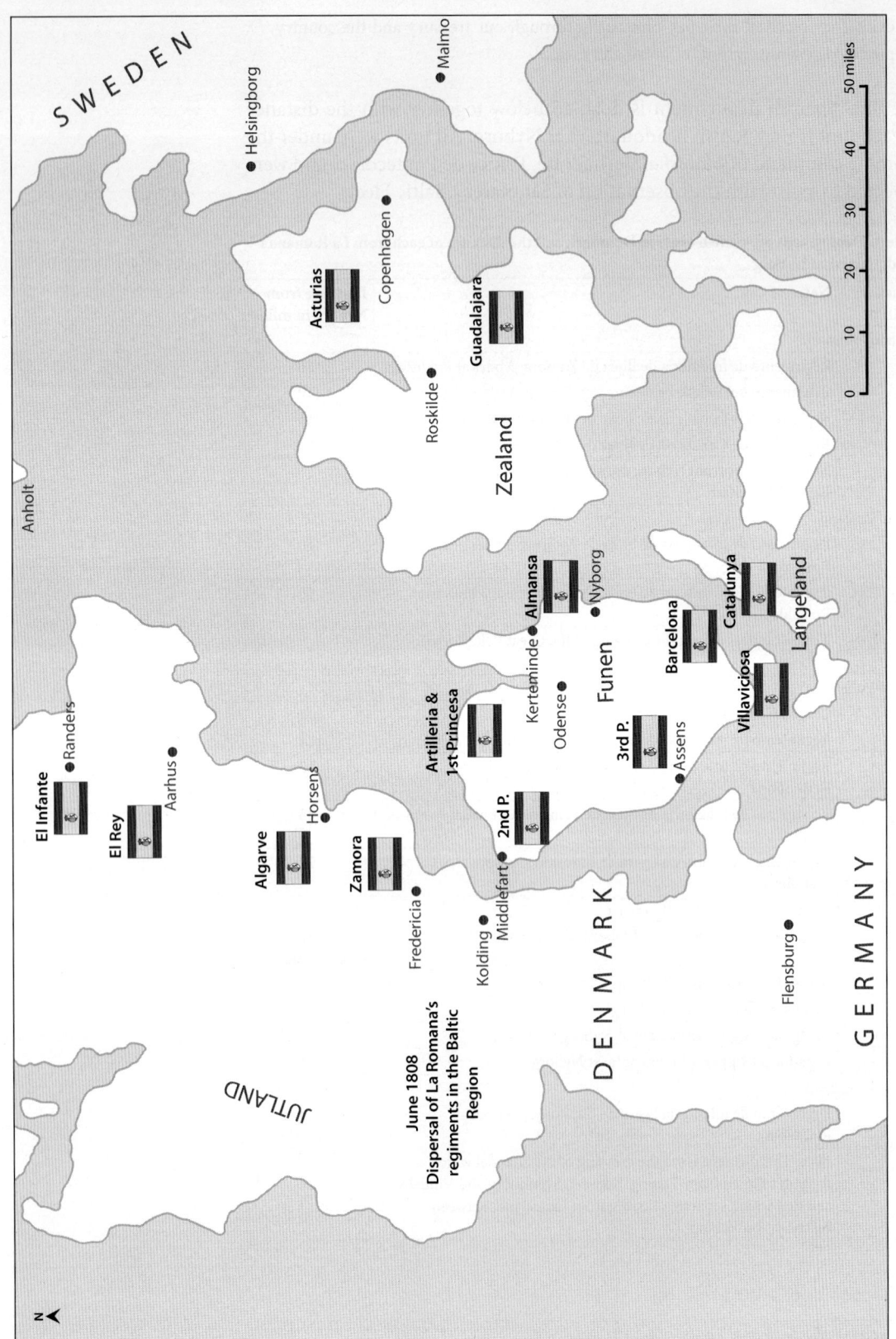

Dispersal of La Romana's units in the Danish Baltic territories, June 1808.

The bleak Baltic climate may not have been to their liking but there were some compensations for the Spanish soldiers whilst they were in Denmark, as they were to enjoy far better conditions of service than those they were accustomed to at home. For instance, they were paid regularly and provided with plenty of campaign experience whilst being provided with regular rations, all of which was a novelty to them. In fact, their pay was generous as well as regular and on a par with that of their French counterparts, usually being extracted from, or willingly paid, by the authorities of the towns they took or were billeted upon. According to Don Estanislao Sanchez Salvador, Secretary to the Headquarters of the Spanish Army in Denmark, each subaltern, in addition to his daily accommodation expenses, received four and a half pesetas for food and subsistence; a captain nine pesetas, a battalion commander 18 pesetas and a colonel 30 pesetas, rising in proportion to seniority up to the rank of general-in-chief, such as Kindelán, who received 250 pesetas and noted that the French, 'Tried to please [me] by any and all means.'[28]

In the next chapter we will examine the story of Brother James Robertson, a Scottish monk who had spent many years with the Benedictine Order in Regensburg, Germany, during which time he had become fluent in German. His language skills made him a possible candidate for a mission to the Baltic, where it was thought he might be able to make contact with La Romana and offer him a way out of his troubles. Before we move on, however, it might be worthwhile to look at an interesting and entertaining account of the impressions so far made upon the Danes by their guests from the south. It would appear that the rather staid, some may say dour, inhabitants of the Jutland Peninsula and the Danish Baltic Isles were somewhat taken aback by the appearance of the Spanish troops when they first arrived; so much so that a number of them were moved to write about the impressions they formed of La Romana's men during their presence amongst them. One young boy, who grew up to become Bishop Jacob Daugaard of Ribe, on Jutland, described his impressions of these strangers in his book, *Souvenirs*, and his daughter, Christine, included them in a book she later dedicated to her father's life entitled, *Biskop Daugaard*. This is part of what the bishop wrote:

> In 1808, three regiments of cavalry arrived in Randers; two continued their journey northwards towards to Aalborg, the third remaining in the town under the command of *General* Kindelán. It all happened one Sunday evening and the townsfolk, terrified at the thought of what these foreigners might be capable of, could not be separated from their fear of the scenes of cannibalism [which took hold in their imagination].
>
> The women and children fled, and after barricading their front doors the men hid themselves in the cellars of their homes … However, the good order and discipline of the Spanish soldiers combined with their daily attendance at evening prayers in the town square, in which the whole regiment took part and exhibited a great deal of reverence, eventually had the effect of dispelling the early fears of

---

28 *AGMM, Bailén 7272.2, Memoria de Estanislao Sanchez Salvador* (henceforth, *Memoria de Salvador*) Appendix 1o, final page of document.

the people. Soon their concerns began to subside and small favours, offered on one part or the other, quickly resulted in the establishment of a great degree of friendship between Danes and Spaniards.

The farmers of the surrounding area often came to have their animals treated by the regimental *maréchal–ferrant* [farrier] who they considered to be a better vet than those practising in the area, thus lending substance to the old proverb.[29] However, the children of the town [at that time the friends of the young Daugaard] were most struck by the drummer of the regiment and the manner in which he sat upon his big white horse whilst frenetically waving his drumsticks about …

In the course of time, via the means of a few German words picked up during their marches and the occasional use of a little mime or pantomime, the Spaniards were able to make themselves understood; and in the more difficult situations that arose they would consult the little dictionary which was always available at the house of the seed merchant …

To the Danes the Spaniards displayed an astonishing amount of gaiety and vivacity, showing great affection towards the local children and always happy to play with them. During the hours of day–light they would hunt for birds and by night they set traps for cats. Later they would sit around in groups, roasting their catch as they smoked their cigarettes and played cards. However, when the day arrived on which they were to be forced to swear an oath of allegiance to King Joseph, their gaiety soon disappeared …

Eventually they left us, and on the day of their departure from the town there was a moment of general sadness amongst the population, an indication of how the Danes regretted the loss of the liveliness those exuberant southerners had given to their little settlement.

The future Bishop Daugaard, then but an infant, found himself, 'Moved by the distress of poor Rosalia, the wife of a soldier lodging at the house of [my] parents, who was possessed of a terrible fear of the sea and hated the thought of having to abandon the donkey that belonged to [my] family.'[30]

Another Dane who mixed freely with the Spanish soldiers in the summer of 1808 was F. Schierne, who later wrote of his experiences when describing the Spanish cantonments, and in a detail from his work there is more evidence of the amicable relations which were established between Spaniards and Danes. The villagers with whom they were cantoned, he wrote, 'Kept, for a long time after they left, the little objects – amulets wrapped in silk – that the Spaniards wore about their chests and gave away as presents.' Schierne also spoke for many years of how much the Spaniards suffered in the particularly severe winter of 1807/08, and of their hatred of the French with whom there were often quarrels, which sometimes ended in stabbings. Nevertheless, he says, 'Bernadotte made great efforts to gain their affection and learn to speak their language. Being a native of Gascony served him well in this instance, and he

---

29 The bishop was probably referring to the proverb, 'No man is a prophet in his own land'.
30 Christine Daugaard, *Biskop Duagaard* (Copenhagen: Unknown, 1896) reproduced in French in Boppe, *Les Espagnols*, pp.45–47.

made sure always to have several companies of Spanish soldiers amongst his personal guard.'[31]

Another author, M.J. Kornerup, later wrote a history of the town of Roskilde on the island of Zealand, where the Spanish regiments of Asturias and Guadalajara were based, dedicating a whole chapter of his work to contemporary accounts of the time the Spaniards were there in 1808, all left by its inhabitants. He refers to the 'colourful entry into Roskilde made by the two magnificent [infantry] regiments of Guadalajara and Asturias', and goes on to describe how 'the old brigadier [of Asturias], Dellevielleuze,[32] then aged seventy-four and riding upon his white horse at the head of the column, reminded one eyewitness of the heroes of Cervantes.' The troops, noted Kornerup:

> Had a fierce appearance despite the light-footedness of their march; the men being short, slim and narrow-waisted, with their brilliant black eyes and shining white teeth contrasting sharply against their brown skin. They made a most remarkable sight ...
>
> Nevertheless, these magnificent troops were of a less martial appearance than those of the French regiments. One saw many guitars hanging from their haversacks, and bringing up the rear [of their column] there was [invariably a] long convoy of carts mixed with a crowd of 'not so attractive' women and children belonging to the soldiers. The former seated upon their mules, lady-fashion, their spirit such that they laughed [heartily] at the jibes of the youngsters. It all made for an amusing spectacle.

It was also a great surprise for the Danes to see the Spaniards smoking cigarettes with hardly a halt, and they followed them everywhere taking great care to ensure that their discarded butts were not the cause of fires.

Obviously, there were difficulties in communication and for the first few days, at least, there was need of an interpreter:

> In Zealand, as in the other provinces, the villagers quickly bonded with the Spaniards to the extent that they would visit them at their cantonments. Their politeness and their good manners were always much remarked upon, but the spectacle that really filled the people with a respectful admiration for them, was the manner in which they held mass without the existence of a Catholic church. It was celebrated in the open air to the sound of military music, the soldiers formed in good order and in pious contemplation around an improvised altar, the men kneeling, bare-headed, holding musket in right hand. In contrast the wives of the officers were richly dressed in silk and velvet, with their head covered by a mantilla as they received their benediction from the regimental chaplain, who was assisted by two children of the choir ...

---

31 Frederik Schierne, *Spanierne i Danmark* (Denmark: Unknown, 1835) reproduced in French in Boppe, *Les Espagnols*, p.47.
32 This is a further reference to Dellevielleuze who, in different places, is variously referred to as '*brigadier*', '*coronel*', '*brigadier-coronel*'.

During the evenings the local people never missed an opportunity to observe the Spanish as they danced the fandango to the sound of the guitars and castanets, and to listen to the serenades often sung beneath the windows of attractive Danish women. However, their food occasionally introduced a hint of sourness to the usually cordial relationship. For instance, the Spanish refusal to eat 'black' bread meant that the bakers were forced to procure the wheat necessary to satisfy their demands …

The colonel of Asturias, a grand old gentleman with superior looks of great distinction, never failed to put on silk stockings and silver-buckled shoes when returning from manoeuvres, and always asked that his hostess prepare a Spanish dish far removed from anything the Danes were used to. Nevertheless, the resulting nostalgia, combined with his hatred for the French, soon became clear when, on the odd occasion, he would murmur, *'Carajo los franceses, kaput Franzos, a mort les Francais.*[33]

---

33   J. Kornerup, *Roskilde, Ancient Town of Denmark on the Island of Zealand* (Copenhagen: Unknown, 1892) reproduced in French in Boppe, *Les Espagnols*, pp.47–49.

Army return for La Romana's expeditionary force, 1 March 1808, as provided by Agustín de Llano.[34]

---

34 AGMM, Bailén 7272.2, Memoria de De Llano.

2

The Story of Brother James Robertson, British agent

The story of Brother James Robertson, briefly alluded to above, was published by his nephew, Alexander C. Fraser, in 1863. In the account of the Baltic mission he undertook, the cleric would claim credit for establishing a direct communication between himself and the Marqués de La Romana on the Danish island of Funen in late June or early July 1808. He had been commissioned to travel to Denmark to deliver a message from the British government to the Spanish commander offering to evacuate his army from the Jutland Peninsula and its neighbouring islands in the Baltic. The plan was to embark the troops and transport them to Spain by employing the resources of the Royal Navy and a fleet of merchant transports. We have already seen how La Romana's host came to find itself so far from home and why, in the summer of 1808, its commanding officer was looking for a means by which he could extricate his force from its state of *de facto* captivity, we shall now see how that means became available to him.

At an earlier time in his life, Robertson had taken orders as a Benedictine monk at a monastery in Ratisbon (Regensburg) Germany. The building where he practised survives to this day under its more recent name of the Schottenkirche (Scottish church). In his story, Robertson says that he left Germany some time before 1804, returning to his native Scotland before moving to Ireland, where he became familiar with the Duke of Richmond whom he had met when the latter visited Ratisbon some years earlier. During a conversation which passed between the two, Robertson offered his services to 'the public' in any way which Richmond might feel they could best be used. In doing so he was probably hinting that he would be prepared to act as a British agent in continental Europe, where his language skills might be of greatest use. Initially nothing came of his offer, but sometime later he was introduced to Sir Arthur Wellesley, then Chief Secretary for Ireland, to whom he repeated his willingness to be of help to the British government should the need ever arise. Several weeks after their initial meeting Robertson received an invitation from Wellesley asking him to make his way to London, and when they met the cleric was informed that his offer of public service might soon be taken up.

All then went quiet for a period before Robertson received a letter from the Irish Office in the spring of 1808 inviting him to call upon Wellesley once more, this time at his house in Harley Street. It was there where Wellesley asked the cleric if he would be willing to travel to Denmark and make contact with La Romana. He readily agreed, and was introduced to Canning on 10 May 1808 who, during the discussion of Wellesley's proposal, became convinced that the Scot should indeed undertake the mission offered him. Once arrangements were underway, a Mr Hammond was delegated to provide Brother James with his instructions, which were as follows:

> You will inform the Marqués Romana that our transports shall be at his orders to convey him and his troops to any place or country he chooses. We ask nothing in return: we do not require that they should fight for us; we simply desire to put it in their power to withdraw from their present situation. We offer to carry them free of cost to South America, to Minorca, to Canada, to England or to Spain, at their option. Tell him Mr. McKenzie waits at Heligoland to receive his determination: that if Spain is resolved to resist the Usurper, we are ready to cooperate with her by every means in our power: that our cavalry were never better mounted, our artillery never better served, that our soldiers of every rank long for an opportunity to measure themselves with the French on land: that we consider Spain as the fairest field of action, and thereupon await the invitation of its oppressed inhabitants.[1]

McKenzie's task was to remain on Heligoland to act as intermediary between Robertson and the government in London whilst the Scot was in Denmark and Germany, he was just one of a network of spies established in northern Europe by the British government during the Napoleonic era.

The instructions detailed above were provided by Bartholomew Frere (younger brother of John Hookham Frere) who had acted as a representative of the British government in Spain some five years earlier. In fact, both Wellesley and Frere had been personal acquaintances of La Romana in earlier times, and it was via Frere's personal connection with him that a means of convincing the Spaniard of Robertson's authenticity as a British agent was concocted, in the event that Brother James ever succeeded in encountering him. It involved a hand-written scrap of Latin text from Frere, together with some (verbal) details of a private conversation he had had with the marqués during his time in Madrid.

Robertson leaves for the Baltic

Robertson left London for Harwich on 4 June 1808, and two days later he was placed ashore on the North Sea island of Heligoland. Two smugglers were then enlisted to take him to the mainland, and after many scares in the night as they attempted to avoid being apprehended, they were eventually

---

1   James Robertson. Alexander C. Fraser (ed.), *Narrative of a Secret Mission to the Danish Islands in 1808* (London: Longman, Green, Longman, Roberts and Green, 1863), pp.12–13.

caught and taken into custody by Customs officials. Once aboard their boat it became apparent to the three 'prisoners' that the officials were in the pay of the free trader, or blockade-runner, who was awaiting the arrival of the smugglers and their cargo. This was to be the first of many such slices of luck enjoyed by Robertson, who then simply made himself comfortable as he was ferried to the German coast. Once put ashore it was 'British gold', claimed Robertson, that smoothed his way across the continent as he was moved from safe house to safe house, eventually arriving in Bremen.

The clergyman soon recognised the need to acquire a false identity, and he claims to have written to the parish priest of a German village where one of his fellow Benedictines, then resident in Ireland (a fact unknown to the parish priest) was born. In his letter, under the assumed name of his German colleague, he told the priest that after such a long absence he wished to return 'home' and requested that 'his' birth certificate be sent to him. Once the document arrived our agent felt free to move about without attracting suspicion, having become a fluent speaker of German during his time in Ratisbon. However, when he later applied for a passport his cover was almost blown by making an elemental error when he began to write his true name, rather than his adopted one, on the passport application form he was asked to complete. By a bit of clever explanation to the clerk at the counter, so he claimed, he was able to undo his forgetfulness and avoid suspicion. With his passport in hand he then travelled to Hamburg, and upon presenting a letter of credit for payment in cash to a merchant sympathetic to the British, he learned from him that La Romana was then at Nyborg on the isle of Funen. Robertson also discovered that the Spanish sick were being held at a hospital near Altona, west of Hamburg, and that they were always attended there by a Spanish priest.

When Brother James met with the priest he was referred to a Spanish junior officer, then a patient at the hospital. After explaining his urgent need to make contact with La Romana neither priest nor officer felt they were in a position to help. As a result, the Scottish cleric decided it would be better to return to Bremen and then proceed to Lubeck. It was there where he obtained a passport that would allow him to enter Denmark and travel to Kiel whence, after some negotiations with local people and sailors, he was ferried to the town of Assens on the west coast of Funen. Posing as a merchant, he went about the town taking orders for wine, chocolate and cigars so as to convince people that the purpose of his visit was purely commercial. Here Robertson's story becomes a little confused as he goes on to explain how he later took a ferry from Assens to Funen; but Assens is a small harbour town actually located on the west coast of Funen. He may well have been on the island of Aroe, which is just a short distance off the east coast of Jutland, rather than in the town of Assens, whilst he was going about the business of taking orders for luxury goods. We may perhaps put this lapsus down to a failure of memory at the time of writing his story, or whilst dictating it to his nephew.[2]

---

2   Robertson, *Narrative of a Secret Mission*, p.56.

After finding accommodation at an inn, he had a chance encounter with a colonel belonging to one of La Romana's regiments. Keeping up his pretence to be a merchant in search of customers, the colonel was happy to direct him to places where he might find some of his fellow Spanish officers who would be happy to trade with him, telling him at the same time that La Romana had his headquarters at Nyborg. By another slice of luck on his arrival at Nyborg, Robertson happened to find accommodation at the same inn as that being used by La Romana and his staff.

Robertson's meetings with La Romana

The Scot claimed that he passed a note to the Spanish commander in chief via his French servants, after introducing himself as a merchant, in reply the Spaniard asked to see some samples of the goods he traded in. When they met, Robertson exposed his true identity to the marqués, telling him that he was a Catholic priest sent on a mission to make contact with him. He then spoke to La Romana about their mutual acquaintance, Mr Frere, revealing certain aspects of the long–passed conversation between the British diplomat and the Spaniard, which Frere had revealed to him as a means of convincing the general of his credentials. Robertson then delivered his message and La Romana, seemingly unconvinced of the Scot's authenticity, asked him to return a few days hence for a second interview. At their subsequent meeting the Spaniard insisted that he was ignorant of recent events at home, the cause, he said, being the withholding by the French censors of all personal letters coming from Spain. Unfortunately, Robertson has left us no accurate record of the dates on which the salient events of his adventure occurred, making it difficult to corroborate.

We know that he left England on 6 June 1808, and we are aware that the party of Asturian deputies which sailed for England in the aftermath of the Madrid uprising, left Spain on or about 24 May. We may therefore safely assume that the 12 or 13 days separating those two events provided time enough for the deputies to have travelled to London; as such, when Robertson claims to have mentioned to La Romana the presence of the Spanish deputies in England, we may allow him some credence. We should note however, that he was unable to provide the marqués with the correct names of the Asturians – but claimed that La Romana recognised the ones that he did provide.

The marqués, Robertson tells us, made mention during their conversation of the 'arrival of Joseph' in Spain, and we can only infer from this that the Spaniard was aware of Joseph Bonaparte's proclamation as king of Spain, which took place on 6 June 1808, the day Robertson left England. This may well be the case, knowing as we do that those Spanish officers in regular contact with their French counterparts in Hamburg were able to read in the French press of events passing on the Iberian Peninsula. Having confessed to have heard about the proclamation of Joseph, we may not be far wrong in believing that La Romana must have had at least an inkling of the events which took place in Madrid on and after 2 May. Something does not quite add up; if La Romana knew of Joseph's coronation then surely he would have known something about the events which led to it. Either the cleric was mistaken in claiming that La Romana was aware of Joseph's proclamation as king, or La Romana was not being fully frank with his interlocutor about how much he knew of the recent events in Spain.[3]

In any event, Robertson appears eventually to have convinced La Romana that he was a genuine agent. The Spaniard did not commit himself to anything during this, their second meeting, but promised to write to the Scot at an address in Hamburg, thinking he was about to commence his return journey to England. At the end of the interview Robertson asked if there were any means by which he could be conveyed to one of the British ships then patrolling the nearby waters. The marqués replied that he was unable to help, and at that point their meeting was concluded.

The Scot then goes on to enliven his story with the tale of another close escape. Determined to hitch a ride home with the Royal Navy, he took to walking along the shores of Funen waving his white handkerchief in as surreptitious a manner as possible, in an attempt to catch the attention of the patrolling British ships. In the course of one of these escapades he was apprehended by members of the Danish militia, taken to the local military authorities and interrogated. Once again, he was able to throw off suspicion and was set free by his captors.

According to the cleric, he and La Romana were to meet once more a short time later when the marqués summoned him to his private rooms. It was at this meeting, so the cleric informs us, that the Spaniard gave notice of his formal acceptance of the British plan before bidding his final farewell to the Scot.

The above is but a short précis of Robertson's interesting story, with a little added discussion of some of the many interesting details contained therein, but we may say that our immediate interest in what he had to say has been satisfied; the message he brought from the British government was successfully delivered to La Romana, so we are given to believe; the Spaniard signalled his acceptance of it and the two men met no more. Robertson, though, still had to make his escape from French–occupied Europe, and in his story, he goes on to tell how he made his way to England via a somewhat circuitous route, thus providing the reader with descriptions of the many interesting and amusing incidents which occurred along the way.

Of course, we do not have to take Robertson's account at face value, and to obtain a different perspective of how things unfolded in Denmark during the summer of 1808, we turn to the historian, Elizabeth Sparrow, for an interpretation of events.[4]

---

3   It is worth noting that La Romana's adjutant, Agustín de Llano, having been sent to Madrid on 8 March, left that city on 7 May and arrived back in Nyborg on 24 June 1808, bringing with him news of all events that had passed up until the time of his departure from Spain. We do not know the date of Robertson's meeting with the marqués, but if it happened after the 24 June, then La Romana would have been aware of much that had happened in Spain, certainly up to, and a little beyond, 7 May 1808.

4   Elizabeth Sparrow, *Secret Service. British Agents in France* (London: John Wiley & Sons, 1999).

A Second British Agent in the Baltic

In her version of the story just related, Sparrow claims that Canning was unhappy about the fact that 'outsiders' had interfered in Foreign Office matters by arranging for Robertson to go to Denmark. As a result he decided to engage a third party, a Mr McMahon, on exactly the same mission as that given to the cleric, after the former wrote to him on 24 June 1808 claiming that he had, '… some particulars relating to the Spanish troops in the north of Germany which you and the rest of His Majesty's Ministers may deem worthy of some attention.'[5]

By this time two Asturian deputies, Don Andres Angel de la Vega Infanzon and Don José Maria Queipo de Llano, Conde de Toreno, had arrived in London after escaping from Spain. Knowing this, McMahon suggested that it might help his mission if one of them would provide him with a letter of introduction to some of the Spanish officers they might know to be with La Romana in Denmark, a suggestion they seem to have complied with, and on 15 July Canning provided McMahon with a signed contract for the use of his services.

The newly-contracted agent then travelled to Denmark via Sweden, receiving assistance from the British Consuls in Gothenburg and Helsingborg as he went. He was carrying letters for La Romana from Canning and the Asturian deputies, and it appears that in the course of his wanderings he may well have succeeded in meeting with the marqués before Robertson arrived in Nyborg. In this respect, we should note here something which Robertson claims he asked of the Spaniard on the occasion of their first meeting:

> Excellency, now permit me to ask if any other agent from the British Government has anticipated me, and especially whether any declarations of the Spanish nation have reached your army? I ask this because a person whose domicile is on the continent claims the credit of having conveyed those declarations to your quarters and has actually received the reward which was offered for that service.[6]

From this it would seem that the Scot had an inkling of McMahon's possible presence in Denmark before he himself arrived; how otherwise could anyone have claimed the reward for making contact with the Spaniards in Denmark? Robertson gives the marqués's reply as follows, 'Be assured, there is no truth in this assertion. If any such papers had been dispersed among my troops, they could not have escaped my notice. Yours is the first and only communication of this kind that has reached me either from England or from Spain.'[7]

It would seem that La Romana's reply to Robertson's question was false, and if so, perhaps it was only to be expected. For all he knew, the Scot could easily have been an agent of the French. Robertson and McMahon eventually met in Hamburg, when the Scot was informed by the other that his mission could now be regarded as a success; the Spanish troops, or the greater part

---

5   Sparrow, *Secret Service*, p.363.
6   Robertson, *Narrative of a Secret Mission*, pp.70-71.
7   Robertson, *Narrative of a Secret Mission*, p.71.

of them, by then having been successfully embarked and removed from the Baltic.[8]

We shall see later on that, apart from Robertson's own testimony, there is little evidence to support his claims that he met with the Spanish commander in chief and succeeded in delivering to him the message from the British government. Communication between Rear Admiral Keats and the Spanish forces in Denmark was indeed established, but that came about via the individual efforts of a Spanish junior officer, as we will see. Amongst Keats's papers held at The National Archives in Kew there is no mention of James Robertson, nor is there any suggestion that he was instrumental in bringing the rear admiral into contact with La Romana.

However, there is just one tantalising piece of evidence which might support Robertson's case. *Capitán* Don Agustín de Llano, adjutant to La Romana at Spanish headquarters, includes a footnote to his statement written for the *Comisión de Jefes* in which he states, '*En primeros de Julio, se presentó en Nyborg un emisario inglés disfrazado de capellán ... le preguntó si quería comprar café ...*' ('In early July, an English emissary disguised as a chaplain arrived in Nyborg ... and asked [La Romana] if he would like to buy some coffee ...'). De Llano goes on to describe how the marqués and the 'chaplain' spoke privately and that the subject of their conversation was the message which the 'chaplain' had been commissioned to deliver to the Spaniard, which was that the British were ready to evacuate his army should he wish to cooperate. Further on in his footnote de Llano states that, 'This story was not made public until it had appeared in the English press.' Unfortunately, de Llano is not clear about whether or not he knew of the story before it was made public. In other words, he is unclear about whether or not he witnessed Robertson's visit, or simply read of it sometime later.[9]

---

8   Sparrow, *Secret Service*, p.367.
9   *AGMM, Bailén 7272.2, Memoria de de Llano, 3a* footnote, p.38.

3

The Revolt of La Romana's Army in the Baltic

Bernadotte demands that La Romana's army swear an oath of fealty to Joseph Bonaparte

In Chapter 1 we learned how, on leaving their winter cantonments during the spring of 1808, La Romana's regiments were dispersed to several locations on the islands of Funen, Tassing, Zealand and Langeland, with four units remaining on the Jutland Peninsula. We shall now begin to piece together the sequence of events relating to the revolt of the Spanish forces in the Baltic, making substantial reference to the statements submitted by some of La Romana's officers to the *Comisión de Jefes*, and where appropriate we shall include any interactions they had with British naval forces in the Baltic, whilst attempting to maintain a chronological order to it all.

We shall begin with an extract from the statement of Jose O'Donnell, first adjutant to the Marqués de La Romana:

> At the beginning of June 1808, Bernadotte moved his headquarters from Odense on Funen to Rendsburg in Schleswig, taking with him the regiment of French infantry which had accompanied him in the former place. It was as though our lucky star had inspired him with such an idea in order to open the way for us to return home, as his actions left us in more or less full control of the islands of Funen and Langeland, there being no more than a regiment of Danish infantry on the former and just a regiment of Danish cavalry on the latter, the great bulk of the Danish army being stationed on the island of Zealand.
>
> As the French newspapers continued to circulate amongst us in abundance, we were able to read what they said about the events which had taken place in Bayonne, that is the renunciation of the Spanish crown by Fernando; the scenes of horror [which had occurred in Madrid] on 2 May 1808; the internment of our royal family in France and about the nomination of Joseph Bonaparte as King of Spain … Then, from about the middle of May, we noticed that the few letters which reached us from home had all been opened but did not contain any news that might alarm us. However, it was at that time when the British began furtively to send us newspapers which provided us with more detailed news.

Once Bernadotte discovered what was going on he did all that he could to stop it, ordering that even an approaching flag of truce should be fired upon by the shore batteries, which were garrisoned by Danish troops.

This was the state of things when, in mid-June, a messenger sent from Bernadotte's headquarters arrived at La Romana's residence, bringing with him some items of 'official' news together with some documentation relating to the recognition of Joseph Bonaparte [as king of Spain] and the swearing of an oath of fealty by the members of the *Cortes de Bayona* to the intruder, as he was known to the Spanish nation.[1] The courier also brought an order from Bernadotte that La Romana's troops must take an equivalent oath of fealty to their new king.

The resultant crisis was both delicate and awful ... The idea of La Romana rejecting Bernadotte's demand out of hand would have been be the same as rendering both himself and our troops prisoners of war. As such he wanted to temporize; to entertain Bernadotte with observations and evasive answers, but there was to be no remedy, he would have to order his men to take an oath of fealty. The marqués then published the news [on Funen and Langeland] together with the order he had received from Bernadotte, and sent copies to Kindelán on Jutland in order that he force the troops under his command to take the oath as stipulated. [Kindelán carried out his orders in the face of] many instances of open insubordination and signs of discontent amongst his men.[2]

Bernadotte's order to La Romana read as follows:

Sr. Marqués,
I have the honour to send you twenty copies of the Spanish Constitution approved by the Junta [de Bayona] and the [new] king. His Majesty received the swearing [of an oath of fealty] during the most recent session of the Junta, and has since left [Vitoria] for Madrid. He was [earlier] escorted to the Spanish frontier, and as his journey [into Spain] continued he was received with great acclamation ...

According to the orders I have received, we will be doing the right thing in having all of the troops of your division swear an oath of fealty to King Joseph Bonaparte ... You will prepare a script for each ceremony [one for each of the scattered units of La Romana's army] ... The [version of the] script to be followed by the staff at your Headquarters will take a particular form ...

[Once the individual ceremonies have been completed,] all of the [signed] scripts will be sent to my Headquarters.[3]

As we can see from the order above, La Romana was expected to draft a document defining both the oath and the form of the ceremony by which it would be taken.

---

1   *Cortes de Bayona*: the assembly of Spanish deputies gathered to witness and sign a new Spanish constitution dictated by Napoleon and Joseph Bonaparte.
2   AGMM, Bailén 7272.2, *Memoria de O'Donnell*, pp.5–7.
3   Author's translation of Bernadotte's order to La Romana as reproduced by Cassinello in *El Capitán General*, pp.69–70, under ref. T. C10 (49). Note, from the format of the reference identifier it would seem that the article referred to is held in the La Romana family's private archive, to which Cassinello had access whilst writing his life of the marqués.

THE REVOLT OF LA ROMANA'S ARMY IN THE BALTIC

Fernando Mijares provides a similar picture of events at Spanish headquarters to that of O'Donnell:

> Accounts of the events surrounding 2 May came to us via the newspapers, and by that same source we came to know about the movement of the Royal Family to France. By this time our correspondence from Spain had been completely stopped …
>
> A few days later we found out about the nomination of Joseph as king of Spain, and of the oath of fealty that had been taken by the so–called Court of Bayonne. This was quickly followed by a demand from Bernadotte that all of the Spaniards in Denmark should take the same oath …
>
> The Marqués de La Romana confided his feelings amongst a very small number of his officers, and although he wanted to refuse the oath outright, sheer prudence obliged him to entertain Bernadotte with some evasive replies in order to play for time, however this delaying tactic did not last for long, and on the arrival of a second letter he found within it an unconditional order to have his men take the oath without further procrastination …[4]

Realising that he would have to submit to the French demands, La Romana and his staff decided to draft a document which would avoid a full and explicit pledge of fealty to the new king, and Miguel Paez de la Cadena, *Auditor* of the army, inserted a clause stating that the Spanish troops would take an oath only of the kind which the 'Greater and most sane part of the Spanish nation' would be willing to take. Once this change had been inserted, copies of the document were sent out to each of La Romana's units.

In his statement to the commission, Agustín de Llano is somewhat more expansive in his explanation of events at this juncture. He mentions his return from Spain on 24 June in company with Don Martín de la Carrera and *Teniente-Coronel* Aylmer of Zamora, all three having been eyewitnesses to the events in Madrid on 2 May. He then informs the commissioners of Bernadotte's obsequiousness when communicating orders to La Romana that he have his troops swear an oath of fealty to Joseph Bonaparte:

> [For most of the month of July 1808, the army was resting quietly in its cantons, and that's how things were] when the Commander of Bernadotte's Personal Guard, Franco,[5] arrived [at headquarters in Nyborg] bringing with him the *Croix de la Légion d'Honneur* for La Romana, having already delivered another to Kindelán on the Jutland Peninsula; both awards having been conferred upon the officers by Napoleon. Franco also brought with him a superb pair of pistols which were a personal gift to La Romana from Bernadotte,[6] but the real items of business he brought were strict orders from Bernadotte that the marqués should make no attempt to open communications with the British …

---

4   *AGMM, Bailén 7272.2, Memoria de Mijares*, pp.5–7.
5   Bernadotte retained a personal guard made up exclusively of soldiers from the regiment of Zamora a unit belonging to La Romana's army.
6   La Romana later presented the pistols to Rear Admiral Keats when he went aboard HMS *Superb*.

A few days later we received news of the arrival of Joseph Bonaparte at Vitoria after having travelled from Bayonne, and a little later Bernadotte sent orders to the marqués that, in imitation of the *Junta de Bayona* which represented the national will [of Spain], he should follow his earlier instructions and have his army take an oath of fealty to King Joseph, and that the act of doing so should be executed with full solemnity …

The same orders were sent to the regiments of Asturias and Guadalajara on Zealand and also to Kindelán on Jutland so that they could be carried out by the troops under his command, these were the regiments of Zamora, Rey, Infante and Algarve. But Kindelán did not inform La Romana that he had received orders directly from Bernadotte, let alone that he intended to carry them out. The first the marqués knew of it was when he heard that the units on Jutland had carried out the extrajudicial order without opposition, Kindelán having told them that La Romana, his staff at headquarters and his troops [on Funen], had already taken the oath without raising any objections, adding that there could not be any complaint against such a just cause. Deceived in this way, what alternative did Kindelán's men have? Nevertheless, there was a strong reaction from his troops and there were signs of imminent subordination to such an extent that, if Kindelán had not issued a delicate reminder to them of their duty to La Romana, things would have gotten completely out of hand, thus exposing our whole plan [of escape] to the risk of complete disaster. In fact, when Franco [still present on Jutland after delivering Bernadotte's order to Kindelán] attempted to pacify the troops, he was forced to flee for his life …

But who could deny that providence had taken a hand in this affair? In the end the men of Zamora, Rey and Infante were able to return to Spain, but had their disobedience continued, surrounded as they were by strong French forces, they could have been subjected to the most terrible punishment in very short time, and lost for ever.[7]

It is worth noting that Mijares claimed that, after dispatching the orders for the ceremony to his units in the field, the marqués began to think that, should the troops put up any resistance to the demands placed upon them, they may well react in a way which would put an end to any hopes of salvation. This was probably the reason why he decided to visit several of his formations in person in an attempt to ensure their compliance with his instructions. In fact, Mijares claims that the troops on Jutland, who were not visited by La Romana, behaved in precisely the manner the marqués feared they might, but were brought to order before things got entirely out of hand, as described in his statement above, which continues:

The marqués, [unaware of what had taken place on Jutland] began to worry that his troops [on Funen and Langeland] might put up some measure of resistance to the idea that they take an oath of loyalty to Joseph, depending on the circumstances under which it was asked of them. As such, he sent his most trusted adjutants (I myself having the honour of being amongst them) to the cantons where they were

---

7 *AGMM, Bailén 7272.2, Memoria de de Llano*, pp.9–10.

to be found, each carrying orders to let it be known, carefully, to the local chiefs and officers, that the oath was of no great importance, but that a refusal to accept it would be to deny, absolutely, all hopes of our being able to return to Spain.[8]

The reader will have already noticed some subtle differences between the various statements submitted to the *Comisión de Jefes*, which is only to be expected when one considers that they were written some ten years after the events which took place in Denmark. But as we continue with our story, we will see that such differences tend to be in the fine detail, rather than the main substance of their content – with one exception, which we shall now examine by introducing a somewhat controversial figure into the Denmark story.

Ambrosio de la Quadra was the *sargento-mayor* of the 1er Catalunya, a rank which was equivalent to that of a major in the British army of today. Despite playing a significant role in the successful evacuation of La Romana's army from the Baltic, Quadra was not invited to submit a statement to the *Comisión de Jefes* in 1818, and there may be good reasons as to why that was the case. Shortly after his return to Spain from Denmark he wrote an account of events in the Baltic. Signed and dated 12 December 1808 it now resides in the *Archivos Generales de Servicio Histórico Militar* in Madrid. A complete facsimile of the document was published in two parts in the 1992 editions of the *Revista de Historia Militar* (a bi-annual publication produced by the *Gobierno de España, Ministerio de Defensa*). Quadra's missive provides a less than heroic picture of the state of things at La Romana's headquarters during the early stages of the revolt by the Spanish troops, and deserves some scrutiny.

His account of the Denmark operation begins by citing an order sent by La Romana to all of his units in Denmark which, in essence, informed his troops that the Bourbon Kings of Spain had decided to abdicate in favour of Joseph Bonaparte, and as a consequence the Spanish army's oath of loyalty to Carlos IV no longer applied, but, continued La Romana, Spain would prosper greatly under its new king. The order (a copy of which is attached to Quadra's statement) ends with a request that, after reading it, all senior officers should reply to the marqués, informing him of their own response to its content and the reaction of their subordinates to it. At this point in his statement Quadra opines that, judging by the sly and underhanded manner of both the content and intent of the order, and bearing in mind the eventual conduct of La Romana, one could see the flawed ingenuity that was the hallmark of the *Intendente*, Lazero de Heras, at work, together with that of his nephew, the *Escribiente del Estado Mayor* (Scribe of the General Staff) stating in a footnote to his document that, 'The dominance that the *Intendente* had over the marqués was of public notoriety …' But as he proceeds with his statement he does begin to express some doubts about the strength of La Romana's character.

Quadra goes on to say that, during the days which followed, Bernadotte's courier, *Colonel* Viliat, arrived at Nyborg bringing a 'suggestion' that La Romana issue a proclamation of loyalty to Joseph in the name of the Spanish troops. Despite the strong opposition of many at Spanish headquarters to

---

8   *AGMM, Bailén 7272.2, Memoria de Mijares*, p.6.

such a proposal, Heras suggested that marqués should produce a statement, 'full of adulation [for Joseph] along with other falsities,' knowing that the intention was to have it published in Hamburg. It was at this point, claims Quadra, that the spirit of the those present began to turn and La Romana, he admits, refused to make the proclamation suggested by Heras, composing instead a somewhat anodyne version, which Bernadotte was still happy to publish in the Hamburg press.[9]

Quadra claims that this initial obsequiousness of La Romana was the cause of Bernadotte's next demand, which was that the Spanish troops take an oath of fealty to King Joseph. This process, he says, was set in train when Don José Jacinto Franco of Zamora was sent from Hamburg to Kindelán's headquarters on Jutland, bringing orders for him to carry out the swearing of the oath by all Spanish troops on the peninsula. After a conversation between Franco and Kindelán one of the latter's officers, Don Luis Ciran, was ordered to present the same order to La Romana at Nyborg with regard to the troops on Funen and Langeland, before going on to deliver the same message to Spanish headquarters on Zealand. There is not much that is new here, but what Quadra says next is the crux of the matter, when he claims that 'the fatal influence of Heras, his ambition and the weak character of the Marqués' were, from this point on, almost the cause of the total humiliation of the army in Denmark:

> [T]hese men, wanting only to please the French, from whom they thought there was much to fear and more to expect, intended to carry out all [of Bernadotte's demands] with the utmost precipitation and no less reserve ... They locked themselves away together with the scribe and the general's secretary, and put together a paper which would serve as the formula [for the swearing of the oath] which was then circulated to the troops, together with an order to carry it out. Within three hours of his arrival, Ciran had been sent on his way to Zealand with a copy of the order for the Spanish units there based, such was the hurry [to conform with French demands].'[10]

La Romana visits his units on Funen and Langeland

Whilst Kindelán was haranguing his men on Jutland, La Romana was visiting his own units on Funen and Langeland to oversee their swearing of the oath. This must have been a difficult duty for the marqués, forced, as he was by Bernadotte's orders, to wear his formal uniform which was by then emblazoned with the *Légion d'Honneur*, and knowing that any expression of

---

9   Ambrosio de la Quadra, *Memorias de los Acontecimientos en el Ejército de Dinamarca, desde los Primeros Rumores de la Abicación de la Corona de España y Congreso de Bayona, hasta la Salida de las Tropas Españoles de aquel Reyno* (henceforth, *Acontecimientos de Quadra*) *Revista de Historia Militar* (Valladolid: Simancas Ediciones, no.72, 1er semestre, 1992 and no.73, 2o *semestre*, 1992) (henceforth RHM, no.**, ** *semestre*, 1992) no.72, 1er semestre 1992 pp.233–234.

10 *Acontecimientos de Quadra*, RHM, no.72, 1er semestre, 1992, pp.239–241.

antagonism towards the French on his part could result in the loss of all hope of escape, surrounded as he was by a number of French spies.

When the Conde de San Román demanded that the men of the 1er batallón de Princesa, one of his own battalions then based at Nyborg, take the oath, there was much insubordination, and there would be a similar reaction from the men of the Artillería on the following day when La Romana and his retinue visited them at Kerteminde. The regiment of Almansa showed an even greater level of disgust when assembled at Odense to take the oath, some of the men making threats of violence towards the significant number of French who were looking on. News of what was happening began to run ahead of the marqués and his staff, and when they arrived at Middelfart to demand submission to the oath from the 3er batallón de Princesa and the company of Zapadores who were stationed there, the mutiny almost ran out of control. San Román, a much-respected officer, was again present but not even he could impose himself upon the situation, having to suffer the ignominy of open insubordination and threats. When it came to the turn of the Zapadores they simply marched off, fully armed and equipped, to take possession of the small islet where they had been carrying out some works. They had earlier secreted some small boats there which they then boarded and went off in search of the ships of the Royal Navy. In almost every case, the only means of getting the various units eventually to comply was to make alterations to both the oath and the form of the ceremony.

There was to be no sleep for La Romana that night. He was in an unenviable position, the situation was fraught with danger and he must have been wondering when the French would react, knowing as he did that Bernadotte would by now be fully aware of the events of the last two days. De Llano claims that, on the following morning, the marqués was visited by 'an extraordinary Spaniard' who had been despatched by Urquijo from Bayonne with the definitive news that Joseph Bonaparte had been crowned King of Spain.[11] At this point La Romana must have been thinking that things could not get any worse. Later that morning he travelled the short distance to Assens where the 2o batallón de Princesa was cantoned, and once he had set eyes upon his soldiers and read in their faces the abject resignation to their situation, his spirits fell. The oath of fealty was dragged from them, but once again only after some amendments had been made to the formal text, the men agreeing to swear loyalty only to '…that power which the whole nation would recognise and swear loyalty to.'

In an effort to avoid, or at least delay, the inevitable reaction from Bernadotte, La Romana wrote to him in an attempt to mitigate the behaviour of his men when pressed to take the oath, and after despatching the courier he moved on to the south-east corner of Funen with the intention of pressing the oath upon the regiment of Villaviciosa at Faaborg and the 1er de Barcelona which was at Svendborg, only to meet with more resistance from

---

11 Don Mariano Luis de Urquijo y Muga had by this time been appointed as King Joseph Bonaparte's Minister of Exterior Relations. It is thought that the despatch he sent to La Romana contained reiterated demands that the marqués force his men to swear the oath of allegiance to the new king.

the troops and their officers. This left only the 1er de Catalunya to visit and they were cantoned on the nearby island of Langeland. The marqués and his staff made the short crossing and forced yet another adulterated form of the oath of fealty from the lips of the Catalans, this in full view of the French commander, Gauthier, and with two artillery pieces loaded with shrapnel aimed at the ranks of the men.

Exhausted and demoralised, the Marqués de La Romana led his party of officers and adjutants back to headquarters at Nyborg. It was now time for them to take the oath, as insisted upon by Bernadotte. After an emotional meeting a final and yet again altered form of the oath was taken by them all.

Quadra's description of what happened on Funen and Langeland as La Romana attempted to get his troops to agree to take the oath is similar to the generally accepted version presented above, but with a few important caveats. He agrees that the reactions of the various units had resulted in a variety of local versions of the oath having to be drawn up, but goes on to claim that when La Romana returned to headquarters with the various doctored versions of the document, after his second day spent touring the headquarters of his battalions, Heras took fright and decided to draw up yet another version of it, this one for the officers of the *Estado Mayor*. It was at this point where things began to go badly wrong for the marqués and Heras. As soon as the Conde de San Román, *Coronel* of the 1er Princesa, became aware that the *Estado Mayor* had signed a version of the formula that was different from that signed by his men, he threatened to rebel should he or his men be held to the formula adopted by La Romana's staff. At this, the marqués demanded that all formulas in circulation be handed in and that a new one be written which would be acceptable to all of his regiments.

When Bernadotte discovered what had happened, he sent Viliat to Nyborg once again, demanding that La Romana put all in order and have his men sign a new and final version of the formula without restrictions or deletions. Sensing the seriousness of the situation they were in, claims Quadra, La Romana fell into a state of dismay, 'declared himself to be ill and retired to his private quarters, refusing to see anyone.'[12] It was not long before Heras adopted a similar line, terrified at the thought of how things might evolve:

> Everywhere there was uneasiness and silence. The melancholy and taciturnity at the general's table, from which both the marqués and Heras were absent, was palpable and noted by Viliat, who felt himself threatened by those around him. In this situation there were plenty who, seeing the state of things and aware of how tumultuous would be the results of any of the measures which might be taken, searched for a way to talk to La Romana, who was by then was depressed, extremely deflated, self-absorbed and indecisive. [His officers] tried to convince him that there was no need for such irresolution and that it was not the time to give up hope. As his staff attempted to get him to think about what he should do next, Paez was the one, on this occasion as on many others, who advised La

---

12   *Acontecimientos de Quadra*, RHM, no.72, 1er semestre, 1992, p.249.

Romana that he should always follow the most decorous path ... The marqués, as usual, readily agreed with his ideas. Though Paez's wise propositions remained in favour with La Romana only until his next meeting with Heras.[13]

From this point on Quadra's account of events is in almost full agreement with those who submitted statements to the *Comisión de Jefes*. But before deciding just how truthful Quadra's description of things at Nyborg was, it is as well to point out the he was not present at Spanish headquarters during the time that the events he describes above took place, as he was with his own regiment on Langeland. And then there is the question of his activities during the eventual execution of the operation to evacuate the Spaniards. As we shall see, it would seem that he made a significant contribution to the success of the mission, but does his self-told story exaggerate his achievements? Quadra's commanding officer and chief of the 1er Catalunya, *Teniente-Coronel* Dionisio Vives, whilst in communication with another veteran and senior Spanish officer some ten years after the events, felt so strongly about what his fellow correspondent claimed was Quadra's role in the Denmark story, in fact an almost verbatim repetition of the claims made by Quadra himself, that he corrected him, pointing out that it was he who did some of the things Quadra claimed the credit for, and there is some incontrovertible corroboration of Vives's version of what actually happened on Langeland, as we shall see when examining the statement made by Fabregues for Keats.

When it was clear that any further attempts to extract an oath of loyalty from lips of the Spanish soldiers would fail, spirits at headquarters sank lower than ever. The various units were scattered across large areas of the Danish Baltic provinces, in many cases separated from each other by wide tracts of water, and Bernadotte had some 26,000 men at his immediate disposal, ready and waiting for any signs of insurrection from their erstwhile allies. All of this at a time when those of the Spanish contingent based at Nyborg had the British frigates in full view, as they lay at anchor in the approaches to the harbour. It was, as Agustín de Llano described it, 'a unique and terrible situation.'[14] In this state of desperation Bernadotte decided to turn up the heat on La Romana, but before continuing with the situation on Funen and Langeland, we shall turn to the events which took place on Zealand when the Spanish troops there were instructed to take the oath.

Events on Zealand according to Santiago Miquel

When looking at events on Zealand we shall refer to the statement submitted to the *Comisión de Jefes* by *Teniente* Santiago Miquel of the regiment of Asturias, and to the personal accounts of what took place there written by *Sargento* Manuel López, also of Asturias, and *Capitán* Rafael de Llanza of Guadalajara. Neither of López's and Llanza's stories come in the form of a statement to the *Comisión de Jefes*. In López's case testimony is to be found

---

13 *Acontecimientos de Quadra*, RHM, no.72, 1er semestre, 1992, p.249.
14 AGMM, Bailén 7272.2, Memoria de de Llano, pp.11–15.

in a paper he wrote, which was later to be submitted to the French national archives by *Maréchal* Soult in 1840.[15] In Llanza's case testimony comes from a diary he kept during and after his service with La Romana's Ejército del Norte (Army of the North, as the Baltic Spaniards were sometimes referred to) extracts from which appear in *Un Español en el Ejército de Napoleón. Diario de Rafael de Llanza y de Valls*, published in 2008. We shall begin with Miquel at the point where he talks about, 'The critical situation of the two regiments of the vanguard present on the island of Zealand' when:

> A Frenchmen employed at Bernadotte's Headquarters, who had formerly been in the Spanish services as an officer with the regiment of Asturias,[16] arrived carrying a collection of documents for *Général de Brigade* Fririon.[17] As soon as he entered the town of Roskilde, he became surrounded by some of his erstwhile fellow officers, all of them keen to discover if he had brought any news from Spain, and attempting to discover the reason for his visit. His replies to their promptings were both insignificant and mysterious, and created a sense of suspicion. The documents he was carrying were soon inspected and an order dated that same day, 31 July, was discovered amongst them. This contained instructions for Fririon to have the regiments of Asturias and Guadalajara formed behind their colours at midday on the following day, 1 August, so that all could take an oath of fealty and obedience to the new king, Joseph Napoleon. It is impossible to describe the level of general irritation caused amongst the Spaniards by this discovery, and as word spread quickly to the camp and to headquarters, a kind of revolution had begun to develop by four o'clock that afternoon.[18]

Miquel goes on to describe how, despite the best efforts of the *brigadier-coronel* of Asturias, Dellevielleuze, who tried to calm the men by telling them that the same orders had been received and carried out by the Marqués de La Romana with respect to the rest of the regiments of his division, they could not be brought to a state of order. Dellevielleuze then resorted to the threat that any soldiers found on the streets after regimental prayers that evening would be shot, something which only intensified the anger of the men to such an extent that he was forced to make a dash to Fririon's headquarters to warn him of the impending danger, as his men, fully armed, followed behind. During the tumultuous scenes which then followed at French headquarters, two of Fririon's junior subalterns, Laloy and Marabail, who strayed unknowingly into the melee, were immediately set upon. Before they could gather their wits and attempt to escape, Laloy was killed and Marabail badly injured by the enraged Spaniards; their officers unable to intervene

---

15 Manuel López, *Précis historique des actions ou se sont trouves les 2e et 3e bataillons du Régiment Joseph–Napoleon avec la 2e division du 1er corps de la Grande Armée dont ils on fait partie pendant la derniere campagne*. Although Boppe informs his readers that López's *Précis* was submitted to the French Archives de la Guerre, the author's efforts to trace it have so far been fruitless. The search will go on, but in the meantime all subsequent references to López's work will take the form: 'López's précis as cited by Boppe in *Les Espagnols*, pp.x–y'.
16 Identified as Don Luis Ciran, Conde de Yoldi.
17 François Nicolas Fririon, in command of French and Spanish forces on Zealand, 1808.
18 *AGMM, Bailén 7272.2, Memoria de Santiago Miquel*, pp.3–4.

to prevent the excesses. In fact, at one point, Dellevielleuze himself was threatened as he tried to appease his men, appealing to them from the open windows of Fririon's chateau and assuring them that the order to take an oath of fealty to Joseph Bonaparte had been revoked, but they reacted by calling for him to come out as they readied themselves to storm the building.

Fririon, in no doubt about the danger he was in, decided to make his escape. After gathering his staff together, the group of Frenchmen made their way across the roof of the chateau to an adjoining chapel, all the time under fire from the Spaniards below. There they managed to acquire some Danish uniforms, which they donned as quickly as they could, before being helped on their way to Copenhagen to seek refuge and inform the King of Denmark of what had happened. Miquel continues:

> Knowing that Fririon had escaped, the Spanish troops conceived the idea of making their way to the nearest port where they thought they might be able to embark, despite the fact that they were some 500 leagues from home; that the rest of the division was not in a position to help them; that they had had no communication with the British, and that there was a Danish army of some 30,000 men on the island. They had not travelled very far when they came up against a Danish division sent by the king to re-establish order at Roskilde, after he had heard of the events which had taken place there … Some Danish officers came forward and told the Spaniards that their king had some sympathy for them, was pleased that the Spanish had respected his subjects, and that henceforth they may consider him to be at their service, offering them his protection should they return peacefully to their encampment…
>
> Three days later, on 3 August, we struck camp on the orders of the king of Denmark and the three battalions [of Asturias] were directed to the towns of Ringsted, Soro[?], Slagel[se] and their neighbouring hamlets, where they were later sub-divided into companies and half companies on the pretext of finding them suitable accommodation.[19]

Events on Zealand according to Rafael de Llanza

Rafael de Llanza left Barcelona on 3 January 1806 as a captain in the infantry regiment of Guadalajara, his unit having been selected to participate in La Romana's expedition to Denmark. It would be some eight years before he saw his beloved homeland of Catalunya once more. Thankfully, he has left us the story of much of the latter part of his service during those eight years.[20] He also kept a diary detailing the early days of his service under La Romana which, he claims, amounted to some 300 pages and covered all of the time he spent in Denmark. Sadly, this was lost during his transportation to France as a prisoner of war in 1808, during the aftermath of La Romana's escape from the Baltic. We will be revisiting his story in later chapters, but before we do

---

19 AGMM, Bailén 7272.2, Memoria de Miquel, p.5.
20 Ignacio Fernández de Bobadilla (ed.) *Un Español en el Ejercito de Napoleon. Diario de Rafael de Llanza y de Valls* (Madrid: Almena Ediciónes, 2008).

so we shall examine a few words from him relating to the days leading up to and immediately following the Royal Navy's embarkation of the Spanish troops at Nyborg in August 1808. They describe the events which took place on Zealand up to and immediately after the sacking of Fririon's headquarters:

> The King of Denmark made arrangements for the six battalions [of Guadalajara and Asturias] to establish camp in the vicinity of Roskilde during the months of July and August [1808], and it was to become more a place of diversion for the royal family and court than a military camp. Exercises, games, banquets and dances were regular events at our base.
>
> It was during this time that the Spanish people were struggling to break free from the chains which their allies were attempting to place them in, but we knew nothing about it, as the French press was presenting a picture that reflected a desire of the Spanish population to place themselves under the yoke. In light of this, and despite our situation, our spirits became more restless with each passing day, and it was in this state of anxiety that the Marqués de La Romana was to receive an order that [his] regiments swear an oath of fealty to the King of Spain, that is, to Joseph Bonaparte.
>
> [Spanish headquarters at Nyborg distributed the order to all outlying units, and it] arrived [at Spanish headquarters, Roskilde] at midday on 31 July. At three o'clock our troops attacked the palace being used by *Général de Brigade* Fréant [*sic* for Fririon] as his headquarters…[21] When the Danish king received notice of what had happened … he set off from Copenhagen with a force of 10,000 men … to halt the Spaniards, believing that they were marching on the city…
>
> On 2 August an order was received instructing our commanders to strike camp and send the battalions to different points in the north of the island … Once at their destinations they were divided into companies before being dispersed to various locations on Zealand; my eventual destination being the palace of Kregerup [*sic* for Kagerup]. This was how we were to remain until the 11th, ignorant of any news from the Isle of Funen where our general was stationed, and fearing his arrival at any moment with the intention to impose severe punishments upon us for the events of 31 July when we had refused to obey his orders. Then, very early on the 11th, we received orders to re-assemble the battalion and march it to a given location so that it could be inspected by His Majesty … When we arrived at the stipulated place, we discovered five or six thousand [Danish] infantry and a corresponding number of cavalry and artillery awaiting us.
>
> We formed the battalion in order of battle and almost immediately General the Prince of Hesse intimated that, by order of the king, we were to surrender our arms. This piece of news came as a shock to all of us. We obeyed his directions and then asked under which cause, or for what crime, he had placed us in such a situation. He replied that, 'His Majesty has taken the right to make reprisals against you because the Marqués de La Romana has surrendered the isle of Funen to the enemy [the British]. He has also surrendered himself and his army. However, His Majesty, in consideration that you have taken no part in that enormous crime,

---

21   Llanza mistakenly uses the name Fréant in his diary. It is more than likely that he was confusing the names of *Générals* Fririon and Friant, having served under both: Fririon in Denmark and Friant in Russia.

THE REVOLT OF LA ROMANA'S ARMY IN THE BALTIC

has promised that you will be treated with the greatest respect.' With these words the Danes forced us aboard a number of wagons and took us [the officers] to the town of Risted [*sic* for Ringsted] the men of the battalion being marched to the Arsenal at Copenhagen.

The men of Asturias and Guadalajara were to remain in their present situation on Zealand for some days to come, so we shall leave them for now and return to events on Funen and Jutland, before learning what next became of them.

The Reconnaissance Mission of *Capitán* Fernando Mijares

It would seem that, after witnessing the reaction of his troops to the idea of taking an oath of allegiance to Joseph Bonaparte, La Romana realised that he might be forced to mount an operation to remove his army from Denmark, if not there would be a strong possibility of a clash between the Spaniards and the overwhelmingly superior forces available to the French and Danes. The widely dispersed situation of his units would weaken La Romana's ability to fight a viable action, and if they could not be concentrated his enemies would be able simply to attack each isolated corps in turn and destroy the Spanish army in detail. If he had to fight it would be better to unite his forces, and in making such a move, should it be successful, it would also facilitate an embarkation of his men if he could come to an agreement with the British. There is ample evidence in Fernando Mijares's statement to the *Comisión de Jefes* to suggest that the marqués was already thinking along these lines by 1 August:

> Very early on the morning of 2 August, I was summoned by La Romana and he said to me the following words, or similar. 'Last night I advised the Conde de San Román that I would like to make a trip to Middelfart and Bogense to inspect the second and third battalions of his regiment, in order to observe how their spirits were after the stormy scenes relating to the swearing of the oath. My aim, in reality, is not this, but to charge you with a commission which you must carry out with the greatest success and secrecy. To achieve all that I want it is necessary that you, as a friend of the Conde de San Román, manage the affair in a manner such that the license I am actually seeking, he will ask me for,[22] but under any circumstances be [back] here by lunch time so that the affair can be more easily handled; supposing, that is, that San Román would like to lunch with me.'
>
> It didn't take much to convince San Román to allow me to accompany him on a journey to have lunch with La Romana, a journey he would otherwise have had to make by himself, and [on the way to Nyborg] I proposed to him that he ask La Romana if I could carry out the planned inspection of his second and

---

[22] That is to say, La Romana needed San Román to ask him if Mijares could review his troops, rather than put himself to the trouble. If La Romana were to ask San Román to allow Mijares, a junior officer, to review his troops, it would represent a huge breach of etiquette. Essentially, La Romana simply needed a pretext for sending Mijares on a secret mission, and he needed San Román to inadvertently ask for that pretext – so that he could send Mijares to the west of Funen without attracting suspicion – by asking him if Mijares could inspect his troops in place of the marqués himself. Note, the underlining in the text is the author's emphasis, it does not appear in the original.

third battalions instead of La Romana himself. When, during our lunch together, San Román made his proposal, La Romana feigned disgust at the suggestion that he should give me such permission, [pretending that he wanted to carry out the inspection in person] but in the end 'acceded' to San Román's request. The marqués then granted me the necessary license to leave headquarters but only for four days – apparently at the insistence of San Román with some support from O'Donnell who, I supposed, was party to the secret mission I was about to undertake, as he rightly commanded the utmost confidence of the marqués.[23]

Once lunch was over [and we were alone] La Romana said to me, '[whilst you are away] I want you to reconnoitre the coast of the Little Belt from Middelfart to Bogense, noting with care those points which will allow for an easy disembarkation, particularly opposite Fredericia, and also the number of boats, more or less, to be found in Fredericia. I charge you to work in the utmost secrecy and exactness during your reconnaissance, and to carry it out without giving away any sign of what you are doing.'[24]

Obviously, it would have been impossible for La Romana to have carried out such a mission without attracting suspicion, hence his convoluted plan to place Mijares in a position to do it in his place. By the time Mijares returned from his mission, some four days later, he would find that La Romana's somewhat sedate progress towards instigating a plan for escape had been overtaken by events.

Bernadotte demands that the Spanish troops re-take the oath of fealty

On 6 August an adjutant of the Prince de Pontecorvo arrived at Spanish headquarters in Nyborg, presented himself to the marqués, and handed him a letter from Bernadotte which was full of threats. The French prince had heard of the insubordination of the Spaniards when instructed swear loyalty to Joseph Bonaparte, and was having none of it. He demanded that La Romana have his men re-take the oath in its official and formalised structure, without alterations or restrictions of any sort. He then issued a direct criticism to La Romana, telling him that generals do not make excuses (he had obviously read the letter which the marqués sent him whilst at Assens) and suggested that the application of firm discipline would not allow such disobedience. He then went on to say that he was aware of the causes of the trouble and reminded the Spaniard that he should make an example of those responsible if they did not mend their ways. The marqués now found himself in a most awkward situation; how was he going to tell his troops to submit, wholly and finally, to the French yoke? This was his darkest moment, and with all seemingly lost he was about to be the recipient of some startling news.

---

23   It would seem that this was a ploy to ensure Mijares's swift return to Nyborg to report on his findings.
24   *AGMM, Bailén 7272.2, Memoria de Mijares*, p.9.

<u>Cuerpo auxiliar ó División del Norte</u>

Estado q.e manifiesta la fuerza aproximada de cada uno de los Cuerpos que lo componian, y la posicion que ocupavan en Dinamarca a fines de Julio 1808.

Cuerpos	Fuerza aproxim.^d hombs.	Cavallos	Situacion
Reg.to Infant.a de Zamora	2.160		Sus tres Bat.s estavan en Fredericia en el Jutland, con el Gen.l Kindelan
Reg.to Inf.a de Guadalaxara	2.160		En la costa occidental de la Isla de Seeland, con 6 Batallones.
Reg.to Inf.a de Asturias	2.160		
Reg.to Inf.a de la Princessa	2.160		1.er Bat. en Nyborg – 2.o en Kierteminde, y 3.o en Middelfart; todo en Fionia.
Bat.on Ligero 1.o de Cataluña	1.200		En Rudkiobin, Isla de Langeland
Bat.on Ligero 1.o de Barcelona	1.200		En Swemborg, Isla de Fionia.
Reg.to Cavall.a del Rey	560	500	En Aarhuus, en el Jutland
Reg.to Cavall.a del Infante	560	500	En Randers, Id.m
Reg.to Cavall.a de Algarve	560	500	En Horsens, Id.m
Reg.to Dragones de Almanza	560	500	En Odensé, Capital de Fionia
Reg.to Drag.s de Villaviciosa	560	500	En Faaborg y Assens – Id. de Fionia
Una Comp.a de Art.a a Cavallo con 6 piez.	90	70	De estas 18 piez.s las 6 estavan embarcadas p.a pasar a la isla de Seeland, 6 en Swemborg, y las restantes en el Quart.l Gen.l
Dos Comp.s de Bat.on con 6 piez. cada una	180		
Una Comp.a de Zapadores	100		En el Quart.l Gral de Nyborg.
Total	14.210	2.570	

<u>Plana Mayor</u>

General en Jefe............El Ten.te Gral Marques de la Romana
General en 2.o............El Mar.l de campo D.n Juan Kindelan......En el Jutland

1.er Ayud.te Grales del E. M.
Cor.l efectivo de Infant.a D.n Ign.o Martinez Vallejo; encargado del E. M.
Cor.l ef.vo de Cavall.a D.n Juan Cavallero.
Brig.r de Artill.a D.n José Montes Salazar
T. Coronel de Ingen.s D.n Mig.l Rengel

2.o Ayud.te Grales del E. M.
El Ten.te Cor.l efecto de Infant.a D.n José O'Donnell
De Cavall.a D.n N.
El Cap.n de Art.a D.n José Guerrero de Torres
El Cap.n de Ing.s D.n Juan de la Vera.

Comand.te de Artill.a El Ten Cor.l D. Mariano Bresson
Com.te de Ingen.s El Brig.r D.n N. Hermosilla, q.e estava en Hamburgo donde quedó prisionero
Intendente.....D.n Lazaro de las Heras
Auditor de Gr.ra D.n Juan Mig.l Paez de la Cadena

La Romana's army return for the end of July 1808, as provided by José O Donnell. Note that the document includes La Romana's staff officers (*Plana Mayor (PM)*) and that the location of each of his units is listed in the right–hand column.[25]

---

25   *AGMM*, Bailén 7272.2, Memoria de O'Donnell.

Teniente Rafael Lobo, Spanish naval officer, arrives in the Baltic

At half past four on the evening of Monday 25 July 1808, the following entry was written in the log of the brig-sloop, HMS *Mosquito*, then at anchor in the Yarmouth Roads: '4:30 p.m. came on board a Spanish officer for passage to the Baltic on a mission.'[26] The officer in question was Rafael Lobo, another of those who was to submit evidence to the *Comisión de Jefes* in 1818. He was a lieutenant of the Spanish Navy and had been sent to London in charge of a set papers from the *Junta Suprema de Sevilla* to be delivered to the group of Asturian deputies then established in the British capital.[27] He also brought orders and papers for La Romana, but before continuing his journey to the Baltic he was given a further set of instructions for the marqués by the deputies, together with some papers from the British authorities for Rear Admiral Keats, commander of one of Vice Admiral Saumarez's squadrons. Lobo's statement to the *Comisión de Jefes* has the heading: 'Report of the events which occurred during the mission to rescue the Spanish troops from Denmark, charged to Naval Lieutenant of the Royal Armada, Don Rafael Lobo, by Don Adrian Jacome and Don Juan Ruiz de Apodaca, Deputies of the *Junta Suprema de Sevilla* (henceforth, *Junta Suprema*) in England.' It begins as follows:

> Having set sail for the Baltic from Yarmouth at three in the afternoon on 25 July [1808] in the brig [HMS] *Mosquito*, we anchored alongside the British warship [HMS] *Dictator* on 4 August in front of the port of Nyborg, which is on the island of Funen.
>
> Whilst with *Dictator* her captain informed us that Vice Admiral Saumarez had recently arrived in the Baltic, and went on to tell us the story of a Spanish officer belonging to the garrison of Langeland who had taken it upon himself to make an escape to the British ships. When he succeeded in getting aboard one of these, he told the officers present that the reason for his escape was to propose that British naval forces should protect an attempt by the Spanish troops to escape from the island of Langeland. The captain also told us that, because of what the Spanish officer had said, he had been placed aboard [HMS] *Edgar* which was [at that time] anchored off Langeland making attempts to establish communication [with the Spanish] in order to attempt to put the officer's plan into effect.[28]

We should note here that the Spanish officer from Langeland was Antonio Fabregues, who had been stationed on the island with his battalion, the 1er de Catalunya, and that his intentions were to ask the Royal Navy to embark the men belonging to his unit.

---

26   The National Archives (TNA) ADM 51/1828, Log of *Mosquito*.
27   The *Junta Suprema de Sevilla (aka Junta Suprema Central, Junta Suprema and Junta de Sevilla)* was initially set up in May 1808 in the absence of the Spanish king; it relocated to Seville in September of the same year and was Spain's official governing body until its dissolution in January 1810.
28   *AGMM, Bailén 7272.2, Memoria de Rafael Lobo*, p.1.

THE REVOLT OF LA ROMANA'S ARMY IN THE BALTIC

Teniente Antonio Fabregues visits the ships of the British fleet

The following entry for 1 August 1808 appears in the log of the sloop, HMS *Edgar*, then on station in the Great Belt off the east coast of Funen: '4:30 p.m. sent barge and cutter in chase of a boat … Boats returned with a Spanish officer and soldier who had given themselves up.'[29] Thus, is recorded the rescue of Antonio Fabregues by the Royal Navy; the soldier accompanying him was his servant or valet. We now return to Agustín de Llano's statement for an explanation of how Fabregues managed to place himself aboard a British warship:

> On Langeland, once the excitement relating to the taking of the oath had died down, Gauthier asked the *sargento-mayor* of the 1er de Catalunya, Don Ambrosio de la Quadra, if he could recommend to him a trustworthy junior officer who could be relied upon to deliver some letters from Bernadotte to the French general commanding on the island of Zealand, *Général de Brigade* Fririon. These were almost certainly the prince's responses to the letters he had received about the recent behaviour of the regiments of Guadalajara and Asturias [on Zealand].
>
> It was at about this time that Don Rafael Lobo, a Spanish naval officer, had arrived in the Baltic from London, and was with Admiral Keats's squadron. He was carrying orders for the British that they should protect our escape and subsequent retirement [from Denmark] and return us to Spain. He also brought letters for La Romana and Kindelán from the *Junta Suprema*, [Tomás] Morla and other persons, which described the state of things in Spain and the hopes of the nation … but these were quite out of date, some of them having been written as early as 20 May …
>
> *Teniente* Fabregues of Catalunya was the man selected by Quadra to carry the documents to Zealand. This young man, once aboard the small boat [commissioned to ferry him to Zealand], threatened to kill the members of its crew if they did not put him aboard one of the British warships. [Once he had succeeded in his aim, he was eventually brought before Keats and] he told the Admiral [what it was he was hoping to achieve] …[30]

In the course of their conversation, Keats told Fabregues of the recent arrival of Lobo and his reasons for coming to the Baltic, and said that he would now do all that was in his power help with the Spanish evacuation. Fabregues replied that, with his acquired knowledge of the Baltic isles, he would willingly assist as much as he could, and when the conversation was over Keats sent a signal from HMS *Superb* to the ship in which Lobo was by then sailing away, ordering its captain to return the Spanish officer to him, and when he went back aboard *Superb* Lobo was delighted to discover Fabregues awaiting his arrival. It would seem that Lobo must have left *Superb* once he had spoken with Keats, in order to go in search of Vice Admiral Saumarez. It is said by one of the Spanish sources that after Lobo had initially informed Keats of the expectation that he should take the initiative with regard to an

---

29 TNA, ADM 51/2336, Log of *Edgar*.
30 *AGMM, Bailén 7272.2, Memoria de de Llano*, p.16.

embarkation of the Spaniards, Keats replied that he could not see any way in which he could act with effectiveness and sent him in search of Saumarez aboard what was probably HMS *Mosquito*, the ship which brought him to the Baltic. Hence the need for the rear admiral to request Lobo's return whilst HMS *Edgar*, which had brought Fabregues to Keats in the meantime, stood off the admiral's flagship.

After much discussion about how to conduct matters from that point on, it was decided to place Fabregues back ashore at a secure location on the coast of Langeland, in possession of all of the papers necessary to convince his comrades of the arrival of Lobo and the news that he brought.

According to Quadra, when Fabregues came ashore with the set of documents given to him by Lobo and Keats, he could hardly contain himself, informing his *sargento-mayor* that he went about the island telling almost everyone he met where he had been, and that the British were about to evacuate his regiment from Langeland. As chance would have it, claims Quadra in his statement, his path crossed with that of Fabregues on the isle of Tassing, as the ferry from Funen dropped him off on his return journey to Langeland, having travelled to Svendborg on Funen to pick up the latest orders concerning the swearing of the oath of fealty. It was when the ferry coming from Langeland arrived that he met with Fabregues, the latter disembarking as the former was embarking, Luckily, Quadra asked Fabregues what he was up to and when he learned of what had happened he took the junior officer back with him, realising that he had to try to contain the news he had spilt.

Once on Langeland, Quadra went to see Gauthier and immediately realised that the French commander knew all, in fact he was in the act of writing a report on matters to Bernadotte, having just sent off a messenger to him on Jutland informing him of what was happening, when Quadra entered his office. Before the Spaniard could speak, Bernadotte asked him why he and his men wanted to return to Spain! At that Quadra knew the game was up, so he went off to organise the transfer of Fabregues and his papers to Nyborg.

With only 100 French soldiers on the island, Gauthier knew he would not be able to confront the 1,200 or so men of Catalunya until help arrived. The commander of the 1er Catalunya, Dionisio Vives was 'nowhere to be seen' claimed Quadra, so it was then that he decided to take matters into his own hands, placing Gauthier under arrest after agreeing to allow his 100 men to sail to a nearby uninhabited island once they had been disarmed, which still left an antagonistic Danish force to contend with on the island. These were mollified by a truce agreed with the Spaniards after negotiating with Quadra. This still left Quadra with the problem of what to do with Fabregues, his news and his documents, all of which had to be presented before La Romana in Nyborg without a moment's delay.[31]

In agreement with other versions of the story, Quadra had Fabregues disguise himself and go to Nyborg in the company of *Teniente* Felix Carrera, taking all papers with them and an instruction not to pass them to La

---

31 *Acontecimientos de Quadra*, RHM, no.73, 2o *semestre*, 1992, p.218.

Romana until they were sure he was in support of the plan for embarkation they contained.

A detail from the above was later confirmed by Fabregues himself. According to an article published in the *Gazeta de Sevilla* on 15 November 1808, Fabregues wrote to his brother on 29 August, whilst aboard HMS *Edgar*, informing him of the recent events in Denmark. The article included a transcript of Fabregues's letter and we reproduce some lines from it immediately below, translated into English:

> I had the great fortune one night to get aboard a British ship off the coast of Langeland without being seen. [Later I returned ashore and] went to my commanding officer [Vives] who sent me in disguise to the commander in chief [La Romana]. I gave him the documents and everybody was delighted.[32]

This passage confirms Fabregues's actions. De Llano says that both men arrived at headquarters in Nyborg on the night of the 6/7 August, but O'Donnell and others say it was the 5/6 August.

At this point we may look to Jose O'Donnell's statement which contains some small but not wholly insignificant differences from that of de Llano. For example, he states that whilst Fabregues was aboard HMS *Edgar*:

> He offered to take the documents ashore if they would secretly disembark him one night at a point on the isle of Langeland to which he would direct them. That is what was done, and the honourable deserter went ashore with great risk to his life should things not work out as he wanted. But despite all that his comrades did to shield him, news of his return soon reached *Colonel* Gauthier … Fabregues was quickly discovered by the French and placed in a dungeon,[33] but by then the documents which he brought ashore were in the safe hands of *Sargento–Mayor* Ambrosio de la Quadra, who had hidden them … [Later] Quadra was able to overcome Gauthier's vigilance and remove Fabregues from prison by disguising him as an ordinary soldier, before sending him to Nyborg accompanied by *Teniente* Don Felix de la Carrera, to whom he gave the documents.[34]

O'Donnell continues: 'After midnight on the night of the 5/6 August, Carrera and Fabregues arrived at headquarters in Nyborg, and from there they went to the quarters of an officer belonging to the staff of headquarters. This officer took the documents straight to La Romana.' The officer referred to was O'Donnell himself, who explains in a footnote to his statement, 'The two officers arrived at my house after midnight and entered through an open window. This put me in a position to present to the Marqués de La Romana that very night the sublime, patriotic sentiments.'[35]

---

32 *Gazeta de Sevilla*, edition of 15 November, 1808, p. 390, at: <http://www.cervantesvirtual.com/obra/gazeta-ministerial-de-sevilla-ano-1808/> (accessed, 11 March 2021).
33 Quadra does not mention this in his first–hand description of events.
34 *AGMM, Bailén 7272.2, Memoria de O'Donnell*, p.9.
35 *AGMM, Bailén 7272.2, Memoria de O'Donnell*, p.10.

La Romana receives the intelligence brought by Lobo to the Baltic

When La Romana was presented with the papers Fabregues had brought ashore, which included a letter from Keats in which the British admiral expressed his willingness to contribute all that he could to achieve a successful embarkation of the Spaniards, he lost himself in a brief moment of sheer happiness before being brought back to earth when the enormity of the task now facing him began to dawn upon him, something which the slightest accident could upset. His units were scattered far and wide and were surrounded everywhere by strong French and Danish forces. He was in no doubt that Bernadotte would by now be aware that Fabregues had made contact with the British, in fact Gauthier had sent a message to Bernadotte to that effect as soon as he knew of it, and this meant that the marqués would have very little time to put an effective operation into motion. Any inkling of a plan for escape which he may have already formed in his mind would have required not just the assistance of British warships, but also the availability of a significant number of naval transports. Those extra resources the British would undoubtedly be capable of providing, but in the absence of any advanced warning it was clear that the necessary ships were currently nowhere to be seen. After taking a few moments to gather himself, La Romana began to piece together a plan which might just bear fruit, and his thoughts may have been influenced by the contents of Keats's letter. It was clear that, whilst in conversation with Lobo and Fabregues aboard *Superb*, the beginnings of a plan had taken shape and the two main tenets of it were that, firstly, La Romana would have to gain possession of a suitable harbour, and secondly that, in what was beginning to look like a two-phase operation, his units on Jutland and Funen, if not those on Zealand, would have to be removed to Langeland where, after securing the island, they could await the arrival of British transports before being re-embarked for Spain. It would seem that the marqués had been thinking along similar lines, as he had already formed an idea about how he might be able to take control of Nyborg and its port, and he was about to set things in motion. We take up the story with O'Donnell:

> Without any further hesitation La Romana decided to cross the Rubicon, not to bring blood and fire to his own country, but to be victorious or perish with her.
>
> On that same night, and without suffering any more intervention from Bernadotte's secretary [Viliat, who was still awaiting La Romana's response to Bernadotte's orders to have his men repeat the oath of fealty] the general dictated a circular for the chiefs of the four regiments on Jutland, as well as an order for Kindelán under whose immediate command they remained. All chiefs were given a resumé of the content of the documents we had just received, with an additional note to the effect that the motherland, iniquitously oppressed, called upon the valour and spirit of all good Spaniards to come to her defence; that her ally, Britain, would offer to facilitate a withdrawal or embarkation to Spain … [There was a further note for Kindelán detailing the] particular precautions to be taken when hurrying the movement of his men to join the concentration of Spanish units on Funen, together with a confidential letter detailing the motives

upon which the expectation of a successful outcome for the operation were based … The colonels of the cavalry regiments were also ordered to have their horses shot should it be impossible to find transports [to ferry them across the Little Belt to Funen].

These orders left headquarters on the morning of the 6 August, carried by three artillery officers chosen to travel by post under the pretext that they were on their way to buy some horses required to haul the guns of their regiment. The importance of their mission was stressed upon them to the extent that, should they encounter any local chief who refused or showed reluctance to accept the orders they brought, they should encourage the men to mutiny against him by informing them of the reason for his mission.[36]

Unaware of recent events, Fernando Mijares (who, as we saw earlier, had been sent on a mission to the north-west coast of Funen) returned to Nyborg from his reconnaissance of the crossing points between Jutland and Funen on the evening in question, just as O'Donnell was dispatching the marqués's orders to Kindelán's units, and he describes what happened when he went to report his findings to La Romana, as follows:

I returned on the evening of 6 August and went to see La Romana, and after reporting on the findings of my mission he told me, full of happiness, that, 'When you left here I had only the faintest hopes that your work would be useful to us; but now, thank God, I know it will be. This morning I gave orders that the division concentrate here so that we may begin our journey to Spain. Keep this to yourself and be prepared to leave here with some documents at five in the morning.[37]'

La Romana determines upon taking possession of Langeland

If we return to O'Donnell's statement, we may now begin to discern the various strings to La Romana's plan, especially that of obtaining possession of Langeland:

It was of the greatest importance to avoid the consequences which could result from the critical situation in which the 1er de Catalunya found itself on Langeland. With this in mind La Romana sent another trusted officer to Faaborg and Svendborg to inform the colonels of the regiments of Villaviciosa and the 1er de Barcelona of the situation, and to pass on the marqués's orders that those two corps should cross to Langeland …

Orders were also sent to the Dragones de Almansa [who were at Odense, some twenty-two miles from Nyborg] and the 2o batallón de Princesa [who were at Kerteminde, some twelve miles from Nyborg] to make their way to Nyborg, and

---

36 *AGMM, Bailén 7272.2, Memoria de O'Donnell*, p.11 and p.21, *Nota 3a*. The three artillery officers were *Capitán* Joachin Lamor, and *Tenientes* Pablo Ventades & Manuel Zacares. The latter was arrested by the Danish authorities at Kerteminde when returning from his mission and made a prisoner of war.

37 *AGMM, Bailén 7272.2, Memoria de Mijares*, p.9.

the marqués did not forget to inform Rear Admiral Keats of all his plans and dispositions, telling him that he would signal to him from Cape Knudshoved when the time was ready for his ships to enter the harbour at Nyborg.[38]

Once all these measures had been taken, it was on the morning of 8 August that the marqués publicly announced that all of his units on Funen were to be concentrated at Nyborg, in compliance with the instructions of Bernadotte, in order that they re-take the oath of fealty. He then gave official notice of what was planned to Baron Gooldingkrona,[39] governor of the fortress at Nyborg, in order that he might not be surprised or become worried by the increase in the number of our troops in the vicinity of the town. Neither this chief, nor the Danish garrison, nor the inhabitants of Nyborg, became at all suspicious of our motives until the moment came for us to take possession of the place.[40]

The Spanish take control of Nyborg

It is now time to see how La Romana's risk-strewn operation to take possession of Nyborg was carried out with great success, and we shall refer once more to the statement of an eyewitness to events, *Capitán* Don Estanislao Sanchez Salvador:

> The [possession of the] town of Nyborg ... was absolutely necessary to realise our project; without it and its port, the British would not have been able to help us and neither would we have had the boats necessary to execute our escape. It was therefore of the utmost importance that the need for its speedy occupation figured strongly in our plans, and to succeed in this task would require a combination of the greatest subtlety and care. The place itself was strong due to its position and its state of defence, which included a garrison of two Danish line battalions, and to add to our difficulties one must state that at no time were we ever permitted to have more than two companies within its walls. To increase that number under any pretext would awaken suspicions on the part of the Danes. On the other hand, it was necessary for us to take advantage of anything that came to mind, knowing that if the Danish authorities were to see through the reasons we gave for the concentration of our troops [in the vicinity of Nyborg] ... they would be able to frustrate our aims. Fortunately, an imperative order had arrived from the Prince de Pontecorvo insisting that all of our troops on Funen should retake [the oath of fealty to King Joseph Bonaparte] without any restrictions or conditional clauses. This offered us a plausible pretext [for our concentration at the town] and the hope of success in our ultimate aims.
>
> Things got underway when we began to spread the word that our regiments on Jutland had taken the oath [at the first call of asking] without any complaints whatsoever, and that they would be coming to Funen to persuade, or oblige, those of our troops on the island to submit to what was desired of them. The ploy produced [better than] expected results, because not only did it acquire credence amongst the Danes, but also the Spaniards, with the consequence that, in order to

---

38 *AGMM, Bailén 7272.2, Memoria de O'Donnell*, pp.11–12.
39 This is the first of several different spellings of his name found in the statements of La Romana's men.
40 *AGMM, Bailén 7272.2, Memoria de O'Donnell*, pp.11–12.

take the fullest advantage of the opportunity, the Marqués de La Romana ordered that our various corps concentrate on a plain which lay to the east of Nyborg on the 8 or 9 of August, in order that he could personally harangue and exhort the whole to submit to the re-taking of the oath.

At dawn on the given day the regiments of Princesa, Almansa and all of the Artillería, were to be found in the immediate vicinity of Nyborg. To our great joy the people of the area had not yet discerned our intentions, and as such put up no resistance to our troops passing through the town in order to take the shortest route to the field selected as the venue for the ceremony. When some of the infantry, cavalry and artillery had passed through the gates, and we had more than 2,000 men of all arms within the walls, the mask was allowed to slip, and *Teniente-General* José O'Donnell, together with a company of Grenadiers, went to the house of the Danish governor, Baron 'Guildencrown' to explain our intentions and that in achieving them we wanted to avoid any bloodshed amongst the Danish citizenry. At first, he was overcome by surprise and not quite in control of himself, asking us to desist in our temerity; but in the end he realized that now was not the time to remedy his lack of foresight, and he agreed to put his signature to the order handed to him by O'Donnell (which had been pre-written in Danish by Don Julio O'Neill) to the effect that the posts within the town, together with the coastal batteries, be handed over to us so as to allow the British to enter into the harbour.

All of this was carried out to the amazement of the inhabitants as well as the Port Commander, an officer of the Danish Navy in command of two brigs of war lying in the harbour who, perhaps for having had more time to think, or simply because of his decisive and determined nature, firmly declared that he would sooner see his boats smashed to pieces than allow the British to enter the port. In an attempt to overcome his obstinacy, we threatened to turn the shore batteries against him and thus destroy the brigs within a few minutes, but all was in vain; and seeing that our negotiations were using up precious hours of time, we eventually decided that the British should enter by force.[41]

In his statement to the *Comisión de Jefes*, Jose O'Donnell describes some of his own contributions to the operation to take control of Nyborg (written in the third person as was the Spanish convention for official documents at that time):

At dawn on 10 August the troops were formed in Nyborg under the pretext that they were to re-take the oath, and it was then that La Romana sent an officer of his headquarters staff [O'Donnell himself] to the house of the Danish governor. The officer was carrying orders written in Danish from the marqués, which he was expected to sign. These would confirm to the Danish commanders [of the various posts within the town as well as its external coastal batteries] that they were to hand over their positions to the Spanish troops, who were standing-by in overwhelming numbers with the aim of subduing any sign of resistance. It was at this moment that the governor realised we were determined to return to Spain with the help of the British naval forces which were about to enter the port. This

---

41   *AGMM, Bailén 7272.2, Memoria de Salvador*, pp.1–2 of document no. 3.

elderly and honourable soldier, who we appreciated for his virtue, took some time to make up his mind about how he should respond, weighing the necessity to cede to superior forces against the admiration he felt for the patriotism and daring of the Spanish. Eventually he tried to convince us that our plan, although noble, was impractical due to the lack of transports, victuals and etc., and that the French would arrive to throw it into disarray; but in the end he admitted that any kind of resistance on his part would not only be useless but impossible, as he could not even leave his quarters. Eventually we were able to take possession of the nearest shore batteries without opposition.[42]

Spanish units from Jutland join the concentration of the army at Nyborg

We will leave the statements of Salvador and O'Donnell at this point, as they begin to touch upon elements of the Royal Navy's operation to embark the Spaniards which we shall look at later, and with the Port of Nyborg secured by La Romana on the evening of 8 August (O'Donnell says on the 10th) we will now turn our attention to the Spanish units on Jutland, who were under the command of *Mariscal de Campo* Kindelán, to see how successful they were in their attempts to join the concentration of the marqués's troops at Nyborg. Firstly, we should note that the Spanish dispositions on the Jutland were as follows: the bulk of the cavalry regiment of El Infante was stationed at Randers in the north of the peninsula, with a detachment some 50 miles further to the north at Aalborg. The cavalry regiment of El Rey was at the port of Aarhus to the south of Randers, and the last of the cavalry regiments on Jutland, that of Algarve, was at Horsens, some 30 miles south of Aarhus. Each of these regiments had a strength of about 600 troopers and officers. Finally, there was the infantry regiment of Zamora with a strength of some 2,150 men, and these occupied the southernmost position of the Spaniards on the peninsula, at Fredericia, and controlled the main crossing point of the Little Belt between Jutland and Funen. The availability of that crossing would be crucial to the Spaniards in order to afford them the shortest sea passage to Funen, should they retain control of it. However, this was always unlikely to be the case; once the French and Danes had got wind of La Romana's intentions to bring all of his troops to Nyborg, their first movements would be directed toward gaining possession of the harbour at Fredericia.

The size of the task facing the Spanish cavalry units may be judged by looking at the distance each would have to cover if they were to head for the crossing point at Fredericia. From Randers, El Infante would have some 75 miles to cover; El Rey from Aarhus about 60 miles; Algarve from Horsens 30 miles. The infantry of Zamora was best placed, being stationed at Fredericia itself. Just to make life a little more difficult for the cavalrymen, and indeed the infantry of Zamora, was the fact that they would need to acquire the use of significant shipping resources to get them across the water to Funen, and

---

42   *AGMM, Bailén 7272.2, Memoria de O'Donnell*, p.14.

this would almost certainly involve the pressing into service of local Danish seamen. Things must not have looked at all promising to them.

The story of the regiments of Zamora and Algarve

We have already seen that, once the story of Fabregues's communication with the British was revealed to La Romana he sent orders to his units on Jutland that they begin their movements to Nyborg immediately, and we shall now see how they fared. Firstly, we return to O'Donnell's statement to see what became of Zamora and Algarve, those units located closest to the favoured crossing point between Jutland and Funen:

> Whilst La Romana waited with impatience for news of the results achieved by the orders sent to Jutland, his second in command, *General* Kindelán, who was at Fredericia with the three battalions of the regiment of Zamora, was preparing an act of treachery which the marqués could never have judged him capable of, and which could have thwarted our noble plan if he had behaved with more coherency, more firmness and more daring. After receiving his orders from *Capitán* Lamor, he read them with deep concentration and repeated what they said without removing his gaze from the paper; no doubt giving himself time to compose his facial expression in order that he didn't give away his thoughts. He then calmly asked if all of the difficulties [associated with the plan] had been considered, as well as the means of overcoming them, and when Lamor answered that all had been prepared and put in motion, he said that he would obey with gusto the voice of his chief and of the motherland.
>
> Whilst still in the presence of Lamor, Kindelán called for the chiefs of Zamora and ordered them to hurry their march. He then made as though to prepare his personal baggage and (in order to appear even more convincing) sent off a horse of little value along with a traveling chest (which was later found to be half empty, the rest of the space taken up with old clothing) with the men of Zamora, saying that he would follow on immediately. Zamora made their short march to the crossing point of the Little Belt and made the passage without difficulty. A few hours later Kindelán left Fredericia in his berlina, but on arriving at the crossing point and seeing the opportunity he was hoping for, he set off for Hadersleben [*Sic* for Haderslev some 40 miles to the south of Fredericia] to inform the French of what, without doubt, he would have called an act of treachery. The result was that by the evening of the 9th the crossing point of the Little Belt was occupied on the Jutland side by part of the French vanguard.
>
> Word of Kindelán's betrayal soon spread to headquarters at Nyborg, where there was much concern for the regiments of El Rey and El Infante, which were the units at greatest distance from the Little Belt crossing point, but the general staff were quite sure that Algarve would be able to get from Horsens to the crossing before the French. Unfortunately, for reasons difficult to fully understand, this is not what happened, and the whole regiment was taken prisoner.[43] It was later

---

43 AGMM, Bailén 7272.2, *Memoria de O'Donnell*, pp.11–12. In a footnote to his statement O'Donnell says that, 'There were reasons to suspect that the Regiment of Algarve was lost

discovered that a captain of the regiment, who went by the name of Costa (a French émigré to Spain from the early days of the revolution) tried, though somewhat tardily, to make his way to Nyborg together with some fellow officers and about 100 troopers, but ran into superior French forces which were blocking the approach to the Little Belt. Costa, at his wits end, surrendered on obtaining an agreement that his men would be well treated, before shooting himself in full view of all present.[44]

The Story of the Regiments of El Rey and El Infante

The two cavalry units in the north of Jutland, El Rey and El Infante, decided that they would be running far too risky a course if they were to attempt to reach the crossing point of the Little Belt at Fredericia. Instead, they chose what might seem to some as being an even more dangerous option, that of making a sea-crossing to Funen from ports on a more northerly part of the east coast of Jutland, and they may well have been helped in arriving at their decision by what was said to them in La Romana's orders. We may now turn to the statement made to the *Comisión de Jefes* by *Teniente-Coronel* Joachin Astrandi of the Regimiento de Caballería Ligera del Infante, which was based at Randers and at Aalborg on the northern tip of the Jutland Peninsula, to see how his regiment made its way to Funen; but firstly, it might be instructive to examine La Romana's orders for the cavalry chiefs of Rey and Infante, which were are follows:

> I have just received, from the hands of a Spanish officer, at set of documents from the *Junta Suprema* de Galicia and *General* Don Tomas Morla, which inform me that the provinces of Andalucia, Galicia, Valencia, Catalunya, Extremadura, Castilla [and] Aragon have taken up arms in defence of the liberty of our country, and that in a short time a squadron will arrive in these waters which will embark us so that we will be able to take part in the just cause they defend.
>
> I am determined to embark with those troops that I command and who wish to follow me, and I am counting upon [my belief that] you, your officers and the rest of the individuals of the regiments which you command, will want to participate as good Spaniards in the glory of our nation. For this reason, it will be best if you take advantage of the moment and march with the regiments at your command, taking the shortest route by which to arrive on the island of Funen. Make use of the boats at Aarhus and other ports, taking possession of them by force if necessary. To disguise the real reason for your action, you will tell the Danes that your troops are required [on Funen] in order to take the oath demanded of them. If possible, embark all of your horses, but if not take only the best of them.

---

through the fault, or at least the indecision, of its chiefs, who took too long to make up their minds [about what to do] and lost [a lot of] time waiting for the return of some of its officers who had been sent to discover what El Rey and El Infante were going to do. *Capitán* Costa, seeing that the moment was being lost, mounted his horse [and set off] with all those were able to follow him, but by then it was too late.'

44   *AGMM, Bailén 7272.2, Memoria de O'Donnell*, pp.12–13.

Make all efforts to take with you all of the stores and rations which have been established [at your camp] and embark them for Funen, but if in doing so it will cause you much delay, then leave them behind; but in any case, it is indispensable that you take advantage of the moment and that you cross with the least delay to this island [Funen].

The officer [charged with] giving you these instructions will inform you, more or less, of the news which has inclined me to take this action.

Nyborg, 7 August 1808.

Marqués de La Romana

P.S. I recommend to you, very particularly, that you make your troops observe the most exact discipline, your officers and sergeants making sure that they do not commit the slightest extortion or damage, not only to the innocent inhabitants of the country, but also to the French you may encounter.[45]

Astrandi added the following note at the foot of his copy of La Romana's orders, starting at the margin heading, '*Prim.a nota*', which in its final paragraph overlaps a little with the content of his main statement. The note reads as follows:

I received this order at 10:45 p.m. on 8 August, at which hour I asked the Danish commander at Randers if I could use the boats [in the harbour] to embark the whole of my regiment (something he absolutely refused to allow, saying that there were no suitable boats available at the time, and that it wouldn't be possible to provide them, nor to find crews for them, as quickly as we might like). Seeing his obstinance and bad intentions (he seemed suspicious despite us having told him that the purpose of our voyage to Funen was to go to the assistance of the Marqués de La Romana because the regiments at his immediate disposal did not want to take the oath of fealty to King Joseph. Those of us on Jutland had already taken the oath, but that was because *General* Kindelán had tricked us into doing so by telling us that the whole of Spain had taken it and that tranquility reigned across the whole of the nation). I then asked the commander for a dozen carts in which to transport our baggage, a request he complied with, thus enabling me to carry off the sick belonging to the regiments of El Rey, Algarve and my own from the hospitals, leaving only two men behind because of the seriousness of their condition.

At one o'clock in the morning of 9 August the regiment marched for Aarhus, some seven leagues distant and the place where the regiment of El Rey was cantoned, which meant that there would be no accommodation for my own men, who were therefore forced to stay at places some one, two or three leagues away, where they awaited my orders.

I went to the town of Aarhus to make preparations for the embarkation of my regiment and found that El Rey had not yet made their own embarkation, but had begun their preparations for doing so at midday. My own regiment followed suit at four in the afternoon, when they appeared and formed themselves on the

---

45 AGMM, Bailén 7272.2, *Memoria de Astrandi*, page headed, *Copia del oficio del Exmo. Sr. Marqués de La Romana, No. 30*, p.1.

quayside together with their baggage and arms, having left behind only their horses and saddlery.[46]

Astrandi's (main) statement to the *Comisión de Jefes* comprises several separate sections, but most of his eye-witness testimony is contained in the section headed, '*Contestacion a los 6 puntos que comprende la aclaración que solicita la tercera sección de jefes y officiales al Ministerio de la Guerra*,' and describes how the regiments of El Infante and El Rey made their way from the Jutland Peninsula to Nyborg:

> [A]t a quarter to eleven on the night of 8 August, whilst I was at Randers, I received an order from an adjutant of the Marqués de La Romana, and at one o'clock on the morning of the 9th I began the march of the regiment to Aarhus where, after stabling the horses at places one, two and three leagues from the town, I gave the order that the troops should concentrate with only their baggage and arms on the quayside at that town. It was there where all of the officers worked stubbornly alongside the men in an attempt to prepare the dismantled boats which we found there, in order that they be of use to us. After informing the governor of Aarhus that we had received orders from our general in chief that we should travel to Nyborg to help bring to obedience the regiments which were refusing to take the oath of fealty to King Joseph, he decided to do all that he could to supply us with the boats we needed, and we were able to make sail some five hours before a unit of French troops arrived to prevent us from leaving. An express [courier] had arrived at four o'clock that afternoon carrying two letters from *General* Kindelán, each addressed to the governor with orders that he pass [one of] them to the colonel of El Rey and [the other] to me, with the aim of upsetting our plans. However, it did not prevent our embarkation, which we completed at midnight on the 9th. The letter which the governor was to pass on to the colonel of El Rey, who had sailed at midday, was received whilst he was at sea.
>
> Both corps were forced to leave their horses ashore, as we were required to make as swift a passage as we could, but the arrival of Kindelán's letters for the governor of Aarhus contributed more than anything else to the difficulty in our obtaining the boats we required, as he was the person we had to depend upon for their procurement...
>
> At ten in the morning [of 10 August?] I arrived with my regiment at Kerteminde which, according to the orders from La Romana, was where we had to disembark, but as our army had already evacuated the place, we were instead greeted by canon fire. It was then when a British cutter approached and asked us if we wanted their waters[?] to which we answered in the affirmative and went on to anchor in the Bay of Nyborg, where we found the division already embarked.[47]

---

46   *AGMM, Bailén 7272.2, Memoria de Astrandi, Prim.a nota.*
47   *AGMM, Bailén 7272.2, Memoria de Astrandi*, page headed, *Copia del oficio del Exmo. Sr. Marqués de La Romana*, [sub-heading] *Contestación a los 6 puntos que comprende la aclaración que solicita la tercera sección de jefes y oficiales a la Ministerio de la Guerra, 3erPunto, p.1.*

THE REVOLT OF LA ROMANA'S ARMY IN THE BALTIC

The reluctance of the governor of Aarhus to supply boats to Astrandi is understandable, after him having to procure four boats for the regiment of El Rey earlier in the day. Ultimately, three more boats were found but, as was the case with El Rey, Astrandi then began to insist that the owners of the boats be pressed into service in order to take him and his men to Kerteminde on Funen, a sea crossing of some 60 miles and an impossibility for the Spanish cavalrymen to make without the help of experienced sailors.

When the seven boats bearing El Rey and El Infante arrived at Nyborg, Keats assigned them the identifiers, X1–X7, and it is worth noting that, as well as their Danish crews, these small craft were crammed with some 1,200 Spanish cavalrymen, including officers. As we shall see, when Keats later used the same boats as troop carriers in a situation where he was short of shipping, he placed less than half that number aboard X1–X7, albeit for a longer sea passage. All of which suggests that the sea crossing from Aarhus to Nyborg must have been extremely uncomfortable for the Spanish troopers.

The letters from Kindelán referred to by Astrandi above contained an order which ran contrary to the order both he and the commander of El Rey had earlier received from La Romana. It read as follows:

> Illegitimate obedience, infamy and dishonour. That will be the case if you obey the orders which have been dictated to you by the Marqués de La Romana. Blind passions and personal interests!
>
> The very secretary of state and the minister of war, who are our authorities, have ordered you to take the oath of fealty to the king, to the constitution and to the law. You and your regiment have taken it, and a man of religion and honour, such as you, knows well how sacred the oath is. This is the true proof of a good Spaniard and of love for the motherland; not a low obedience to this fury of rebels who pretend to stand in royal authority and exhale the pestilential breath of dishonour over troops who have always been characterised by their fidelity and their military virtues.
>
> I charge you then, in the name of the king, in the name of honour and of the motherland, that you ignore such perfidious insinuations, and instead instil in your troops, fidelity and discipline … and give notice, without a moment's loss, to HRH the Prince de Pontecorvo, so recognised by his many titles as a lover of the Spanish…
>
> 8 August 1808,
> Juan Kindelán
> P.S. French troops are no doubt now in movement to quash the treachery.[48]

Such was the flavour of Kindelán's patriotism!

---

[48] *AGMM, Bailén 7272.2, Memoria de Astrandi*, page headed, *Copia del oficio del Mariscal de Campo D. Juan Kindelán. No. 4.*

The Capture of Langeland

With the concentration of La Romana's units at Nyborg underway, it was necessary to set in motion the second phase of his plan for evacuation, that of gaining possession of the island of Langeland and securing it against any attempts the French might make to land on its shores in pursuit. The French had only a weak garrison of some 100 grenadiers on the island under the command of Gauthier, but there were stronger Danish forces available to him, including a regular cavalry regiment and larger units of Danish territorials, which comfortably outnumbered the 1,100 or so men of the 1er de Catalunya under the command of Don Francisco Dionisio Vives; coincidently the officer given the task in 1818 of obtaining the statements from his former comrades which we are currently examining.

We have already learned of the daring actions taken by *Teniente* Antonio Fabregues of Catalunya to make contact with the ships of the British fleet and of the strength of character, not to say initiative, of the *sargento–mayor* of that battalion, Don Ambrosio de la Quadra, who intervened to take control of the delicate situation which arose when Fabregues returned from the British ships, Dionisio Vives, the battalion's senior officer, seemingly incapable or unwilling to show the leadership qualities demanded in such critical circumstances. From what we are about to discover it would seem that there were no bounds to Quadra's self-assuredness, and it appears he was quite happy to impose himself upon the men of his battalion during the difficult few days which followed once La Romana set his plan for escape in motion. We begin the story of the struggle for control of Langeland with Mijares, the officer chosen by La Romana to carry his orders from Nyborg to the Regimiento de Villaviciosa and the 1er de Barcelona, both stationed in the south–east corner of Funen, instructing them to cross to Langeland and go to the aid of 1er de Catalunya in their efforts to subdue enemy resistance on the island. We return to Mijares's statement:

> As a consequence of what the marqués had told me on the evening of 6 August, I arrived at his house at four in the morning on the following day. It was then when he gave me the documents for the colonel of Villaviciosa, who was at Faaborg, and for the commander of Barcelona who was at Svendborg. Before I set off, I received verbal orders from him to instruct those corps that, whatever the cost, they were to embark at Svendborg for Langeland in order to provide assistance to the Regimiento de Catalunya which, as he told me, was in a difficult situation.
>
> The lack of boats at Svendborg obliged me to insist that Villaviciosa and Barcelona did not pass directly to Langeland, but that they should first cross to [the isle of] Tassing [which lies at the mid-point of the crossing] in order that they make two short voyages [rather than one long one]. Doing it this way meant that all of the horses belonging to Villaviciosa could pass to Langeland in line with La Romana's orders, with the objective in mind of having a corps of cavalry available to oppose that of the Danes.
>
> Although the embarkation at Svendborg began at ten o'clock on the morning of the 7th, we did not complete the crossing of the troops to Tassing until midday

on the 10th, at which hour there arrived the Artillería with four of their pieces, and these were also embarked.

Once all of the troops were said to have crossed, I went to Svendborg to see for myself that this was the case, and it transpired that the governor there had received notification that, at dawn that day, the Spanish had taken control of Nyborg and the nearby telegraph station. This news, together with the sound of canon fire he had heard, made him suspicious of me. He thus judged that I had not given him the true reason for our embarkation to Langeland and made me a prisoner of war. In return, and with a feigned air of serenity, I told him that his luck would be out when the further three battalions I was expecting arrived at Svendborg. The idea that he might, as a result, end up in Spain as a prisoner of war himself, gave him such a fright that after five hours he gave me back my sword and provided me with a small boat in which to cross to Rudkobing, where I arrived at eleven o'clock that night. It was at that place where Quadra informed me of the events that had taken place at Nyborg after my departure. He also told me that Gauthier had discovered that Fabregues was not to be found in the dungeon [to which he had been earlier confined by the governor after making contact with the British] making it necessary for him [Quadra] to drop all pretence and take control of Langeland [from the French and Danes].[49]

The situation of Catalunya on the island had remained critical until the arrival of Barcelona, and for four consecutive days and nights [whilst Villaviciosa and Barcelona were making the crossing from Funen] the Catalans had stood with their arms at the ready as the only means to avoid being 'insulted' by a nearby regiment of Danish cavalry ...

On 13 August 1808, the Marqués de La Romana arrived with the troops he had embarked at Nyborg, the ships carrying them anchoring on the east coast of Langeland at a point close to a shore battery garrisoned by Danish troops. This was later occupied by our soldiers; its garrison did not resist.[50]

There are just a few things to say about Mijares's statement at this point, Firstly, the story about Fabregues having been detained by Gauthier: from what Quadra said as a direct witness to events on Langeland, it would seem that Mijares is mistaken. By the time Quadra brought Fabregues before the Frenchman, the Spaniards were in control of the island and, as we know, Fabregues was later sent to Nyborg, meaning he could not have been in detention.

Secondly, the crossing from Svendborg to Tassing is about 500 yards wide, that from Tassing to Langeland about three miles, though there is an island in mid-channel. According to Quadra, the only boats available at Svendborg and on Tassing were all very small craft, which meant the troops were able to make both crossings in 'penny packets', but that the horses belonging to the Dragones de Villaviciosa had to swim the shorter crossing to Tassing and wait for some larger boats to be brought from Langeland in order to complete their journey. All of which explains why the crossing from Svendborg to Tassing took four days to complete, as claimed by Mijares.

---

49 Mijares makes the same point as O'Donnell with respect to Fabregues being detained by Gauthier.
50 *AGMM, Bailén 7272.2, Memoria de Mijares*, pp.10–11.

Barón de Armendáriz, colonel of Villaviciosa, was one of the recipients of the orders Mijares brought from La Romana, and in his statement to the *Comisión de Jefes*, after a short preamble in which he explains the importance of taking possession of Langeland if the marqués's plan was to have had any chance of succeeding, he goes on to provide us with the following account of events which occurred in the south-east corner of Funen during the operation to secure it – all in the third person:

> [T]he small island of Langeland, situated to the south-east of Funen ... [was] very fertile and had an abundance of cereals, legumes and livestock; as such it was seen as a place where a base might be established in order to ensure the success of La Romana's great plan for embarkation and escape. The 1er de Catalunya was already established there, and the marqués's orders were that the 1er de Barcelona and the Regimiento de Villaviciosa ... should take possession of the island ... in order to ensure our escape from Denmark ...
>
> The 1er Barcelona was able to succeed in making the crossing to Langeland, but the Barón de Armendáriz and his regiment [Villaviciosa] were not able to do so without having to overcome some great obstacles and inconveniences. As well as having to make their march [from Faaborg] to Svendborg – whilst flanked by a number of Danish gunboats – in order to make their embarkation for Tassing, an island in mid-channel between Funen and Langeland, they also found themselves deprived of all resources required to enable them to make the crossing. This was due to the activities of the Danish authorities and the local populace, who had hidden all available boats. ... In this situation the barón allowed his troops some rest before instructing some of them to swim the [narrow] channel to Tassing, but realising that it would be difficult to have the whole of his regiment make the crossing in this manner ... and impossible for the Artillería ... he decided to do all that he could to overcome the situation...
>
> Eventually he collected the sum of some 300 pesos from the men of his regiment to pay for the use of three sizable boats in which to pass his unit to Tassing. Once on the islet the barón's mind began to focus on the more difficult task of crossing the wider channel between Tassing and Langeland. His first thoughts were to gain the sympathies and confidence of the islanders, but the people were found unwilling to offer him their assistance in fear of the retribution they might receive from the French, and began to remove themselves to various hiding places. It was impossible to find more than five or six of them, but after handing over another 300 pesos they agreed to provide us with some boats. Eventually they delivered just two small craft before disappearing from sight. Night was falling, so there was no choice but to begin our crossing with what we had. The barón decided to send one of his adjutants, Don Manuel de Mojó, to Langeland in order to inform [*Sargento-*] *Mayor* Quadra of the situation and request him to provide all of the help he could to allow us to complete our crossing. Mojó returned at midnight bringing some boats with him and assured us that more were on their way, thus guaranteeing our passage. He also brought a message from Quadra asking that the barón cross immediately and take command of the Spanish troops on the island.[51]

---

51   AGMM, *Bailén* 7272.2, *Memoria del Barón de Armendáriz* (henceforth, *Memoria de Armendáriz*), pp.1–11.

Armendáriz goes on to explain that there was a considerable Danish force on Langeland, which appeared 'disgusted and uncertain' about the aims of the Spanish, having observed that Quadra had disarmed some 100 French grenadiers, part of the island's garrison, and locked up its commander, Gauthier. Thinking that he might have some trouble from the Danes and that there was no time for negotiations, Armendáriz ordered his men to arms and succeeded in bringing the them to terms by making it clear that he was willing to use full force to gain control of the island. The Danes were later disarmed before the arrival of the convoy from Nyborg which brought La Romana and his troops.

Once the Spaniards from Funen had been disembarked, the work of fortifying the island against the possibility of a French attack was put into motion, whilst this was going on, the ships which had brought the troops from Nyborg were re-victualed and watered should they be needed to transport the army without delay. All the time they were on the island, explains the barón, Danish gunboats kept up a series of attacks, mostly at night, upon the posts constructed and manned by his men along its western shore. These were all repulsed without loss to the defenders.[52]

Before we move on, it might be worth looking at the apparent inaction of Francisco Dionisio Vives as events were unfolding on Langeland. Some historians have questioned how it was that Quadra felt himself justified in taking on such an influential role in matters on Langeland when Vives, nominally in command of the 1er de Catalunya, was present. The implication would appear to be that he was either unwilling to act against the French or simply too weak to impose himself in his role as commander of the battalion. It would seem that Vives had later become aware of some of the things that had been said about him during the operations in the Baltic, and that it still rankled with him at the time he was collecting statements from his former comrades for the *Comisión de Jefes*, some 10 years later. We are allowed a glimpse into Vives's mind in an attachment he made to Armendáriz's statement; no doubt after he had read in the barón's testimony of how it appeared to him that Quadra was the man in command of the Catalans on Langeland, as he struggled to bring his own regiment ashore. In fairness to Vives, we have included the content of his attachment below. It is a copy of what he wrote in reply to Armendáriz after receiving his statement, and before he sent it (and the attachment) to the *Comisión de Jefes*:

> Your Excellency,
> I have received [your] memoir relating to events concerning the Spanish troops in the North under the command of the Marqués de La Romana during 1808... I would like, therefore, to provide Your Excellency with my opinion about the story related in the said memoir. I have read it with particular attention, and I find it to be written with the steadiness and delicacy that one should expect, and with the accuracy and impartiality associated with Your Excellency. I have found no essential equivocations in its content other than that which appears

---

52   *AGMM, Bailén* 7272.2, *Memoria de Armendáriz*, pp.6–11.

in relation to the actions of Don Juan Antonio Fabregues. This officer did not provide *Sargento-Mayor* Don Ambrosio de la Quadra with the least information about the documents provided to him by Lobo until after he had disembarked [on Langeland] and had agreed with me that he should go to see the Marqués de La Romana. [In fact] Fabregues encountered Quadra whilst making his journey to Nyborg, and forced him to return [to Rudkobing] when he became aware of the importance of the documents he was carrying, and to whom they were addressed. Quadra then selected an officer to accompany Fabregues [before sending him off once again on his journey to see La Romana] & etc. & etc.

The plan to establish contact with the British was actually put together by me and Fabregues, when I found myself both in command of our coastal posts on the island of Langeland, and of Gauthier's confidence, the man in command of all troops belonging to the garrison of the island (he was 1st adjutant at Bernadotte's headquarters). As such he was in a position which allowed him to commission a courier to take some documentation to Zealand. I was the one who nominated Fabregues for the commission and agreed with him [Fabregues] that [whilst in the course of executing his commission] he should look for a means of establishing contact with the British and arrange for them to embark the detachment of the 600 men under my command, & etc. & etc.

It is not surprising that Your Excellency has suffered this equivocation, because at the time you arrived ashore on Langeland you found Quadra in charge of the arrangement for the first deployments on the island, by order of La Romana.[53] This circumstance could have given rise to your supposition that he was the author of the plan I refer to.

This is all I would like to say to you in reply to your submission.

To: His Excellency, Barón de Armendáriz.

30 January 1819.[54]

Much of what Vives says above is supported by the content of the statement given by Antonio Fabregues to either Captain MacNamara, when he was taken aboard HMS *Edgar*, or to Rear Admiral Keats when he was subsequently transferred to HMS *Superb*, as we shall see in the next chapter.

A Summary

Having moved some 10,000 of his 15,000-strong army to Langeland to await re-embarkation to Spain, we can say that La Romana had planned and executed an outstandingly successful operation in very short time; acting decisively when unexpectedly faced with the news of Fabregues's initiative late on the night of 5/6 August. Knowing that to hesitate for a moment would have spelt the end for the hopes of his army to return to Spain, he formulated the basis of a plan for escape and delegated the task of framing the orders for

---

53 It is likely that La Romana, when sending Felix de la Carrera on his return journey to Langeland on the night of 10 August, instructed him to place Quadra in command of the arrangements for the arrival of the convoy bearing his troops to the island.

54 *AGMM, Bailén 7272.2, Memoria de Armendáriz*, attachment by Vives.

its execution to José O'Donnell. Those orders then had to be sent to distant locations, carried by hand–picked men of sufficient intelligence, guile and determination who could be trusted to deliver them and act as they saw fit to ensure they were obeyed without delay.

Whilst O'Donnell grappled with the task set him by his chief, La Romana himself had to lay plans for securing the port of Nyborg with hardly any time to spare, and at the same time keep up a continuous communication with the British fleet. The unexpected triggering of the operation meant that there would be two phases to plan and implement, as the naval transports required for carrying the Spanish army home had not yet been martialled in England, let alone set sail, at the time the marqués was forced to act. To have any chance of success a haven had to be found for the Spanish whilst they awaited the arrival of the merchant shipping and La Romana, perhaps in conversation with Keats, decided that the place most suited to that purpose was the island of Langeland. It would require bold action on the part of the Spanish troops to secure the place, and La Romana came up with a plan to ensure their actions would prevail. Its essence was that whilst a number of his units were obeying his orders to concentrate at Nyborg, he sent further instructions for the men of Villaviciosa and Barcelona to make their way to Langeland in whichever way they could. Once established there they provided a huge reinforcement for the single battalion of the Regimiento de Catalunya already present, the combined force was then able subdue any resistance from the French and Danes, thus ensuring the security of the imminent disembarkation of all those then aboard ship at Nyborg. All of this was carried out in enemy territory where the forces ranged against the Spanish were considerably superior to their own. True, La Romana had been unable to extricate the regiments of Guadalajara and Asturias from Zealand, and he had lost the cavalry regiment of Algarve on Jutland, plus a few more soldiers at some of his hospitals, some various small detachments and a group of officers who had been amongst the French at Hamburg celebrating Napoleon's birthday as the marqués launched his operation. Against all the odds he had avoided a confrontation with the enemy, one he would most surely have lost, and managed to concentrate the bulk of his force on Langeland without alienating the Danish populace or fighting any actions against its regular or territorial forces. Let there be no mistake, this was a brilliant success by any measure.

We shall now leave the Spaniards on Langeland as they await the arrival of the naval transports from England. There was still much to be done to ensure the final success of the operation, and most of the responsibility for that was to fall upon the shoulders of another who rose to the challenge in the Baltic during the summer of 1808, Rear Admiral Richard Goodwin Keats. In the next chapter we shall examine the Royal Navy's contribution to events in Denmark.

4

The British Naval Operation to Rescue La Romana's Army

Had things gone to plan, La Romana would not have made his move upon Nyborg until the Royal Navy had accumulated sufficient shipping in the Baltic to accommodate the Spanish army and its equipment. The purpose of Lobo's mission to the Baltic was to oversee the establishment of communications between British and Spanish forces, as this would be a necessary precursor to the formation of a local plan of evacuation in anticipation of the arrival of the naval transports. The Spanish emissary had barely been introduced to Keats before his thoughts were thrown into disarray due to the unauthorised and precipitate action of Fabregues which, as we have seen, resulted in the need for an immediate invocation of the operation to embark La Romana's army. In the previous chapter we saw how the marqués rose to the challenge and instigated the necessary movements of his forces to secure the port of Nyborg. Keats too was alert to the new set of circumstances and wasted no time in coordinating his actions with those of the Spaniards, sending his gunboats into Nyborg harbour to quash Danish resistance whilst La Romana's troops secured the fortress town and its batteries. Luck was on the side of the allies in that a quantity of somewhat-less-than-perfect shipping was discovered in the port, which would just about suffice to remove the waiting Spanish units to Langeland, seen as a secure staging post where a comprehensive concentration of La Romana's army could be made before its evacuation from the Baltic. In this chapter our focus will shift to the British efforts to make the most of the situation they were presented with, and to see how they overcame some significant difficulties in rising to the challenge, due mainly to the initiative and energy displayed by Rear Admiral Keats.

We begin with reference to an intelligence report compiled for Vice Admiral Saumarez by Captain Peter Paget of HMS *Goliath*, whilst his ship was on station between Danzig and Riga during the period 26 June to 6 July 1808. It contains the following passage:

> Masters of merchant ships from Memel [Lithuania] had informed the captain of *Goliath* of the presence of 15,000 Spanish troops. These had been divided [as follows]: one third to Copenhagen, one third to Poland and one third to Holstein under Bernadotte.

THE BRITISH NAVAL OPERATION

On 29 May, American captains out of Copenhagen had told of barracks being provided there for the Spanish …[1]

A second report, this from Captain Dickolman of the cutter, *Prince Gustavus*, dated 28 July 1808, informed the British Baltic forces that, 'Accounts from Spain and Portugal had reached Stralsund [but I have] received no intelligence about the Spanish troops.'[2]

So much for the British; but the French were also employing their intelligence services to keep a watchful eye upon the situation in the Baltic. It would seem that by the end of July 1808, their agents had become aware of British hopes to solidify their newly formed alliance with Spain, by focussing upon the possibility of offering assistance for the removal La Romana's army from its *de facto* captivity in Denmark. The following letter, addressed to Bernadotte and apparently written by the Commissioner General of Police in Antwerp, Jean Francois Bellemare on 16 July 1808, provides evidence that the French had gained some knowledge of British intentions:

Anvers [Antwerp], *le 16 Juliet 1808.*
[From:] *Le Comissaire Général de Police Anvers.*
[To:] *M. le Prince de Ponte Corvo.*

Sir,
Considering the position that I presently occupy and the measures I have been allowed to take, it is possible for me to obtain an understanding of English intentions and of the situation within England itself. On the occasions that I receive intelligence which I believe to be of such a nature that it might be of interest to you, I will ensure that you are provided with it.

I am assuming that at the present time Your Highness is aware of an attempt that might soon be made by the English to remove all or some of the Spanish troops under the command of the Marqués de La Romana. He appears to be in tune, perhaps too much in tune, with the ideas of the English government. He is also suspected of being against the interests of France and is seemingly willing to align himself with the policies of England. He is a man whose behaviour, words and correspondence should be kept under observation judging by the high opinion in which he is held in London. I am able to make these assertions from the content of specific reports I have received.

I am confident that Your Highness has taken all precautions necessary to locate the Spanish troops out of reach from any English expeditionary force, whose aim it would be to remove them.

My only intention in offering you this advice is to help you to provide the necessary security against such an incursion by the English.

With my greatest respects,
Bellemare.[3]

---

1 TNA, ADM 1/6/(352–353) Letters from Commander in Chief, Baltic, Nos. 1–169.
2 TNA, ADM 1/6/(365). Note: It would seem that Dickolman was referring to news of the Spanish uprising of May 1808 and the Franco–Spanish invasion of Portugal which preceded it.
3 Bellemare to Bernadotte, 16 July 1808, TNA, ADM 1/6/(438).

Two copies of this letter are available at The National Archives in Kew, but it is not clear if they are copies of Bellemare's letter made by someone associated with Britain's network of spies on mainland Europe, or the genuine article itself, intercepted *en-route* to Bernadotte who was then in Hamburg. At the time the letter was written Brother James Robertson had been operating in the Baltic region for several weeks and Mr McMahon had recently left England *en-route* to Denmark, each on their separate mission to make contact with La Romana. Perhaps their presence and purpose had been discovered.

It was on 1 August 1808, the date on which Fabregues was picked up by *Edgar*, that the British were to make their first direct contact with the Baltic Spaniards, and news of it came to Vice Admiral Saumarez aboard HMS *Victory* via Captain Graves of HMS *Brunswick* in the following report:

> Graves to Saumarez,
> HMS *Brunswick* off Sproe[?] 3 August 1808.
> Apologies for the capture of the ship, *Tigress*, by eighteen gunboats between Langeland and Zealand on her passage to you with a letter stating that a Spanish officer was received by the *Edgar* … bearing a message from the commanding officer of the Spanish troops at Langeland that he wished an interview with the English.[4] After consulting with captains MacNamara and Campbell, I dispatched the *Tigress* to give you the information, considering it a circumstance that should be made known to you without a moment's delay …
>
> Captain MacNamara [HMS *Edgar*], being appointed to that station, I conceived to him the prospect to hold that interview and desired him to undertake it. The variable winds … have not enabled him to reach the rendezvous appointed by the [Spanish] officer at the time of writing this.[5]

The Spanish officer referred to by Graves was, of course, Antonio Fabregues, whose story we have already related, and despite the unfavourable conditions mentioned by the captain of HMS *Brunswick*, MacNamara eventually succeeded in putting Fabregues ashore on Langeland some days later, after the Spaniard had spent some time aboard HMS *Superb* in the company of Admiral Keats.

When the news of Fabregues's presence aboard *Edgar* was initially received by Keats, he wrote to Saumarez informing him that he was awaiting the details of Fabregues's interview (mentioned in Graves's letter above) before making any decisions about how he should act. However, it would seem that he was already thinking of Langeland as a possible place of assembly for La Romana's forces, should they agree to embark, telling Saumarez that, 'it seems to me that it might under certain circumstances be very advantageous to get them into Langeland.'[6]

---

[4] This is probably a reference to Dionisio Vives.
[5] TNA, ADM 1/6/(401) Report from Captain Graves to Saumarez. The rendezvous point mentioned by Graves is that off the coast of Langeland which Fabregues had agreed with Vives.
[6] Keats to Saumarez, 4 August 1808, TNA, ADM 1/6/(403).

The rear admiral's hopes for mounting a rescue attempt were then given a given a significant boost when *Mosquito* arrived to join him, delivering Rafael Lobo and his papers aboard *Superb* with the Spaniard keen to get the business of rescuing his compatriots underway. It was also the case that the intelligence available to Keats regarding the situation of the Spanish troops on the various islands had been greatly improved via the divulgences of Fabregues. The Spaniard's statement to Keats (or MacNamara) now lies amongst the Admiralty Papers at The National Archives in Kew, it is dated 5 August 1808 aboard *Superb*, and it would seem that it was after he was transferred to *Superb* from *Edgar* that the Catalan wrote his missive, as it appears in Keats's book of memos. It is in French, written in the third person and accompanied by an outline of the Spanish dispositions in the Baltic (it also lists the Danish strength on Zealand) and was dictated to either Captain MacNamara or Rear Admiral Keats.[7] A translation of its content is provided below:

Superb,
5 August 1808

… Don Antonio Fabregues, ensign in the 1er Regimiento de Catalunya, was sent to serve with his regiment on the island of Langeland under the command of a French general. The lieutenant-colonel of his regiment was Don Dionisio Vives, who for some time had been determined to communicate with the English squadron in order to discover the state of things in Spain, and at the same time to know if the English were willing to embark the Spanish troops. Given the opportunity to send some dispatches to Copenhagen, he [Vives] asked the undersigned, Fabregues, to act as a courier for the documents and at the same time informed him that, should an opportunity present itself, he should place himself aboard a ship of the English squadron.

If, having succeeded in doing so, he was convinced that the English would be willing to receive the Spanish troops onboard, he should return to the pre-arranged place [off the coast of Langeland] and, using the pre-arranged signal [to his comrades ashore, indicate to them that they should try to reach the British ship from which he was making the signal]. Indeed, on the day when the undersigned succeeded in placing himself off Langeland aboard HMS *Edgar*, he made the signal, but Vives did not appear, the reason being [as the undersigned was soon to discover] that the strength of the wind was so great that Vives did not want to take the risk of reaching the ship.

The undersigned succeeded in boarding a ship of the English squadron as follows:

[Whilst off the coast of] Langeland in a fishing boat one day, he noticed some English boats chasing a group of small Danish vessels and obliged his rowers to make for them, at the same time waving to them [to indicate that he wanted to join them]. As soon he boarded one of the English vessels he was taken to *Edgar* and placed aboard her, where he remained until this day. He knows for certain that all of the Spanish troops share the same sentiments as those which he himself

---

7   TNA, ADM 1/6/421a. Fabregues's list of the disposition and strength of Spanish units in Demark, as dictated to Captain MacNamara or Admiral Keats.

feels, and that every individual wished for a favourable opportunity to escape from the French.

Signed: Antonio Fabregues Boixa.[8]

Table 4 'Return of the Spanish Troops that are in Dannemarck'.

At Zeeland	
Two regiments of infantry – Guadalajara y Asturias	4,000
There are no French troops, but the Spanish are commanded by a French general. Danish troops about	30,000
At Funen	
Regiment of Princessa, infantry	2,000
Ditto Barcelona, light infantry	1,000
Ditto Almansa, cavalry	400
Ditto Villaviciosa, ditto	300
Artillery with 16 field pieces	200
At Jutland	
Zamora, infantry	2,000
Algarve, cavalry	300
Infante, ditto	300
Rey, ditto	300
Artillery with four field pieces	50
At Langeland	
1º de Cataluña, light infantry	1,100
Artillery with two field pieces	25

From TNA, ADM1/6/421a. This is a verbatim copy of Fabregues's table of Spanish dispositions. From the mixture of languages (see title and penultimate row) it is quite clear that a it was dictated to a British sailor in somewhat informal terms.

The various comings and goings aboard the British ships in the Baltic on 5 August are described in their logs. At 10:30 a.m. on the morning of Friday, 5 August 1808, the following entry was written in the log of *Mosquito*, the ship which brought Rafael Lobo to the Baltic: 'Sent a boat on board HMS *Edgar* … boat returns.'[9] This would suggest that the captains of *Mosquito* and *Edgar* were made aware of the presence of each other's Spanish guest; Fabregues on *Edgar* and Lobo on *Mosquito*. The following entry from *Mosquito*'s log for 13:30 p.m. on 5 August probably marks the transfer of Lobo to *Superb*: 'Joined company with HMS *Superb* Rear Admiral Keats … Sent the Spanish officer on board the Admiral.'[10] These log entries would appear to confirm de Llano's earlier claim that Keats, after receiving Lobo aboard *Superb* from *Mosquito*, had then returned him to *Mosquito* (we know Lobo had left *Superb* by the time Fabregues was delivered to *Superb* by *Edgar*) so that he could go in search of Saumarez's squadron, after telling the Spaniard that he could not see how he could offer his assistance to remove La Romana's men from the Baltic without the permission of his superior. It was only after Fabregues had

---

8 TNA, ADM 1/6/(421–422). Statement from Fabergues to Captain MacNamara or Keats. Note: Fabregues sent his signal each day whilst off Langeland aboard *Edgar* between 1 and 5 August 1808.
9 TNA, ADM 51/1828, Log of *Mosquito*.
10 TNA, ADM 51/1828, Log of *Mosquito*.

later been placed aboard *Superb* by the *Edgar* that Keats changed his mind and sent what would seem to have been *Edgar* in pursuit of *Mosquito*, to tell her captain to return Lobo to *Superb*.

During the course of that busy day aboard *Superb*, 5 August 1808, Keats took the opportunity to strengthen his naval force by taking command of four gunboats which were in company with a passing British convoy, assigning one to each of *Superb*, *Devastation*, *Brunswick* and *Hound*. In a letter to Saumarez dated that day he makes mention of the threat posed by the increasing size of the Danish gunboat flotilla, noting that there were some 18 of those vessels then active in his area of operations.[11]

In another letter of 5 August, Keats makes his first direct communication with La Romana, informing him of the decision taken by the British government that he should offer the Spaniard all the assistance he could to embark his army and remove it to Spain. He goes on to suggest that the widely dispersed Spanish units be concentrated on 'some of the islands of the Belt, for their perfect security' until the expected transports arrive from England, and then states that the details of a concerted plan for the coming operation would have to be settled upon, at the same time requesting a meeting between the representatives of the new allies. There is also a proposal to La Romana that he might like to demonstrate his willingness to meet by sending one of his men out to the ships bearing a copy of his (that is, Keats's) letter, as proof of identity and authority. Failing this, he continues, he will send someone under a flag of truce to the Spanish post at Spodsberg on the east coast of Langeland, to whom the Spanish should give a sign of their acceptance by making some conspicuous signal from the shore at noon on the following day. No doubt this letter from Keats was taken ashore by Fabregues along with the papers from London and Seville, which he received from Lobo whilst both men were aboard *Superb*.[12]

We may note here an entry from the log of HMS *Edgar* for 6 August 1808, confirming that Fabregues was put ashore on Langeland at 2:30 a.m. on that day:

> Came on board the Spanish officer. 2:30 a.m. landed him on the island [of Langeland]. Made the signal to the shore with a gun … Papers by HMS *Superb* answered. Sent a cutter around the island of Langeland, observed a Spanish soldier waving the ship.[13]

With his usual thoroughness Keats, in his letter of the 5th, informs La Romana that he will instruct all of his crews to be on the lookout for any of his men who may thus make an approach by boat. This is confirmed in his message to the captains of his fleet dated 7 August aboard *Superb* off Langeland, in which he reminds them that, should such a happy circumstance arise, the conveying vessel and its crew ought to, 'be received and care taken not to let

---

11   Keats to Saumarez, 5 August 1808, TNA, ADM 1/6/(425–426).
12   Keats to La Romana, 5 August 1808, pp. 17–18, TNA, ADM 1/7/(17–18) Letters from Commander in Chief, Baltic, Nos 170–312.
13   TNA, ADM 51/2336, Log of *Edgar*.

them return, unless a particular desire be expressed to that purpose by the persons received.' Irked by the memory of a similar event in the past in which the 'water taxi' involved was allowed to leave after delivering a messenger, thus creating the need to find alternative means to return him whence he came, Keats was determined not to have a repeat of the incident.[14]

It would appear that the hoped-for communication between British and Spanish forces was successfully initiated at this point, and in his next letter to La Romana Keats refers to a Spanish officer and some papers he had handed over to either himself or Captain MacNamara, which contained a detailed return of the Spanish forces in Denmark (he was almost certainly referring to Fabregues and his divulgences whilst aboard *Edgar* and *Superb*). He also outlines several possibilities for the forthcoming operation, but towards the end of his communique he makes allowance for the case that La Romana's preference might be that of seizing the port of Nyborg.[15]

By 8 August HMS *Mosquito* had been in the Baltic for three days, she arrived from England on the 5th bringing orders from the Admiralty for Saumarez (as well as Lobo and his papers) duplicates of which were passed to Captain Graves (HMS *Brunswick*) to be delivered to Keats. Strangely, in a letter to the Admiralty dated 8 August, Vice Admiral Saumarez makes no mention of Don Rafael Lobo's arrival aboard *Mosquito*. However, he confirms to their lordships that he will provide all the assistance he can to the proposed rescue operation regarding the Spanish troops, but stresses that his priority remains that of protecting the Baltic trade.[16]

The Embarkation at Nyborg

It was also on 8 August that La Romana began his move to seize the port of Nyborg, as related earlier. Once the operation was concluded, Keats, who was aboard HMS *Brunswick* at the time, was quick to congratulate him in his letter of the same date,[17] and sent the *Brunswick*'s Captain Graves ashore to make an assessment of the shipping in the harbour, by then under Anglo-Spanish control.

In a letter to La Romana dated 9 August, the rear admiral points out to the Spanish commander that he can take only 1,500 of his men aboard those of his ships standing off Nyborg, suggesting that the troops be transported only as far as Langeland, where they may await the anticipated arrival of a convoy of transports from England. He explains that he will be sending some of his sailors into Nyborg to man 20 of the Danish smacks taken when

---

14 Book of Orders and Letters of Captain (afterwards Admiral) Keats, Keats to all captains, 7 August 1808, TNA, ADM 80/145.
15 Keats to La Romana, 7 August 1808, TNA, ADM 1/7/(19–20).
16 Saumarez to the Admiralty, 8 August 1808, TNA, ADM 1/6/(415).
17 We should note here that Keats's dates regarding the seizure of Nyborg are a little out of kilter with those of O'Donnell and Salvador (see earlier). Keats's are probably more trustworthy as they are taken from his contemporaneous diaries and logs, whereas O'Donnell, Salvador and the rest of the Spaniards were relying more upon their memories of events some 10 years past when they wrote their statements.

it was occupied; more, he says, will follow as the rest of his ships arrive at the port. He ended his letter by advising that water and provisions for the Spanish troops must be placed aboard all designated troop carriers at the first opportunity.[18]

Before sending his ships into the harbour to help secure it, Keats wrote a letter to the governor of Nyborg in which he asks the Dane not to interfere with the operation to embark the Spaniards, hinting at the possible consequences should he refuse to cooperate:

From: Keats, aboard HMS *Brunswick* off Nyborg.
To: His Excellency the Governor of the town of Nyborg.
9 August 1808

Sir,
His Excellency, the Commander in chief of the Spanish forces in Denmark, having deemed it expedient, under the present circumstances, to take possession of Nyborg, my duty naturally calls me to a cooperation with the troops of that nation, and a constant frequent communication with the town of Nyborg. To place Your Excellency as much at ease as possible respecting the line of conduct that may be adopted in the present event by the English admiral commanding in the Belt, notwithstanding the hostility of this day, I have the honour to inform you, that I have given the strictest orders to all under my command, to observe towards the inhabitants of Nyborg the utmost civility; and it is my wish to abstain from every hostile and offensive act, so long as no hostile and offensive measures are pursued by the troops of Denmark and France against those of Spain; but, if any opposition should be attempted by the Danes or French, to the peaceable and unoffending object in view, namely, the quiet embarkation of the Spanish troops, I shall certainly, take measures which it is to be apprehended might occasion the destruction of the town of Nyborg.[19]

Historians are people with an eye for detail, and by now some of the readers might be asking themselves just how it was that Keats was writing memos aboard *Superb* whilst she was off Langeland on the 7 of August (he actually wrote one as late as the 8 August from *Superb*) and now we see him writing letters to the governor of Nyborg whilst aboard *Brunswick*, off Nyborg, on 9 August, the two places being separated by a distance of some 35 miles by sea. The answer comes from Rafael Lobo's statement to the *Comisión de Jefes*. Lobo was also aboard *Superb* off Langeland on the night of 7 August, Fabregues having been placed ashore on that island just two days earlier. Anxious to hear of any news which might have emerged from Fabregues's meeting with La Romana at Nyborg, Lobo went ashore on Langeland and discovered that La Romana had already set his plan for taking Nyborg in motion, and with that news he swiftly returned to Keats on *Superb*, insisting that all the ships of his squadron should immediately head for Nyborg. Unfortunately, the winds and currents were not favourable at that moment,

---

18   Keats to La Romana, 9 August 1808, TNA, ADM 1/7/(21).
19   Keats to the Governor of Nyborg, 9 August 1808, TNA, ADM 1/7/(23).

so Keats suggested that both he and Lobo make the journey in a *falua* (a type of small sailing boat). Lobo continues in his statement to say that, 'At nine on the morning of 8 August we boarded the *falua* and at eight that night we were aboard the *Brunswick* in front of Nyborg, having rowed 12 leagues in eleven hours.'[20] With that, we may now return to our story.

Despite his keenness to assist at Nyborg, Keats's ships were to discover two Danish gunboats blocking their passage as they neared the harbour entrance, and he was left with no alternative but to enter into action. After a short but lively engagement in which both sides sustained casualties, the way was cleared to continue with the operation on the morning of 10 August 1808. On that day Keats wrote again to the governor, our previously mentioned 'Guildencrown', apparently unaware that he was by then in the custody of the Spaniards, having been arrested by José O'Donnell early that morning:

From Keats, aboard HMS *Hound* off Nyborg.
To His Excellency the Governor of the town of Nyborg.
10 August 1808

Sir,
It must be evident to Your Excellency that, as my entrance into the harbour of Nyborg was hostilely opposed, I am bound by no absolute law or usage to abstain from hostilities, and to respect the property of the inhabitants. But, though neither one nor the other could be better secured than by the word of a British officer, still it must be evident to Your Excellency, that under existing circumstances, the Spanish general has occasion for several of the small craft in port, and that unless the masters and crews of them will lend their aid to equip and navigate the vessels, it may not be in my power to secure them from injury; but, if they will, I pledge myself, after the service on which they are required (and which will be of short duration) shall have been ended, that I will not only use every means in my power to secure them from injury, but grant passports to them all to return in safety.[21]

To allow himself to remain close to the point of action, Keats had placed himself aboard the shallow–draught sloop, *Hound*. She was a much smaller vessel than *Brunswick* and could therefore navigate the shallow waters of the harbour. On 9 August, once he had just about established control of the port, Keats wrote to the captains of *Superb*, *Brunswick*, *Edgar*, *Hound*, *Kite* and *Devastation*, requesting that the first three listed each provide eight crews to man the best of the captured Danish vessels; the remainder each to provide three. This gave a total of 33 crews, each of six men, to supervise the embarkation of troops, baggage, horses and artillery before sailing the vessels to Langeland.[22]

Via a memo of 10 August, a further 70 men from the crews of *Superb*, *Brunswick* and *Edgar* were allocated to help equip the Danish boats (which we shall henceforth refer to as the 'Nyborg transports') and haul them out

---

20   *AGMM, Bailén 7272.2, Memoria de Lobo*, p.2.
21   Keats to the Governor of Nyborg, 10 August 1808, TNA, ADM 1/7/(25).
22   Keats to respective captains, 9 August 1808, TNA, ADM 80/145.

THE BRITISH NAVAL OPERATION

of Nyborg harbour. In another memo of the same day, again to 'respective captains', Keats gives instructions for the soldiers of the Spanish Army to be embarked from Slipshavn, which is situated about a mile and a half from Nyborg harbour at the end of the Knudshoved promontory lying immediately south–east of the port.[23]

The rear admiral did his best to keep his commander in chief informed of his actions, and in a letter to Saumarez of 11 August he provides him with a comprehensive report on the events at Nyborg, putting the number of Spanish troops embarked at 6,000 with a further 1,000 joining by sea, having made their own escape from Jutland. These were the cavalry regiments of Rey and Infante which had sailed from Aarhus. He adds that another 1,000 men, 'Are thrown into Langeland' and by this he was referring to the men of Barcelona and Villaviciosa who, having commenced their movement on 9 August, managed to 'island–hop' their way from Svendborg on Funen to Rudkobing on Langeland via the isle of Tassing, as earlier described (he confirms this movement in a footnote to his letter). He also gives praise to Fabregues, 'the Spanish officer on the *Edgar*,' for facilitating the means of communication between British and Spanish forces, and Saumarez is informed that, although the Danish garrison 'yielded to circumstances, an armed brig of eighteen guns, the *Fama*, and a cutter of twelve, the *Sacorman*' resisted until they were 'reduced' by the *Edgar*. These vessels were soon repaired and taken as prizes, giving good service over the coming weeks as the operation proceeded.

Note is made of the 57 sloops or doggers (Nyborg transports) which were commandeered in the harbour before being fitted out and loaded with the greater part of the artillery, baggage and stores belonging to the Spaniards. All vessels then sailed down to Slipshavn, where the troops were embarked on the following morning. Due praise is given to his officers and men for successfully carrying out the operation.[24]

Details of the naval action at Nyborg

There are but a few brief lines contained in the logs of the various ships which relate to the action at Nyborg, but those that were written do provide some detail of events in the harbour as Keats's action unfolded.

Logs for 9 August.

> HMS *Brunswick*:
> Came on board a boat with two Spanish officers from Nyborg. Sent the barge to Langeland [*sic* for Funen?] with a Spanish officer.[25] Captain Graves (*Brunswick*) and the Spanish Ambassador[?] went ashore to Nyborg at 3:50 p.m. At 4:00 p.m.

---

23 Keats to respective captains, 10 August 1808, TNA, ADM 80/145.
24 Keats to Saumarez, 11 August 1808, TNA, ADM 1/6/(442–443) and TNA, ADM 1/7/(27–28).
25 It would seem that the log writer aboard *Brunswick* had confused Funen for Langeland.

manned the gunboats and launch to engage the enemy in Nyborg. 7:15 p.m. heard the boats engaging; 7:45 p.m. the firing ceased, the enemy having struck.[26]

HMS *Devastation*:
7:40 p.m.: Observed Danish brig open fire on the *Kite* & *Hound* ... 8:00 p.m. Enemy surrendered. Anchored in harbour.[27]

HMS *Edgar*:
Sent all the boats armed into the harbour in Co with the boats of the squadron. At 7:40 p.m. the enemy commenced firing at boats, the firing ceased; at 10:30 p.m. the boats returned having secured the vessels in the harbour.[28]

HMS *Hound*:
Passed by HMS *Superb* & *Brunswick*. *Kite* anchored in entrance to Nyborg harbour. At 7:15 p.m. a Danish brig & [?] commenced firing on us & the gunboats – which the boats returned. At 7:40 p.m. fired once at the Danish vessels when they struck colours and the brig taken possession of by Captain Lockyer. Anchored in Nyborg harbour.[29]

With Danish resistance quashed the work to embark the Spaniards, their equipment and baggage got underway and Keats displayed enormous energy in supervising the task. Temporary crews were assembled for each of the Danish craft captured in the harbour, some of which had to be made seaworthy before they could take onboard men or cargo, and once an assessment of their condition had been made, carpenters were assigned to carry out the necessary repairs. Some indication of the level of activity in the port is contained within the ships' logs.

Logs for 10 August.

HMS *Brunswick*:
Cleaning the fore hold for the reception of prisoners. Barge returned from Langeland [*sic* for Funen?] with one man killed and one dangerously wounded. At 4:00 p.m. sent all boats ashore with parties of men to fit out the Danish prizes. Came alongside, the *GH* victualler. The admiral on board the *Hound* & the Danish vessels getting under weigh in the harbour, joined by a brig & 3 sloops.[30]

HMS *Devastation*:
The captain, 6 officers & 30 seamen went on shore to fit out vessels for the embarkation of the Spanish troops & equipage. Officers, ship's co. & boats employed embarking the equipage, sick and women of the Spanish army on board

---

26 TNA, ADM 51/1823, Log of *Brunswick*.
27 TNA, ADM 51/1957, Log of *Devastation*.
28 TNA, ADM 51/2336, Log of *Edgar*.
29 TNA, ADM 51/1948, Log of *Hound*.
30 TNA, ADM 51/1823, Log of *Brunswick*. Note, it would seem that the log writer is still confusing Funen for Langeland.

the [Danish] Schuyts. Sent a party of men with artillerymen on shore to dismantle the guns in two batteries. Weighed and ran out to outer roads.[31]

HMS *Edgar*:
Sent a party of men to assist equipping the vessels captured.[32]

HMS *Hound*:
At 10:00 a.m. hoisted the flag of Rear Admiral Keats. Fitting out the Danish vessels. Removed 40 Danish vessels.[33]

Logs for 11 August.

HMS *Brunswick*:
Getting ready to receive Spanish troops and storing away provisions. Cleared 4 Danish sloops of Spanish troops. Sent a butt of water and a bag of bread aboard one of the Danish sloops for the Spanish troops. Sent the gunboat onshore to signal the boats still embarking troops from the shore at 12:00 a.m.[34]

HMS *Devastation*:
Sent all boats with an officer in each on shore to embark Spanish Army.[35]

HMS *Edgar*:
Sent all boats and a working party away to bring off the Spanish troops. Received 217 Spanish soldiers.[36]

HMS *Hound*:
Embarked Spanish troops. At noon boats returned having embarked Spanish troops on board 65 vessels. Struck the flag of Admiral Keats at 3:30 p.m.[37]

A report on the action at Nyborg was later submitted to the Danish authorities by General-Adjutant F. Bulow, chief of headquarters of the Danish Army, and it might be worth noting that his list of the ships seized by Keats does not tally exactly with the latter's:[38]

> In the port of Nyborg the enemy seized the brig [*brick de guerre*] *la Fama* (two six-pounders and a dozen twelve-pound carronades) the cutter [*yacht de guerre*] *Soe-Orm* (twelve eight-pounders and eight four-pounders) and the armed pilot

---

31 TNA, ADM 51/1957, Log of *Devastation*.
32 TNA, ADM 51/2336, Log of *Edgar*.
33 TNA, ADM 51/1948, Log of *Hound*.
34 TNA, ADM 51/1823, Log of *Brunswick*.
35 TNA, ADM 51/1957, Log of *Devastation*.
36 TNA, ADM 51/2336, Log of *Edgar*.
37 TNA, ADM 51/1948, Log of *Hound*.
38 It is quite easy to see how the British interpretation of the name of one of the boats, *i.e. Sacorman*, may well have been a confusion of *Soeorm*, especially if the last two characters were indicators of a port of registration, hypothetically 'an' for Anholt, for instance: (*e.g.* Sacorm vs Soeorm, or, adding the hypothetical port identifier: Sacorman vs Soeorm an).

boat, *Laurwig*. These ships were surrendered only after their crews had put up a courageous fight for twenty minutes against a superior British squadron with double their fire power, allied to that of the land batteries occupied by the Spanish.[39]

The Evacuation of the Spaniards from Nyborg to Langeland

With the army's baggage and equipment safely embarked at Nyborg it was time to embark the Spanish troops, and as he moved his ships to nearby Slipshavn, Keats began to focus his mind upon the planned disembarkation at Langeland, an operation he thought might prove difficult and dangerous. In customary fashion he attempted to anticipate problems before they arose, La Romana sending Felix de la Carrera to Langeland on the night of 10 August to warn the Spanish troops there of the intention to disembark the bulk of the army onto the island. Then, in a memo to all respective captains, Keats instructed them to 'anchor as near to the shore of Langeland as the depth of water will allow', and continued as follows:

> If, in the passage to it [the anchorage], any gunboats of the enemy should be met, the men–of–war nearest that can without difficulty communicate with them, will send a flag of truce and inform their commanders [that] the vessels in company are from Nyborg with the Spanish Army, which by convention are peaceably retiring to their own country from Denmark. And if any opposition or hostile measure be adopted on the part of the gun boats, the English admiral will burn every vessel, instead of affording them passports to return unmolested to Nyborg, which otherwise they would have been permitted to do.
>
> *Hound*, Nyborg Harbour, 11 August 1808.[40]

On the same day, the rear admiral circulated a memo to respective captains containing his 'Scheme of Embarkation' for the Spanish soldiers, which was to be carried out at Slipshavn. *Superb*, *Brunswick* and *Edgar* were each to receive 800 troops; *Hound* 200; *Devastation* and *Kite* 150 each and *Minx* 100; thirty *schoots* (Nyborg transports) would each take 150, giving an overall total capacity of some 7,500 men.[41]

Confirmation of the success of the Nyborg operation was conveyed to the Admiralty in a letter dated 13 August, which Keats sent to England with the *Euryalus*, stopped by the rear admiral on her passage home from the Baltic. Their lordships were also informed that all evacuees from Nyborg had been successfully placed ashore on Langeland and that La Romana and the Danish governor of the island had entered into a convention designed

---

39 Bulow's report appeared in *Pallas: eine Zeitschr. für Staats–u. Kriegs–Kunst, Volume 1, 1808*, (Tubingen: J. G, Cotta, 1808), p.454.
40 TNA, ADM 80/145, Keats to respective captains, 11 August 1808.
41 Using the regimental returns for La Romana's army, the numbers awaiting evacuation at Nyborg would have been: Princesa 1er, 2o & 3er bns. (2,282); Zamora 1er, 2o & 3er bns. (2,256 – crossed from Jutland); Almansa cavalry (540); Artilleria (527); Zapadores (100) plus La Romana's staff, giving a total of some 5,710. The cavalry regiments of Rey and Infante were at Nyborg aboard their own transports having sailed from Jutland.

Spanish cart ('tartana') with a soldier of the regiment of Guadalajara and his family. (From the Suhr brothers serie *Sammlung verschiedener Spanischer National-Trachten und Uniformen der Division des Marquis de la Romana, 1807 und 1808 in Hamburg in Garnison*; collection of Markus Stein)

i

Servant of a Catalonian officer in a peasant smock. (From the Suhr brothers series *Sammlung verschiedener Spanischer National-Trachten und Uniformen der Division des Marquis de la Romana, 1807 und 1808 in Hamburg in Garnison*; collection of Markus Stein)

Muleteers transporting forage. (From the Suhr brothers series *Sammlung verschiedener Spanischer National-Trachten und Uniformen der Division des Marquis de la Romana, 1807 und 1808 in Hamburg in Garnison*; collection of Markus Stein)

Line and light infantrymen, with a muleteer. (From the Suhr brothers series *Sammlung verschiedener Spanischer National-Trachten und Uniformen der Division des Marquis de la Romana, 1807 und 1808 in Hamburg in Garnison*; collection of Markus Stein)

Light infantryman of the 1er de Catalunya, with his wife and child. (From the Suhr brothers series *Sammlung verschiedener Spanischer National-Trachten und Uniformen der Division des Marquis de la Romana, 1807 und 1808 in Hamburg in Garnison*; collection of Markus Stein)

Prince of Pontecorvo's Guard of Honour formed by men belonging to the regiment of Zamora, with a Catalan officer, 1807. (NYPL Vinkhuijzen Collection)

to prevent hostilities for the duration of the occupation.[42] In another letter bearing the same date he writes to Saumarez informing him of the landings at Langeland, adding that he will set to work on the following day to begin the task of preparing the best of the Nyborg transports for the purpose of evacuating the troops from the island, should the need arise. He also advises his commander in chief that, in his opinion, the island would not be able to sustain the Spanish troops for more than two weeks.[43]

O'Donnell says that the convoy carrying the troops from Nyborg to Langeland anchored at Spodsberg on the east coast of the island on 13 August, and that once the men were ashore, they crossed to the west coast where they bivouacked and set up defensive posts along the shoreline, making use of some of the heavy artillery they found nearby. Spanish headquarters were established at Rudkobing and La Romana, after initiating talks with the commander of the Danish troops on the island, Count Ahlefeldt Laurwig, obtained his agreement not to engage in hostilities, but nevertheless insisted that the Danes surrender their arms and horses, the latter were then put to use by the Spanish when forming a cavalry unit to help defend the island, should the need arise.[44]

With all going as well as could be expected, Keats ultimately suffered his first setback. In a letter to the Admiralty dated simply, August 1808, he says that he has received correspondence from Gothenburg informing him that the merchants there, in combination, are willing to let their vessels 'only at an exorbitant price.' He then makes a first mention of the idea that he should use his own resources to transport the Spaniards to Gothenburg, rather than await a deal to be struck with the Swedish ship owners.[45] A second letter, sent to the Admiralty on 13 August, illustrates Keats's concerns about the supply of provisions for the 10,000 men of La Romana's army then on Langeland.[46] The *Ann*, a victualler, had recently arrived on the scene, but Keats states that 'much of her cargo has already been appropriated by the officer commanding.'[47] He also informs their lordships that he has had word from Saumarez that two more victuallers have received orders to sail for the island, and reveals his intention to detain the Nyborg transports until the victuallers arrive. The whole together, he suggests, might then suffice to transport the Spanish army to Carlscrona or Gothenburg. They are further informed that La Romana considers the island of Langeland 'tenable' but, as Keats points out, 'the rapid approach of a change of season, and other circumstances, rather incline me to a desire to make an effort to convey them with the least delay to Sweden.'[48]

---

42 Keats to Admiralty, 13 August 1808, TNA, ADM 1/6/(454).
43 Keats to Saumarez, 13 August 1808, TNA, ADM 1/7/(15).
44 *AGMM, Bailén 7272.2, Memoria de O'Donnell*, pp.16–17.
45 Keats to Admiralty, [?] August 1808, TNA, ADM 1/6/(455).
46 To the 6,250 or so to be transported from Nyborg has to be added the 1,250 or so of the 1er de Barcelona together with Villaviciosa who crossed from Svendborg, the men of Rey and Infante (1,080) who made their own crossing from Aarhus via Nyborg, and the Spanish garrison troops on Langeland, Catalunya (1,200).
47 It is not clear if Keats was talking about La Romana or Saumarez.
48 Keats to Admiralty, 13 August 1808, TNA, ADM 1/6/(456–457).

NAPOLEON'S STOLEN ARMY

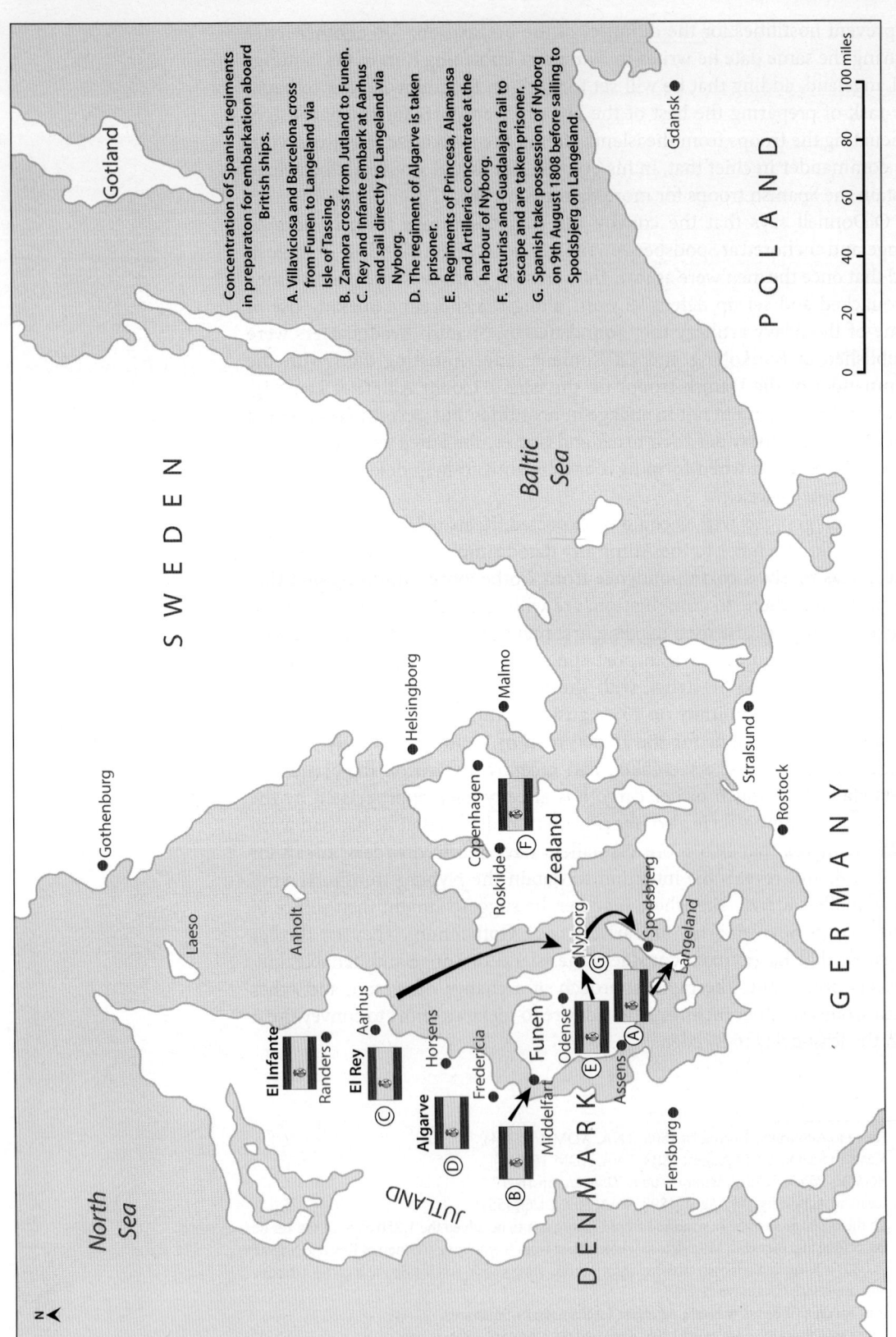

Concentration of Spanish regiments in preparation for embarkation aboard British ships.

A. Villaviciosa and Barcelona cross from Funen to Langeland via Isle of Tassing.
B. Zamora cross from Jutland to Funen.
C. Rey and Infante embark at Aarhus and sail directly to Langeland via Nyborg.
D. The regiment of Algarve is taken prisoner.
E. Regiments of Princesa, Alamansa and Artilleria concentrate at the harbour of Nyborg.
F. Asturias and Guadalajara fail to escape and are taken prisoner.
G. Spanish take possession of Nyborg on 9th August 1808 before sailing to Spodsbjerg on Langeland.

Movements made by Spanish units in August 1808 as they concentrate on Langeland.

Keats Prepares to Evacuate the Spaniards from Langeland to Gothenburg

The rear admiral was obviously not a man to waste a single second if he could avoid it, and his mind seems to have been working in overdrive to formulate a viable plan for removing the Spaniards from their perilous situation at the earliest opportunity. His next memorandum to respective captains, dated 14 August, provides an illustration of Keats's talent for meticulous planning. The captain of each of the capital ships of his squadron is instructed to ensure that each of the transports to which he has supplied a crew is to have painted on its bow and quarter the first letter of his ship *i.e.* a letter 'S', 'B', 'E', 'H', 'D' or 'K'. Each assigned transport will then receive a number to give it a unique identifier. For example, *Superb*'s transports will carry the identifiers: S1, S2 … S20. *Brunswick*'s will carry, B1, B2 … B15, whilst *Kite*'s will have K1, K2 and K3. An inventory template is provided for the captain of each transport so that once their returns were collated into a single document, it would indicate the sea worthiness and readiness of each of the vessels.[49]

In a short memorandum of the same day, Keats mentions the seven boats which had arrived from Jutland (Aarhus) carrying the Spanish cavalry units of El Infante and El Rey, who had pressed their Danish crews into service. These were the *Anna Maria*, *Duen*, *Maria I*, *Kaftine*, *Marie*, *The Three Dames* and the *Rib Marie*.[50] It might be instructive to reproduce in full Keats's next memo of 14 August, in which he includes the final changes to his scheme for the identification and organisation of the vessels he is anticipating will have to be convoyed from Langeland to Gothenburg:

> A lieutenant from each of the ships of the line, and a respectable petty officer from the smaller ships, are to be put into one of the most eligible transports [associated with his ship] who will be considered as the Agent of the whole that are manned by the ship he may belong to. The *Superb*'s are to be distinguished by a red vane; the *Brunswick*'s by a white; *Edgar*'s by a blue; *Kite*'s by a blue with a white ball; *Hound*'s by a half white, half red vertical; *Devastation*'s by a half blue, half yellow vertical.
>
> The Agents are to wear small, broad pendants, the colour of the vane of their division, and they are all to be provided with the printed convoy signals and instructions, and apprised that all signals made [which are] accompanied with a triangular yellow flag, relate to them.[51]

International politics then took a hand in matters, as the Swedes began to prove difficult allies. Saumarez, it seems, had submitted a request to the Swedish government asking for permission to disembark the Spanish troops in Sweden, should there be a delay in the arrival of their transports from England. In a letter to the Admiralty, Saumarez reveals the gist of the Swedish reply:

---

[49] Keats to respective captains, 14 August 1808, TNA, ADM 80/145.
[50] Keats to respective captains, 14 August 1808, TNA, ADM 80/145.
[51] Keats to respective captains, 14 August 1808, TNA, ADM 80/145.

> Saumarez to the Admiralty,
> Dar[?] Head, 14 August 1808.
> I enclose for their lordships' information an extract of a letter which I have this morning received from Baron Toll, governor general of Scania, in reply to mine of the 11th instant requesting to be informed on what part of the coast of Sweden the Spanish troops could be received, should the endeavours to withdraw them from the islands in the Belt prove successful, and so by the Baron's reply, it appears doubtful whether they can be admitted in Sweden, their lordships will be pleased to order a sufficient number of transports to embark them from the island of Langeland.[52]

In the extract to which Saumarez refers there is not much sign of any eagerness on the part of the Swedes to help him. Reading between the lines of Toll's reply, the best we can say is that the baron's referral of Saumarez's request to the King of Sweden smacks of procrastination rather than an outright refusal. Toll's letter, written in French and attached to that of Saumarez's to the Admiralty, forms part of the same reference given above.

Meanwhile Keats, aboard *Superb* off Langeland on 15 August, was busy with his plans and preparations for the anticipated re-embarkation of the Spanish troops. The transports requested from England by Saumarez would take some time to arrive, if they were to arrive at all, and he must surely have been thinking through the possible consequences which chance of circumstance might bring along in the meantime. The French and Danes might cross the narrow channel which separates Langeland from Funen; it may not be possible to keep the thousands of Spanish troops on the island supplied until the transports arrive; the growing menace from the Danish gunboats might put his warships, not to say the expected British merchantmen, at risk and the weather might turn at any time as the nights drew in.

There was also the threat posed by Russia's Baltic fleet, now that the Tsar was in alliance with Napoleon. Saumarez might be able to confine it to the eastern waters of the Baltic using the reduced resources at his command, thus allowing Keats to stand watch over the Spanish Army, but his commander in chief would surely have liked to have *Superb*, *Brunswick* and *Edgar* available for any possible action. Should it be possible for the Spanish troops to be removed to a place of safety, if not directly to Spain then temporarily to Sweden, most of these problems would melt away. Keats began to plan for an early resolution to the Spanish question, and in a memo to his captains, written on 15 August, he talks about the re-embarkation of the Spaniards, adding that since 'circumstances may render such an event necessary at very short notice, all boats are to be kept constantly ready by day and night for that purpose.'[53] He then goes on to define a set of numerical signals to be used should circumstances deem it necessary. These are listed below:

---

52 Saumarez to Admiralty, 14 August 1808, TNA, ADM 1/6/(458–459).
53 Keats to respective captains, 15 August 1808, TNA, ADM 80/145.

Additional signals by day:

701: All boats to assemble on board the *Superb*, or in the direction denoted, to embark or disembark troops.

702: To commence the embarkation or disembarkation.

703: To stop the embarkation or disembarkation.

By night: Substitute signal by night:

41: Boats to assemble on board the Admiral, or wherever previously directed to embark or disembark troops.

42: To commence the embarkation or disembarkation.

43: To stop the embarking or disembarking of troops.

The officers and petty officers intended to be employed on this service are to be provided with copies of these signals.

Keats next turned his mind to his gunboats, and in a memorandum written on the same day as that regarding the signals just described, he wrote another to his captains instructing them to keep their gunboats in constant readiness for service. His communication contained the following set of additional signals.

Additional signals by day:

704: Gun boats to assemble on board the *Superb*, or in the direction denoted.

705: Gun boats to take a position more to the northward. If a particular number, it will be denoted.

706: Gun boats to take a position more to the southward. If a particular number, it will be denoted.

707: Gun boats, or the number of them specified, to proceed in the direction denoted.

708: Gun boats indicated are in a good position.

709: Gun boats not in an approved situation

710: Gun boats to anchor.

711: Gun boats to weigh.

712: To strike, if struck, to get up masts.

713: Recall.

Over the next few days Keats sent out several memos to his captains relating to the watering and provisioning of the various warships and transports standing off Langeland. The scale of this re–victualing task is highlighted by de Llano, when he says that on the 18 August, 'some 200 cattle were purchased as well as 600 tons of rye, 200 tons of peas, 800 lbs. of lard and some beer, all paid for in cash and embarked that day.'[54]

The transports, S10, B3, B6 and B14 were soon sent inshore to pick up the baggage of the army, and on 19 August the transport identifiers X1, X2 … X7 were mentioned by Keats for the first time; these were the seven small ships which came from Jutland ferrying the men of El Infante and El Rey which, as he commented on 15 August, were wholly crewed by Danish

---

54 *AGMM, Bailén 7272.2, Memoria de de Llano*, p.26.

sailors. Also, on the 19th *Edgar* is ordered to provision the prize, *Sacorman*, which was to receive one hundred troops, and to water and provision the victualler, *Mary*, which was to receive one hundred and twenty troops. *Brunswick* is instructed to do the same for the victualler, *British Volunteer*, again for one hundred and twenty troops, and the captain of the transport, *Mary*, was ordered to prepare to take on board the Spanish sick; she too was to be provisioned by *Brunswick*.

It was on that same day, the 19th, that Vice Admiral Saumarez arrived at Langeland in his flagship, *Victory*, and de Llano describes how La Romana went aboard her to have talks with the admiral, as all of the British ships raised the Spanish flag to the top of their mainmasts and fired a 24–gun salute to celebrate the union of the two nations, the Spanish artillery, he says, firing a corresponding salute.[55]

In another memo of that day, Keats expressed his hopes that the embarkation of the Spanish troops would be completed 'tomorrow, when they will proceed to Gothenburg' having been informed by Saumarez that he had received intelligence from Rear Admiral Hood, as well as some Swedish sources, informing him that the Russian fleet had put to sea. He regrets the impossibility of providing enough [transport] tonnage for Keats's operation and stresses his wish to see the Spaniards removed to Gothenburg with all expediency. He also mentions his regrets at not having the services of Keats's squadron at his disposal until the rear admiral's operation is concluded.[56] It is clear, from a subsequent memorandum by Saumarez, that he does not hold out much hope that Keats will find the convoy of transports requested from England when he arrives at Gothenburg, advising him to procure such tonnage as he can, at the best possible price, to transport the Spanish troops to Spain. It is obvious, from what he goes on to say, that he would like to have all of his capital ships available as soon as possible, as he is about to sail to the Gulf of Finland in search of the Russian fleet.[57]

In a third memorandum of the 19th, the British commander in chief includes a comprehensive return of the Spaniards on Langeland, it includes the number of women and children with the troops, which he puts at 116 of the former and 67 of the latter.[58]

Whilst Keats was busy with the preparations for re-embarkation, the Spaniards on the west coast of Langeland were anticipating trouble from the French and Danes. Each night, Spanish officers were sent out into the waters around Tassing and Svendborg in small launches, with instructions to report on all that they might see or hear. As a result, word soon began to arrive that Bernadotte had gathered sufficient forces on Jutland to allow him to cross the Little Belt on 20 August and take possession of the north and west of Funen, before beginning an anticipated move to the south-east of the island towards Svendborg in preparation for an invasion of Langeland. Time, it would seem, was once more working against La Romana and his

---

55 *AGMM, Bailén 7272.2, Memoria de de Llano*, p.26.
56 Saumarez to Admiralty, 19 August 1808, TNA, ADM 1/7/(34–35).
57 Saumarez to Admiralty, 19 August 1808, TNA, ADM 1/7/(46).
58 Saumarez to Admiralty, 19 August 1808, TNA, ADM 1/7/(48–50).

army, and when it was realised that the British naval forces would have great difficulty in operating amongst the shallows in the channel which separates Langeland from Funen, the concerns about a French crossing increased. Spurred on, and still uncertain about a timely arrival of British transports, work continued on the victualing and watering of the ships and boats which had brought La Romana's men from Nyborg, all in the expectation that they would have to be used to transport the army to a temporary place of sanctuary, probably Gothenburg. The wisdom of these precautions was aptly demonstrated when, on the night 22/23 August, there was much activity by the Danish gunboats in the waters between Tassing and Langeland, with several of the Spanish posts being fired upon. On that morning, the 23rd, the order was finally given to re-embark the troops at Spodsberg.[59]

Keats's Convoy Sails for Gothenburg

On 20 August, Keats had placed his men on two-thirds rations, as the victuallers he was expecting from Gothenburg had not arrived. The Spanish troops were placed under the same regimen, and on the 21st, two days before re-embarkation, he issued an 'Order of Sailing and Rendezvous' to all of his ships at Langeland. With the exception of *Superb*, each of *Brunswick*, *Edgar*, *Gorgon*, *Devastation*, *Hound* and *Kite* were to head a flotilla of victuallers, transports, Jutland transports and Nyborg transports. The assignment of the flotillas to their 'mother ship' was almost as it had been earlier; but it would seem that Keats had decided not to encumber his flagship, *Superb*, with the responsibility shepherding the 'S division' to Gothenburg. Instead, rather than issue a new set of identifiers for the little boats, which would have meant a lot of repainting of their hulls, he simply shuffled his earlier configuration by transferring the 'S division' of boats to *Brunswick*; *Brunswick* in turn transferring her 'B division' boats to *Edgar* and *Edgar* transferring her 'E division' boats to *Gorgon*, a newly-designated 'mother ship'. *Devastation*, *Hound* and *Kite* were each to keep their own division (D, H and K, respectively).

De Llano says that the Spanish troops began to concentrate at a point on the east coast of Langeland just a short distance from the coastal battery protecting Spodsberg, by then garrisoned by a strong Spanish force as a precaution that it might have to be used to protect the imminent re-embarkation. He also claims that the four Danish boats 'which had come from Randers carrying the men of El Rey' (they actually sailed from Aarhus) were allowed by Keats to sail for home, but that the four (actually three) which came from Aarhus carrying the men of El Infante were not so lucky. The Danish crews of these three vessels, some 22 men in all, looked on as their craft were victualled for eight days at sea; they were then told that they would be forced to join Keats's convoy, but with the promise that they, together with the crews of the brig and cutter taken at Nyborg, would be

---

59   *AGMM, Bailén* 7272.2, *Memoria de O'Donnell*, pp.17–18.

set free in exchange for an equal number of British prisoners who, it was proposed, should be released by the French and Danes at the same time as the Danish boats were handed back to their rightful owners. The proposal was apparently ignored by the Danish government.[60]

Barón de Armendáriz notes that, during his last few days on Langeland, the Spanish continued to be annoyed by Danish gunboats and the propaganda leaflets introduced onto the island by the French, but that the troops were eventually re-embarked on 21 August (actually the 23rd) and set sail for Gothenburg that day. 'Just one soldier was left ashore,' he says, 'a prisoner who was under a sentence of death, which was commuted to expatriation before his compatriots sailed.' The patriotic Spaniard going on to add that, 'to be deprived of being allowed to return to Spain was, in any case, a punishment far worse than death.'[61]

By the evening of 23 August, Keats had *Superb* off Nyborg on passage to Gothenburg along with his convoy of victuallers and various *pro tempore* transports. In his letter to the Admiralty bearing that date he informs their lordships that La Romana, aware that the French and Danes were gathering forces on Funen with the intention of crossing to Langeland, had encouraged him to embark his troops at the earliest possible opportunity. They are further informed that when Vice Admiral Saumarez arrived on the scene aboard HMS *Victory* he fully endorsed the thoughts of the Spanish commander in chief, and the operation was soon set in motion.

Still of the opinion that no transports had yet been ordered from England, Keats mused upon the possibility of sending some of the troops on to Yarmouth in a single 'division' made up of the best of the vessels at his disposal. He also expressed his concern that the crews belonging to his ships of the line should not be weakened by having a part of them continue to crew the Nyborg transports; especially after having received news that the Russian fleet had put to sea. In the convoy manifesto, which he includes with his letter, he states the number of women and children to be 234 compared to Saumarez's figure of 283. The document itself is another example of Keats's ever-prevailing thoroughness in that it states the number of troops aboard each and every ship and boat in his convoy, and in a footnote to his letter he informs the Admiralty that he has been joined by 18 navy and army victuallers, adding that he is now 'quite at ease on the subject of provisions' and that the newly arrived vessels will 'enable me to clear the crowded transports.'[62] This is confirmed by Rafael Lobo when he says that, 'The army was fully embarked by three o'clock on the afternoon of 20 August [British logs give the 23rd] and made sail towards the north of Langeland. By dawn on 21st [British logs give the 24th] the convoy was at anchor off Nyborg due to unfavourable winds.' He claims it was at this time when a convoy of

---

60 *AGMM, Bailén 7272.2, Memoria de de Llano*, p.28. It would seem that de Llano was mistaken when he claimed that four of the boats X1–X7 were allowed to return to Jutland. Firstly, only seven boats sailed from Aarhus carrying El Rey and El Infante, and not eight as he claims. Secondly, according to Keats's memos it was only X5 that was allowed to go back to Jutland, although it is listed in his convoy manifesto, the rest sailed to Gothenburg with Keats.
61 *AGMM, Bailén 7272.2, Memoria de Armendáriz*, p.9.
62 Keats to Admiralty, 22 August 1808, TNA, ADM 1/7/(56–59).

16 (Keats says 18) transports arrived from Gothenburg carrying victuals for army, 'Keats ordered some them to transfer their cargo into his warships and some of the small boats he was escorting, so that a number of our troops could then go aboard the transports in order to alleviate conditions on our boats, which were badly overloaded.'[63]

Table 5 provides the details of the convoy that set sail from Langeland to Gothenburg on 23 August 1808, and one can see, from the number of troops placed aboard, that many of them were indeed little boats.

Table 5 Manifesto of Keats's convoy which conveyed La Romana's army from Langeland to Gothenburg

Ship Name or Transport Identifier	No. of Troops	Name of Unit	Ship Name or Transport Identifier	No. of Troops	Name of Unit
Superb	945	Villaviciosa, Catalunya, Zamora & Estado Mayor (Staff of HQ)	B7	130	Zamora
Brunswick	937	Zamora & Estado Mayor	B8	80	Zamora
Edgar	860	Princesa & Estado Mayor	B9	145	Zamora
Gorgon	500	Catalunya	B10	22	Zamora
Devastation	158	Artillería & Princesa	B11	60	Rey
Hound	150	Barcelona	B12	78	*not given*
Fama	100	Infante	B13	45	Rey
Sacorman	100	Infante	B14	20	Infante & baggage
Diana, victualler	200	Rey	B15	45	Rey
Ann, hospital ship	200	Rey	E1	95	Princesa
Sincerity	100	Zapadores	E2	115	Princesa
British Volunteer	120	Almansa	E3	30	Princesa
Mary	120	Almansa	E4	95	Princesa
Aetna	200	*not given*	E5	60	Artillería & baggage
Sarah	200	Rey	E6	25	Princesa
S1	115	Catalunya	E7	140	Princesa
S2	100	Catalunya	E8	125	Princesa
S4	115	Almansa	E9	110	Princesa
S5	60	Rey	E10	40	Almansa & officers' baggage
S7	115	Almansa	E11	40	Almansa & baggage
S8	30	Artillería & Barcelona	E12	Reserved	n/a
S9	95	Catalunya	E13	90	Princesa

---

63   *AGMM, Bailén 7272.2, Memoria de Lobo*, p.3.

Ship Name or Transport Identifier	No. of Troops	Name of Unit	Ship Name or Transport Identifier	No. of Troops	Name of Unit
S10	20	Infante & baggage	E14	97	Princesa
S12	60	Infante	E15	90	Princesa
S13	100	Infante	D1	115	Artillería
S14	60	Infante	D2	30	Artillería
S15	60	Infante	H1	77	Princesa
S16	80	Infante	H2	90	Princesa
S18	60	Infante	K1	50	Barcelona
S19	90	Infante	K2	85	Barcelona
S20	75	Infante	K3	105	Barcelona
S21	70	Infante	X1	140	Barcelona
S22	75	Rey	X2	105	Barcelona
B1	145	Zamora	X3	115	Barcelona
B2	120	Zamora	X4	65	Barcelona
B3	20	Rey & baggage	X5	25	Barcelona
B4	140	Zamora	X6	60	Barcelona
B5	30	Artillería	X7	30	Almansa & cattle
B6	20	Zamora & baggage			

Note: In Keats's memo of 31/8/08 (ADM 80/145), *Adventure* is listed as having to disembark 80 Spanish troops, but she does not appear in the convoy manifesto of 22 August 1808 in ADM 1/7/ (58–60).

Source: TNA, ADM 1/7/(59), Keats's convoy manifesto.

As the convoy made its way north through the Great Belt, it passed close enough to Nyborg for the Danish coastal batteries to take a few short-falling pot shots at it. José O'Donnell, who was aboard one of the ships, makes mention of the canon fire, saying that it came from a coastal battery positioned on Cape Knudshoved, south of Nyborg. The flotilla must have looked very much like a smaller version of the armada of 'little boats' that was to embark a much larger army from the coast of northern France some 132 years later; albeit the former was made up entirely of sailing ships.

Before sailing on 23 August, Keats had asked each of his captains to submit a report listing those transports which were 'particularly crowded with troops,' and in his next memo, issued on the same day, he orders that the troops aboard each ship be divided into three watches so that they may be stationed and mustered proportionally. As many as possible are to be kept upon deck, weather permitting. Clothing and baggage are to be well aired, ships are to be fumigated every day, decks are to be scraped and scoured with dry sand, and the '…white–wash brush should always be going.'

To provide for a more robust fleet of troop transports, perhaps anticipating the need to convey the troops to England, Keats had also ordered the provisioning of the victuallers, *Diana* (HL) *Adventure* (HF) and *Lively* (GK) for 150 men each. The respective captains are instructed to ensure that each transport has a competent navigator aboard as well as a copied sheet of the

THE BRITISH NAVAL OPERATION

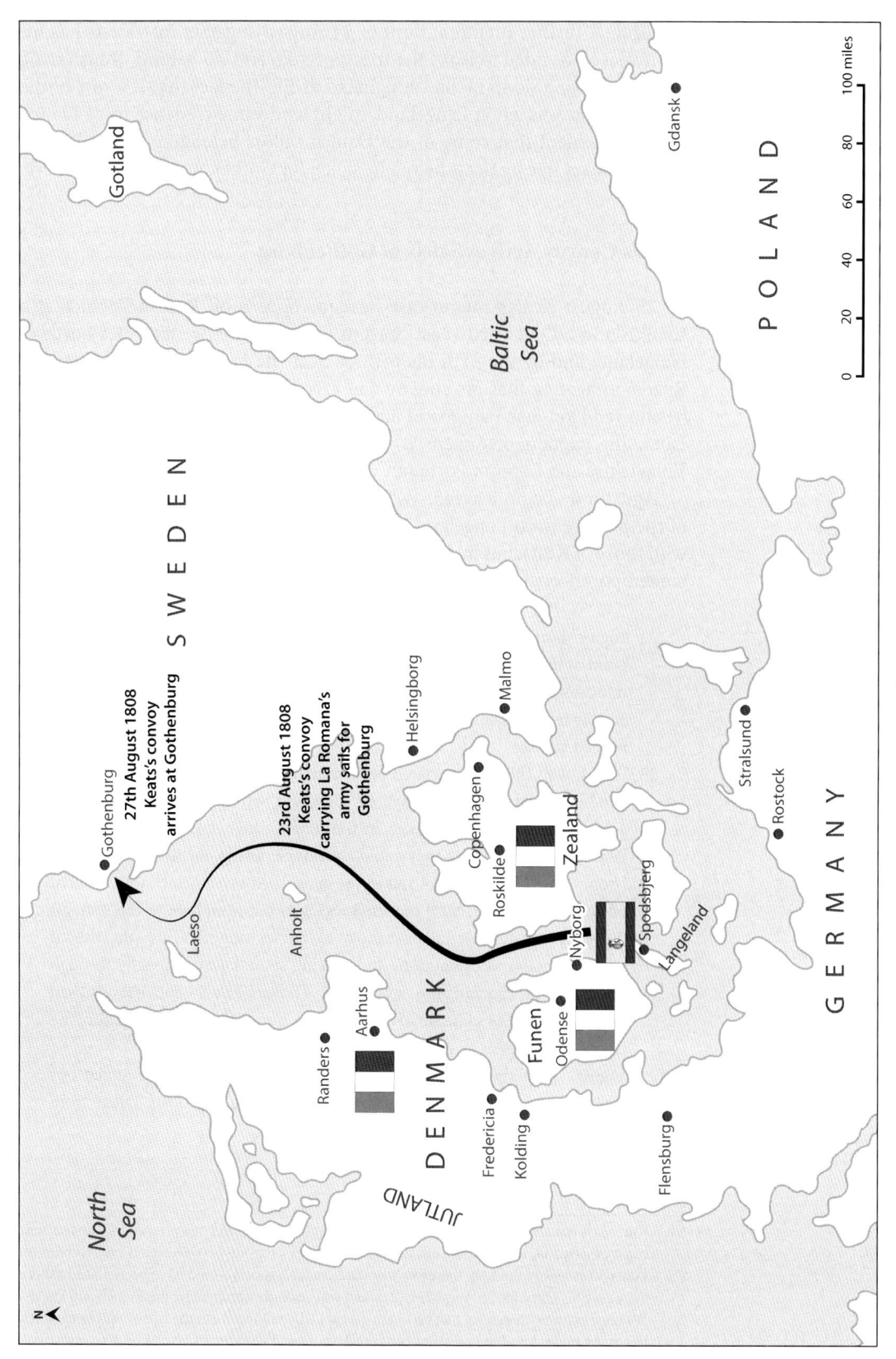

Keats's convoy carrying the bulk of La Romana's army to Gothenburg

Kattegat. A further memorandum of 24 August suggests that Keats has for some reason decided to leave the transports E6 and X5 behind, transferring their troops to a sloop he has designated as EF. The fact that X5, one of the Jutland boats, was left at Langeland, might lend some credence to de Llano's earlier statement that some of the Danish sailors belonging to the Jutland crews were set free by Keats before he sailed for Gothenburg from Spodsberg.

Keats's Convoy Arrives Safely at Gothenburg

By 25 August Keats's memos are headed, '*Superb* off Romsoe', which is a small island off the north–east coast of Funen, some twenty miles north of Langeland, and by the 27th his memos bear the heading, '*Superb*, Flemish Roads', indicating that his convoy had arrived at Gothenburg. On that day he allowed Don José Panigoand and his wife to transfer from X4 to *Gorgon*. Later, the captain of *Superb* is instructed to receive *Capitán* Milans of Villaviciosa and *Capitán* Porta of Catalunya, each from *Gorgon*.

Agustín de Llano leaves us what is perhaps the most interesting picture of the passage from Langeland to Gothenburg. His dates do not quite align with those of Keats, but by their content it would seem that they were written contemporaneously:

> 22 August: last night we anchored at a point three leagues distant from our point of departure. Today we continued our voyage but made little progress, returning to drop anchor in front of Nyborg and joining company with a convoy from England carrying rations, which provided us with some sorely-needed victuals …
>
> 23 August: with the rations shared out amongst the squadron we sailed in light winds. Passing in front of Nyborg the shore battery at Knudshoved fired a heavy cannonade towards us at too long a range, but it was enough to demonstrate to us what they could have done during our first embarkation [from Funen] if we had not spiked the guns … At seven o'clock we anchored off the island of Korsoer,[64] the wind was light but from here to the Kattegat the sea is very difficult, full of shallows so that we cannot sail at night without taking a thousand precautions and making soundings continually through the night. This morning the naval officer, *Teniente* Rafael Lobo, left us to sail for England in the same brig which brought him here, in order to notify the British government … of our famous and miraculous escape.
>
> 24 August: six of the fifteen ships bringing rations from England joined our convoy, allowing some of our troops still aboard the boats taken from

---

64 Korsoer is not an island, it is a small harbour town lying at the end of a promontory on the west coast of Zealand, marking the eastern end of the sea crossing between itself and Nyborg on Funen. It is highly unlikely therefore that the Spanish Sappers would have been placed ashore there (see his entry for 25 August) as Zealand was strongly occupied by the French and Danes. We must assume, therefore, that de Llano was actually talking about the isle of Sprogoe, which lies at the midpoint of the crossing between Nyborg and Korsoer.

Nyborg to be transferred to them. As the winds were strong and contrary, we remained off Korsoer.

25 August: the north–westerly continued and we remained anchored, taking advantage of this opportunity we disembarked our Zapadores onto the deserted island of Korsoer with the aim to sink some wells, which might have provided us with fresh water to replace that which we had consumed in recent days, but the results were not very good.

26 August: at dawn we sailed with the wind to the south–west, and at nine in the morning we had an alarm aboard HMS *Superb* when a quantity of rum caught fire in the hold and spread to some stores of varnish and tar. For a moment there was some confusion, but happily it didn't spread any further because, besides the speedy measures taken, a dragoon belonging to Villaviciosa threw his cape over the flames, preventing them from taking hold amidst the varnish and finally extinguishing them within a few minutes. The soldier was perfectly rewarded with a number of guineas via the hand of Admiral Keats, before being taken to the infirmary to have the burns to his arms and legs treated.

On this day HMS *Edgar* separated from us after receiving orders from Vice Admiral Saumarez, disembarking 800 men belonging to the Regimiento de Princesa, some men of the Artillería and some of the *Estado Mayor* at Helsingborg to the south of us. She then sailed with Saumarez's squadron in search of the Russian fleet, which had left port. The soldiers placed ashore then had to make a meandering march through Scania in Sweden in order to re-join us at Gothenburg.[65]

27 August: at four in the afternoon we anchored at Gothenburg. The coast here is very rocky and close to that of Norway. The harbour is formed of an infinity of rocky islets which make it quite secure, though the entrance is difficult. Because of this hundreds of little boats came out to direct the convoy and its escort despite the strong wind and high sea, which meant that we had to enter by the stern. There is a fort which defends the place and the city is some three leagues distant, it is arrived at by boat along a beautiful fjord.[66]

At this point we should perhaps reflect upon just how arduous the passage from Langeland to Gothenburg must have been for the majority of the Spanish troops. Many of them, perhaps the majority of them, were crammed into small open boats with standing room only. It was late August in the Baltic and darkness must have been approaching by mid-evening, which meant they would have had to prepare themselves for some ten uncomfortable hours each night, with little in the way of sleeping comforts available to them. Food and fresh water would have been in short supply and many of the men would have been living in permanently damp or wet clothing, their feet perhaps immersed in cold sea water. Fortunately, the weather was benign, something O'Donnell thought worth a mention:

---

65 *AGMM, Bailén 7272.2, Memoria de Llano*, p.40. In Note 13a on page 40 of his *Memoria*, de Llano says that the 860 Spanish soldiers made the whole 300 mile journey from Helsingborg to Gothenburg in small carts carrying just three soldiers each!
66 *AGMM, Bailén 7272.2, Memoria de de Llano*, pp.28–30.

We continued on our way with fortune granting us weather which was always favourable, because those little boats, overcrowded with people, would not have survived even the mildest of winds, and many of them would have had to put-in to Danish ports where their passengers would have been taken prisoner.[67]

When the Spaniards arrived at Gothenburg on 27 August the Swedes were still proving to be troublesome allies, insisting that La Romana's men had to remain aboard ship until the British transports arrived. After some days in this situation, and some pleading from Keats, it was agreed that they could go ashore on some of the many small islands in Gothenburg Bay.

By 29 August it is apparent that Keats was in the process of removing all Spanish troops from those of his ships that would be staying in the Baltic, whatever the eventual means by which La Romana's army was to be returned to Spain. It was by this order that some 1,400 troops were disembarked from *Superb, Brunswick, Edgar, Gorgon, Devastation* and *Hound* onto the islands of Branno[?] and Stretsy[?] in the Flemish Roads. In his memo of that day, he also instructs that the men of Zamora aboard *Brunswick's* transports B1, B2, B4, B6, B9, B10 and B12, are to be landed on the islands of Wingo, Cherso[?] and Donso[?].

Three days later Keats wrote to the Admiralty from Gothenburg, informing them of the safe arrival of his convoy of 66 victuallers and Nyborg transports. He informs their lordships of the very crowded conditions in which the Spaniards were held aboard ship, pointing out that he had obtained permission from the governor of Gothenburg for some of the men to be cantoned in the villages of the islands 'contiguous to the harbour.' The number of sick he gives as 300, and he explains that he has sought permission to make use of a building ashore as a hospital.

It is clear that the rear admiral was still not fully convinced of the promise that he would be provided with regular British transports in which to take the Spaniards home. In his letter, he explains that he is about to initiate a works programme to prepare each of the victuallers at his disposal in such a way that it might enable them to be used as something akin to a convoy of troop transports, capable of taking some 2,500 men to England. To accommodate the rest of La Romana's men he was investigating the possibility of hiring some merchant ships, but the Swedish owners, he claims, were still making high demands and were willing only to lease their vessels for a minimum period of three months. However, it would seem that the owners of British shipping at Gothenburg were attempting to drive an even harder bargain with Keats, 'My offers to engage some English ships to convey the troops have been met by proposals very exorbitant,' he informs their lordships.[68]

There is an interesting memo from Keats, written on 29 August, giving instructions to ensure that 'the [Spanish] women and children are victualled in the same manner as the women and children attached to British troops

---

67   *AGMM, Bailén 7272.2, Memoria de O'Donnell*, p.19.
68   Keats to Admiralty, 1 September 1808, TNA, ADM 1/7/(104–105).

when embarked – namely the women at half and the children at one fourth allowance of our seamen.' On the same day, the rear admiral received a memo from Saumarez, the contents of which made it clear that his earlier determination to take the Spaniards off Langeland and remove them clear of the Belt was well founded, and in a letter from Saumarez dated the 22nd, the rear admiral is told that the captain of *Goliath*, Paget, had informed the vice admiral that the Russian fleet consisting of 'thirteen sail of line of battleships besides several large frigates … was at sea, with the probable intention of raising the British blockade of Zealand.'[69]

By 2 September Keats is more relaxed about the promised transports from England. In a letter to the Admiralty of that date he confirms to their lordships the arrival at Gothenburg of two packets from England, providing him with 'strong reasons to believe transports have been ordered from thence for the conveyance of the Spanish troops.' On the strength of this information, he decides to suspend negotiations for the hire of shipping. English merchants were demanding seven pounds per man, exclusive of water, fuel and provisions, to convey the Spaniards, although he does not say if the price related to transportation to Spain or to England. Swedish merchants, he says, have recently submitted a tender to transport the troops, the terms of which were so 'loose' that he had to ask for clarification of the service they were offering. Later in his letter he mentions that he has consented to a contract at 21 pence per man, per day, for the treatment and hospitalisation of the sick. The rear admiral then touches upon the more delicate subject of Anglo–Spanish relations. He begins by providing a picture of the kind of conditions the Spanish troops had endured since they were embarked at Langeland:

> Embarked as this army has been, crowded beyond example, destitute of accommodation, necessaries and conveniences; sleeping on ballast or exposed to the weather, and not speaking our language, it is not surprising if some murmurs or ill–temper have been shewn. The accompanying letter, which I saw necessary to address to the Marqués de La Romana, (from whom I have always experienced the most zealous and ready acquiescence in everything that regards the service) will inform their lordships that some irregularity has occurred…
>
> But their habits of discipline, and perhaps the age and inactivity of their officers, in many cases, do not admit of the same order we find in our own Army. The circumstance appeared to me to demand serious notice and the regiment [Catalunya] has in consequence been turned from the ship; and I am inclined to believe the example will have a favourable effect…[70]

---

69 Saumarez to Keats, 22 August 1808, TNA, ADM 1/7/(77).
70 Keats to Admiralty, 2 September 1808, TNA, ADM 1/7/(130–131). Note: The majority (1,100 men) of Catalunya were aboard *Gorgon*, with small detachments aboard S1 (115 men) S2 (100 men) S9 (95 men) and it would seem that there had been some trouble amongst the Spaniards aboard *Gorgon*.

From this it would seem that the men of Catalunya had been ordered to leave at least one of Keats's ships, probably *Gorgon*, as a result of some form of insubordination.

Keats's next communication with the Admiralty provides us with a brief insight into the sufferings endured by the people of the Baltic islands as the European war dragged on. It bears further witness to the rear admiral's strong sense of humanity and compassion, many examples of which, usually relating to his concerns about the wellbeing of La Romana's troops, may be found amongst the collection of his letters and memos at The National Archives. His letter of 4 September is reproduced in full:

> Sir,
> The persons named in the margin, the master and crew of a small vessel belonging to [the island of] North Farro, captured by the *Fury*, having represented to me, that their island is at present under the protection of the British Government, solicited to be allowed to go to England, and produced testimonials of the extreme distress the inhabitants of that island are suffering for want of provisions.[71] I have thought it right, under such circumstances, to comply with their request and have ordered them a passage with the *Aetna*, for their Lordships' consideration and further direction.[72]

On 6 September Keats's prayers were finally answered when some 35 transports, together with their escorts *Jasper*, *Racoon* and *Sparrowhawk* sailed into Gothenburg. Interestingly, he estimates the total tonnage of shipping then at his disposal, including the 10 victuallers already with him at Gothenburg and earmarked for the voyage to England, worked out at about one and a quarter tons per man [*i.e.* per Spanish soldier] which he seems to think is a comfortable ratio. This was the usual method of calculation employed by the navy when estimating the scale of naval resources required for the transportation troops. In the final paragraph of his letter of that day, he states:

> Conceiving that it may be of some consequence to the public interest that the Marqués de La Romana should have an opportunity of seeing His Majesty's Ministers before he returns to Spain, in which sentiment he coincides, I have ordered Captain Godfrey of the *Aetna* to receive him, part of his suite, and one hundred Spanish troops, and proceed to the Downs without delay.[73]

In fact, the Spanish commander in chief eventually sailed to England with the *Calypso* on 9 September, the day on which Keats wrote to the Admiralty informing them that the 35 transports from England, plus the victuallers from Gothenburg, would take on board the whole of the Spanish army

---

71 The names of the sailors picked up by the *Fury* are listed as follows, though they may have been Anglicised by the writer of the letter: Paul Nelso Masting, Thomas Johnson, Magnus Zachariahson, John Johnson and Daniel Obeson.
72 Keats to Admiralty, 4 September 1808, TNA, ADM 1/7/(141).
73 Keats to Admiralty, 6 September 1808, TNA, ADM 1/7/(159–160).

then in Sweden; the sole exception being that of the regiment of Princesa which, having been earlier disembarked from *Edgar* at Helsingborg, was still making its way to Gothenburg on foot. In his thorough manner he explains that, should the convoy sail before the arrival of Princesa, he would retain the transports, *DT Supply*, *379 Hero*, *P Jane* and *MS John*, aboard which the Spaniards would be embarked.[74]

With an abundance of shipping now available to Keats, Astrandi says that on 6 September the Spanish high command took the opportunity, 'To pay-off the Danish boats and crews our soldiers had pressed into service either by deception or by force, seeing that the sailors were terrified of falling into British hands.'[75] During the course of the subsequent three days, 7-9 September, the Spanish army was embarked and the convoy ordered to sail to La Coruña. Not long after it left Gothenburg the ships were signalled to make for Santander instead, which would be their final destination. As already stated, it was on the 9th that the commander in chief of the Spanish army sailed aboard the brig, *Calypso*, together with José O'Donnell and his personal secretary, all destined to meet with representatives of the British government in London. The entry in her log for that day briefly notes: 'Answered signal for the captain, employed in getting the Spanish general's packages and 38 Danish prisoners aboard.'[76]

As she approached Yarmouth on 16 September, La Romana and O'Donnell were sent ashore. *Calypso*'s log entry for that day captures the event with the words: 'the general and retinue went on shore.'[77] José O'Donnell sums up this phase of the operation as follows:

> On 6 or 7 of September the British transports finally arrived in Gothenburg carrying rations for the passage to La Coruña, which got under way on the 12th or 13th. Whilst at Gothenburg, the Marqués de La Romana received correspondence from the British government requesting him to make a personal journey to London in order to discuss affairs relating to Spain. To make the passage they placed a brig [HMS *Calypso*] at his disposal. He embarked on 9 September with no company other than an officer of his headquarters [José O'Donnell himself] and his secretary.
>
> [When he arrived in the British capital] he was warmly received with demonstrations of the admiration, respect and appreciation his conduct deserved. He obtained all of the help, financial and other, that he requested from the British government, but it was agreed that [on their arrival in Spain] his troops should disembark at Santander rather than in Galicia, as had been [previously] arranged by the general. In consequence, notice of the change was sent out to the convoy, which left Gothenburg on 12 or 13 of September. This was to suffer a rough southerly passage due to a terrible storm that caused the ships to be scattered, forcing many of them to seek refuge in English ports. However, all would

---

74   Keats to Admiralty, 9 September 1808, TNA, ADM 1/7/(170).
75   AGMM, Bailén 7272.2, *Memoria de Joachin Astrandi* (henceforth, *Memoria de Astrandi*), p.2 in section headed, *Contestación a los 6 puntos ...*
76   TNA, ADM 51/1944, Log of *Calypso*.
77   TNA, ADM 51/1944, Log of *Calypso*.

eventually arrive safely in Santander, the majority of them on 9 October 1808, where they came to anchor.[78]

The marqués was to spend just over three weeks in England before continuing his journey to Spain, during which time it seems he may have been introduced to King George III.[79] He may also have met with Castlereagh, then Secretary of State for War and the Colonies, as well as other ministers.

On 1 October 1808, just two days before La Romana sailed from Portsmouth, Castlereagh wrote to the him assuring him that his army would be supplied with the necessary equipment he had asked for, and expressing his wishes that, 'when the army of Great Britain shall have the honour of taking the field in the cause of Spain, it may find itself in immediate cooperation with the brave troops under the Marqués's orders.'[80]

Once La Romana's business in England was complete, preparations were made to return him to Spain after his long absence, he would sail to La Coruña aboard HMS *Semiramis*, then anchored at Spithead. The entry in her log for 3 October reads: 'Received an order from the commander in chief to prepare to receive an ambassador and suite – and also a Spanish general.'[81]

On the following day there are two interesting entries: 'Employed in cleaning ship and fitting up cabins for ambassador and suite. Came alongside a lighter with two hundred and eleven casks of dollars belonging to government.'[82] On 9 October the log reads: '12:30 p.m. the British Ambassador and Spanish *General* de Romana and their suites came on board – saluted with fifteen guns ... At three up anchor and made sail.'[83]

We should note here that the British 'Ambassador' mentioned in the log was John Hookham Frere, who left for Spain under the title, Envoy Extraordinaire and Minister Plenipotentiary.[84] Frere's time on the Iberian

---

78 *AGMM, Bailén* 7272.2, *Memoria de O'Donnell*, pp.19–20.
79 In A. Aspinall (ed.) *The Later Correspondence of George III* (Cambridge: Cambridge University Press, 1970) Vol. V, p.133, there is a letter from Canning at the Foreign Office to King George III, dated 27 September 1808, in which he humbly begs His Majesty's permission to present Mr Frere, '...on his appointment to a special mission to Spain.' He includes an 'Enclosure' with his letter which comprises a list of the following names: Marqués de La Romana, Teniente–Coronel Don José O'Donnell, *Aide de Camp*, M. de las Heras (intendant with the rank of colonel) Genl. Don Adrian Jacome, Adml. Juan Ruiz de Apodaca, Don Adrian Jacome (nephew of Genl. Adrian Jacome) Don Lorenzo Noriega, Don Rafael Lobo, Visct. Matarrosa, Don Andrés Ángel de la Vega and Don Francisco Sangro. In other words, the whole of the Spanish delegation then in London.
80 Lord Castlereagh to La Romana, 1 October 1808, in Marquess of Londonderry (ed.) *Correspondence, Despatches and Other Papers of Viscount Castlereagh* (London: William Shoberl, 1851), Vol.VI, p.461.
81 TNA, ADM 51/1938, Log of *Semiramis*.
82 TNA, ADM 51/1938, Log of *Semiramis*. It may be worth noting that La Romana placed some 500,000 pesos in bullion aboard Victory when she arrived off Langeland during the Spanish embarkation. Later, on 22 August, the money was transferred to *Mosquito* which sailed for England with Rafael Lobo aboard on the same day. Perhaps the gold placed aboard *Semiramis* was Spanish gold after all.
83 TNA, ADM 51/1938, Log of *Semiramis*.
84 John Hookham Frere, elder brother of Bartholomew Frere. Entered the Foreign Office in 1799 becoming undersecretary of state for foreign affairs. In 1800, he went to Portugal as an 'envoy extraordinary'. He was transferred to Madrid in 1802 and returned to England

Peninsula overlapped with that of Sir Charles Stuart who had been sent to Portugal on 20 July 1808 tasked with a 'special mission'. Frere's stay lasted only seven months; he was recalled to England after Sir John Moore's army was expelled from Spain in January 1809. We may note here that both Stuart and Frere were sometimes referred to as the 'British Ambassador'.

On 20 October *Semiramis* arrived at La Coruña, her log for that day includes the following remarks:

> Manned ship for [British] Rear Admiral de Courcy, who came on board to pay his respects to the Ambassador and *General* de Romana. Also came on board the Spanish Governor and suite. At noon they left the ship with ambassador, general and suites.[85]

Interestingly, the *Gazeta de Madrid* records the arrival of La Romana and Frere at La Coruña, giving the date as 19 October 1808 and adding that Lazero de Heras, who is described as the *Ministro de Hacienda* (probably meaning *Intendente* (Treasurer) of La Romana's army) also returned with the marqués, bringing with him the sum of twenty million reales (about two and a half million pesos).[86]

---

in 1804. He again went to Spain in October 1808 as plenipotentiary to the *Junta Central*, returning to England in May 1809. Bartholomew Frere served as Secretary of Legation in Madrid, 1802–1805 and as minister plenipotentiary ad interim in Seville between November 1809 and January 1810.

85 TNA, ADM 51/1938, Log of *Semiramis*. Note: All of the memoranda referred to in this chapter, which are not specifically listed as a footnote, may be found in the document referenced ADM 80/145, held at The National Archives, Kew.

86 *Gazeta de Madrid*, No. 140, 1 November 1808, *Coruña 22 Octubre*, page 1406, at <www.cervantesvirtual.com/discargaPdf/gazeta–de–madrid–140> (accessed 14 January 2019).

List of Spanish units embarked from Langeland on or about 21 August 1808 (10-column table), and list of units left behind in Denmark (4-column table), as provided by Joachin Astrandi. (*AGMM, Bailén 7272.2, Memoria de Astrandi*)

THE BRITISH NAVAL OPERATION

List of Royal Navy ships which took part in the evacuation of La Romana's army, as provided by Joachin Astrandi. Document includes name of captain and duty performed by ship during the evacuation. (*AGMM, Bailén 7272.2, Memoria de Astrandi*.)

5

The Men Left Behind in Denmark

The Men on Zealand – the Regiments of Asturias and Guadalajara

We saw earlier how the infantry regiments of Asturias and Guadalajara were frustrated in their attempt to escape from the island of Zealand. The men were sent into *de facto* captivity at Copenhagen, unlike their officers, who were allowed a greater measure of freedom on giving their word of honour not to attempt an escape, before being dispersed to a number of small towns and villages. All of the Spaniards were denied any form of communication with the outside world whilst their fate was being decided by members of the French and Danish high commands.

We return now to the statement of *Capitán* Santiago Miquel of Asturias at the point where we left off in a previous chapter, as he and his fellow officers were taking up their quarters in the settlements surrounding Copenhagen.

> During these days we heard not the slightest news until the Danish king was certain that La Romana had completed his escape. It was then when the colonel of Asturias, who was acting as brigadier and commander of his own regiment as well as that of Guadalajara, was sent for by the monarch to agree upon a plan to disarm his men ... this was later carried out on 11 August ... [Once the weapons had been surrendered by the first three of the six battalions on Zealand, the colonel] called the men together and informed them that the King of Denmark had ordered him, as chief of the Spanish troops, to notify them of the ruler's sovereign resolution to make them prisoners of war ... Immediately afterwards the men were marched to Copenhagen, whilst their officers were allowed to remain in the town [Roskilde] until they received fresh orders.
>
> At eleven on the morning of 11 August a strong division of [Danish] infantry, cavalry and artillery ... set off to cooperate with another, which was already in position close to the cantons of the remaining [three Spanish] battalions, in order to complete the disarmament process ... Once this was done the men were marched to Copenhagen and the officers to the towns of Roskilde, Ringsted, Soro and Holbaek...

Be it for fear of Napoleon, or for other political reasons, rather than restore our liberty the Danes decided to hand us over to the French. On 3 September the officers of the two regiments were formed up in two divisions and marched off on different routes, escorted by strong detachments; one [division] to the port immediately to the north–west of the capital, where it was embarked on the evening of the 8 September, the other to the port of Corsoe [*Sic* for Korsoer] where it was embarked on the same day. During the passage from that port the Danish commander under whose custody we were placed forced us into the hold [of his ship] and nailed down the hatches, threatening that anyone who put up resistance would be executed. This was how we remained until the evening of the 9 September when the first division [of officers] was disembarked at Aarhus, the second having been put ashore at Kerteminde on Funen at midday. From Aarhus the former group continued their march, being treated with a degree of rigour by their escort until they were handed over to the French at the town of Werthy[?]; the second division suffering a similar fate on their way to Kolding. All were then conducted to the fortress of Sedan, stopping at various castles and prisons on the way.[1]

It may be worth noting that the marching distance from Kolding to Sedan is about 500 miles, that from Aarhus about 600.

Two of the officers who witnessed the events which took place on Zealand during August and September 1808, Manuel López and Rafael de Llanza, have each left us a record of what they saw and of their subsequent experiences throughout out the remaining war years. The accounts of both men relating to the days immediately following the Spanish surrender on Zealand align closely with that of Miquel, in a broad sense, but López provides us with a little more detail. His story begins:

The two regiments of Asturias and Guadalajara were detached to Zealand after having been cantoned at a number of places [throughout the winter of 1807/08]. They established themselves on the island on 8 April 1808…

On 31 July 1808, obeying instructions he had received from the Prince de Pontecorvo, *Général de Brigade* Fririon issued an order instructing both units to assemble at Roskilde on the following day. It was there where they would be ordered to take an oath of fealty to the new king of Spain, Joseph Bonaparte. The troops were not disposed to partake in such an act of submission; and besides, their feelings had already been hurt by the 'bribe' of a measure of rum and some Danish shillings they had been promised; an 'inducement' which would not have been offered had *Teniente-Coronel* Marti, who had recently been detached to Fririon, given the Frenchman the benefit of his understanding of the character and habits of Spanish troops.[2]

At this point López's story reiterates the account of the reaction by the Spanish troops to the news that they would have to swear an oath of fealty to King Joseph, as such, there would be little value in reproducing what he said,

---

1 *AGMM, Bailén 7272.2, Memoria de Miquel*, p.6.
2 López's précis as cited by Boppe in *Les Espagnols*, pp.63–67.

but it may be worthwhile to include a few words about his transportation into captivity in France. His journey began at the point where, after being disarmed, the Spaniards were marched into several Danish towns, where they were secured before being handed over to the French. As mentioned above, the men were separated from their officers and taken to Copenhagen, and López, being an NCO at the time, was to remain with the other ranks before commencing his journey south:

> Once at Copenhagen we saw our fellow battalions arrive, each disarmed and escorted in the same manner as my own. It was whilst I was there that I learned that the Marqués de La Romana had embarked with the British squadron at Nyborg …
>
> [Later] we were united with our comrades at the Copenhagen Arsenal, where I continued to act as an interpreter. From there we could see the ships of the British fleet, which at any moment could easily have sailed to our aid. But to prevent any attempt at revolt on our part, the Danes had threatened to turn the fire of their batteries on us, should we make the slightest movement…
>
> Towards the end of September 1808, the British squadron left the waters of the Baltic Sound and those Spaniards still held at Copenhagen were removed, a company or two at a time, and taken under escort to Korsoer [on the west coast of Zealand] where they were embarked and secured for the crossing to Nyborg. From there they were marched across the isle of Funen to Middelfart, whence they took passage across the Little Belt to be delivered to the French, who treated them with more humanity than did the Danes, the latter having shown them much animosity coupled with a great deal of bad conduct…
>
> As for the Germans, they were just like brothers to us; they came to those amongst us whom they recognised and were generous in their expressions of consolation and friendship. During our passage to Altona, always under close arrest, we met with some of those who had taken part in the mutiny on Zealand and had been arrested before order was restored. I do not know what became of them.
>
> On our arrival in France the remnants the corps were dispersed to a number of depots located at places such as Thionville, Mézières, Charleville and Besancon, where I became interpreter for the five hundred and fifty men sent with me. It was from these elements that the Emperor came to form the Régiment Joseph-Napoleon in 1809.[3]

In his diary, Llanza provides an interesting account of the transportation of the Spanish officers to France, the passage is quite a long one but it is worth noting a few extracts from it.

> On 4 September we set off to cross the Great Belt. We arrived at Korsoer at nightfall, where we expected to pass the night, but were immediately forced aboard ship, the Danes employing a great deal of violence in the process. Once on deck they lowered us into the hatch and battened it down, just as they do when transporting people sentenced to serve in the galleys. The ship we were aboard was escorted by

---

3   López's précis as cited by Boppe in *Les Espagnols*, pp.76–79.

two gunboats, whose captains were under orders to destroy her should there be any resistance on our part, or any attempt by the English to free us.[4]

Llanza continues with his story describing how, once he and his fellow officers arrived at Hamburg, they were constantly threatened with execution until they received the news that Bernadotte had pardoned them for their excesses at Roskilde. That was the signal for them to begin their long march to imprisonment in France, leaving Hamburg on 18 September. By 7 October 1808 they were at Mainz, and after passing through Dijon they arrived at Sedan on the 31st. It was there that the main body of Spanish officers was divided into smaller groups before being dispersed to a number of secure locations across France. It would seem that the governor of the citadel at which they were detained until their dispersal, did not consider himself above the practice of stealing from his prisoners. Llanza refers to him as: 'a great thief [*un grandisimo ladrón*] … I had never seen a man who would stoop to such vile means to rob a group of unfortunate prisoners.'[5]

His physical and moral strength failing, Llanza was not looking forward to the prospect of more long and fatiguing marches, and it seems that he asked to be sent to a not-too-distant location to begin his imprisonment. As a result, he arrived at the castle of Bouillon in the company of 10 fellow officers on 3 November 1808, where he remained until 6 February 1809 when he was transferred to Avesnes in Flanders, arriving there on the 10th. It was whilst he was in Flanders that he and his comrades were visited by a representative of *Mariscal de Campo* Juan Kindelán, the ex-commander in chief of the Spanish troops on the Jutland Peninsula, who informed them of a decree recently announced at Chamartín (in occupied Madrid) on 11 January. The essence of the edict was that the men of Guadalajara and Asturias were to be incorporated into a new regiment of the French army. It would be christened the Régiment de Joseph–Napoleon.

Over the next few months Llanza was to have several meetings with Kindelán, as he went about the business of recruiting the men he considered to be of suitable material for the officer corps of the new regiment. He was to spend various periods of time in Paris, Lille and Avignon as Kindelán's plans grew to maturity, and it was at Avignon, where he arrived in mid–July 1809, that he and his fellow officers began to hear of the actual state of things in Spain. They were somewhat surprised to discover that the situation was not as bad as it had been claimed to be by the French propagandists, whose articles they had become so used to reading. It was then that the spirits of Llanza and his companions soared, as they began to hear rumours of a possible move to Spain once the new regiment was at full strength. However, he tells us, the lax regime under which they were held at Avignon allowed his comrades to pass their time in the local cafes where, as he puts it, 'This news was celebrated too enthusiastically in the cafes and inns of Avignon, where

---

4   Bobadilla, *Un Español*, p.33.
5   Bobadilla, *Un Español*, p.33.

the fumes of the liquid allowed the escape of some expressions which were not to our advantage'.[6]

Orders soon arrived directing that Llanza's battalion be sent to Dalmatia; its sister unit, a second battalion of the new regiment, would be sent to Flanders. It would seem that the loose talk of his comrades had reached the ears of Napoleon who, horrified at the thought of sending a fully equipped regiment of Spaniards towards the frontier, remarked to Kindelán that: 'The Spanish regiment would have left their flags on the peaks of the Pyrenees [and deserted into Spain].' 'In this,' said Llanza, 'he was not fooling himself.'[7] Here we will take leave of Llanza, but we shall return to his story in a later chapter, as Napoleon's armies prepare for the invasion of Russia in 1812.

In Spanish eyes, the regiments stationed on Zealand had distinguished themselves as much as, if not more than, any others. They may have failed in their bid for freedom but they were in a much-compromised situation, being under the direct command of *Général de Brigade* Fririon at the time. To sum up we examine some words from Ambrosio de la Quadra regarding events on Zealand, in which he places much of the blame for what took place on Don Luis Ciran for his obsequiousness towards the French. We will then leave the final words on Denmark to Napoleon. Firstly, Quadra:

> Highly disliked by his regiment he [Ciran] was deprived of promotion due to his despicable conduct. A hated figure of ridicule due to his extravagant appearance, he was the object of much loathing by his comrades, from whom he was forced to flee after obtaining a position at French headquarters, via a process of intrigue, under the pretext that he was an expert in foreign languages. This specimen [continued Quadra] was the dignified courier of the order and the [arrangements for the] ritual [surrounding the taking of the oath of fealty to Joseph] and his presence, his disrepute and his presumptuousness alone, would have been enough to excite the passions of the troops to the point at which they were to make the unfortunate choices that they did.[8]

It was Don Luis Ciran, we will recall, who arrived at Roskilde on 30 July 1808 bearing Bernadotte's orders that the Spaniards on Zealand take an oath of fealty to King Joseph Bonaparte.

Other Units Captured by the French

After the regiments of Asturias and Guadalajara, the next-largest unit to fall into the hands of the French was the cavalry regiment of Algarve. All 600 of its troopers were stopped by a number of Belgian cavalry squadrons, as they attempted to cross the waters of the Little Belt near Fredericia in order to effect their escape to Funen. Another group, the Spanish officers and men of Zamora unfortunate enough to be assigned to Bernadotte's personal

---

6 Bobadilla, *Un Español*, p.35.
7 Bobadilla, *Un Español*, pp.34–35.
8 *Acontecimientos de Quadra*, RHM, no.72, 1er semestre, 1992, pp.241–242.

THE MEN LEFT BEHIND IN DENMARK

guard, stood no chance of escape. As well as these there were the sick and convalescents at various hospitals and a smattering of Spanish officers and men on detachment with the French. In total more than 5,000 Spaniards were marched off to France. On a brighter note, a group of about 140 men belonging to Asturias and Guadalajara avoided being taken prisoner along with their comrades, these were waiting to be shipped from Nyborg to Zealand when La Romana took possession of the port, and were later embarked with the rest of the army.

At the end of it all the French high command felt the need to mollify their new allies, the Danes, and this may be seen in the words of Napoleon's letter to King Frederick VI of Denmark, written on 10 September 1808 in the aftermath of La Romana's escape, it is both a grovelling apology and a slight upon Bernadotte's abilities as commander in chief of French forces in the Baltic:

> Napoleon to King Frederick VI of Denmark,
> 10 September 1808.
> I have received the letter from His Majesty of 11 August. I was extremely angered at the imprudence of leaving [to their own devices] troops who, under the [prevailing] circumstances, must have been considered suspect. I have been even more angered by the trouble that His Majesty has had to bear. I approve heartily of his behaviour and pray that he will accept my gratitude. A few extra battalions gone missing here and there do not really matter; it is the concern that was shown towards an ally who, like Your Majesty, was in need of consolation, that is really important to me. Let Your Majesty rely on my eternal desire to please him and contribute to his satisfaction and to the benefit of his country.[9]

We will return to the stories of López and Llanza in later chapters, but for now we shall leave them as they attempt to adapt themselves to life as prisoners of war, soon to become soldiers in the new French regiment, Joseph–Napoleon, with which they were to witness some of the greatest events of the Napoleonic era.

---

9   Napoleon to the King of Denmark. Bonaparte, *Correspondance*, no. 14312, t, XVII, pp.589–590.

6

The Transportation of La Romana's Troops to Spain and the Battle of Espinosa

The story of La Romana's Baltic army comprises three main strands. In the previous chapters we have covered the first of them: its movement to the Baltic, its revolt against the French and Danes and its partial embarkation and escape from Danish waters courtesy of the Royal Navy. The second strand is the story of what became of the men who were returned to Spain, and the third that of what became of the men left behind in Denmark, which we will discuss later. But now is the time to examine what became of the regiments disembarked at Santander, as they put up what resistance they could to Napoleon's renewed surge into Spain during the final months of 1808.

La Romana's Army Sails from Gothenburg for Spain

On 12 September 1808, three days after La Romana had left for England, a convoy of British transports and victuallers weighed anchor and sailed from Gothenburg for Spain. Its cargo, if we can put it that way, was the 10,000 or so men of La Romana's army earlier lifted from the shores of Langeland. Five days later the ships were within sight of the east coast of England and it was there where Lazero de las Heras, *Intendente* of the marqués's army, was put ashore to join La Romana and José O'Donnell, both already in London. The convoy then continued its voyage to Galicia, its original destination, until bad weather intervened causing many of the ships to be scattered, forcing some of them to make for the most convenient ports on the north coast of Spain.[1] José O'Donnell claimed that the storms were so bad that some of the ships were forced to seek shelter in English ports.

---

1 Arteche, *Guerra de la Independencia*, Vol. III, Ch. IV, pp.253–254.

TRANSPORTATION OF LA ROMANA'S TROOPS TO SPAIN

There is a minor dispute over the number of ships comprising the convoy assembled to take the Spaniards home. We may recall from a previous chapter that Keats said he delegated the 35 transports from England plus the ten victuallers already at Gothenburg to the transportation of the Spaniards, making 45 vessels in total. However, in the log of one of the escorting sloops, HMS *Jasper*, the entry for 14 September 1808 reads: 'Commodore [HMS *Nassau*], *Racoon*, *Sparrowhawk* & 51 sail of convoy in company…'[2]

Before setting out from Sweden the convoy escorts were earmarked to provide passage for some of the senior Spanish officers. On the 8 September *Jasper* welcomed aboard *Coronel* Rengel, *Capitán* Vera, *Capitán* Recaud and *Capitán* Riera. *Capitán* de Llano, *Capitán* O'Neill and *Auditor-General* Paez went aboard *Sparrowhawk*. *Racoon* took on board *Coronel* Vallego, *Capitán* Salvador and *Teniente-Coronel* Caro, brother of the Marqués de La Romana. *Brigadier-General* Montés (third in command of the Spanish troops) had the pleasure of sailing aboard HMS *Nassau*. Last, but not least, on 11 September one Don Antonio Fabregues, the man who had been instrumental in establishing contact with the ships of Keats's squadron, climbed aboard *Jasper* to commence his journey home.[3]

Two days out to sea the convoy was approached by a Danish warship which was chased off by one of the armed merchantmen. The corresponding entry in *Jasper's* log for 15 September reads: 'At 10:30 a.m. observed *Providence* fire several shots at a vessel under the Danish flag.'[4] On the same day *Nassau's* log reads 'Observed cutters & exchanged several shots.'[5]

By 20 September the convoy was at anchor in the Downs close to the South Foreland, and it was there where it parted company with HMS *Nassau* once she had transferred all of her Spanish officers and soldiers to various transports. When the ships set sail once more, they made good speed across the Bay of Biscay towards the coast of northern Spain and on 27 September *Jasper's* log reports her to be just five leagues off Cape Ortegal. It was then that the weather suddenly took a turn for the worse, a heavy storm blowing up which scattered the convoy across the waters of Biscay. It would require several days to re-group them.

On 2 October, whilst *Racoon* was working her way into the harbour at La Coruña, she was approached by the schooner, HMS *Snapper*, carrying dispatches for the commodore of the convoy. These may well have been the orders for the ships in company with her to alter their destination from La Coruña to Santander, as none of them actually moored in the Galician port. Instead, they remained offshore for some time before making for Cantabria.[6]

It was not until 9 October that *Racoon* and *Jasper* finally led the convoy into Santander, where the Spanish troops were disembarked. As mentioned earlier, it was during La Romana's discussions with the British cabinet that Santander was selected as the final destination for the Spanish troops, the

---

2 TNA, ADM 51/1896, Log of *Jasper*.
3 TNA, ADM 80/145, Keats's memos, 8–11 September 1808.
4 TNA, ADM 51/1896, Log of *Jasper*.
5 TNA, ADM 51/1757 and 1946, Log of *Nassau*.
6 TNA, ADM 51/2764, Log of *Racoon*, ADM 51/1845, Log of *Sparrowhawk*.

reason being that, after their crushing defeat at Bailén on 20 July 1808, French forces had withdrawn from south–west and central Spain towards the line of the River Ebro, with the Spanish armies mounting what was claimed by some to have been a far too leisurely pursuit. Nevertheless, they were now facing the invaders at several points along the new front. Santander, being much closer to the expected theatre of further operations, would allow the Denmark veterans a much shorter march before coming to grips with the enemy than that required had their starting point been Galicia. In their state of exhaustion after such a long and uncomfortable sea voyage, the saving of a 300–mile footslog was considered by many to be a godsend. However not all of the Spanish units were to be spared a considerable trek. As will be seen below, a portion of the force, the dismounted cavalrymen of Infante, Rey and Almansa, together with the 1er batallón de la Artilleria, were landed at Ribadeo which lies some 200 miles west of Santander, but by all accounts they seemed to have enjoyed their march south into the Spanish interior in search of re–mounts, their horses having been abandoned in Denmark.[7]

José O'Donnell adds:

> Those who disembarked in Santander were: the men of the infantry regiments of Zamora and Princesa and the light battalions of 1er de Barcelona and 1er de Catalunya; the cavalry regiments of Rey and Infante and the Dragones de Almansa and Villaviciosa, all of them dismounted; the three companies of Artillería with their guns and equipment but without their draught horses; a single company of Zapadores with their staff officers and administrators. In total 369 officers and 8,821 men were returned to Spain …[8]
>
> As soon as the regiments of dragoons and cavalry were disembarked in northern Spain they were marched into the interior in search of horses. At Santander all six battalions of the infantry of the line were to receive new arms and be merged with the light infantry and sappers, in order to form the División del Norte, with *Brigadier* el Conde de San Román at its head. This division, once integrated with the Ejército de la Izquierda [Army of the Left] commanded by Blake, took part in the Battle of Espinosa. In the course of the fighting the division was to lose a quarter of its men killed in action, including its commander in chief.[9]

Once on Cantabrian soil the fugitives from Denmark were re–armed and re–equipped, but they were to be without their father figure, the Marqués de La Romana, who had been nominated to serve as a member of the recently formed *Junta Suprema* with immediate effect. However, the marqués did not sail from England until 9 October, the day on which his army arrived at Santander.

As we shall see, the succeeding events in Biscay and Cantabria would indicate that La Romana's initial plan of taking his army to Galicia might well have been the better course of action. Had he done so his intention was to

---

7   Arteche, *Guerra de la Independencia*, Vol. III, Ch. IV, pp.253–254.
8   The cavalry troopers and some of the artillery were actually disembarked at the port of Ribadeo in Asturias.
9   *AGMM, Bailén 7272.2, Memoria de O'Donnell*, p.20.

use his veteran soldiers as a core around which to build a new army of some 30,000 men, and Galicia, being something of a natural fortress, would have provided the secure environment necessary to do just that. As O'Donnell later remarked, three months spent in bringing the marqués's plan to fruition in Galicia could have provided more advantages to the nation.

Napoleon Prepares for the Conquest of Spain

Dupont's capitulation at Bailén on 19 July 1808 and the subsequent withdrawal of French occupying forces to the line of the Ebro had not been well received by Napoleon, whose attention, meanwhile, had been intensely focussed upon the situation with respect to Russia and its claims on Finland, Wallachia and Moldova. The Convention of Erfurt, signed on 12 October 1808, brought stability to the situation, and once he had restructured and re-directed the Grande Armée to pose a potent threat to Austria and Prussia, he could turn his gaze towards the Pyrenees once more. His Armée d'Espagne was to be hugely augmented with a reinforcement of about 150,000 men, reinvigorated and given a clear and ultimate mandate: the annihilation of Spanish resistance; the subjugation of its peoples; the confirmation of Joseph as king and the expulsion of the British from the Iberian Peninsula. The Spanish armies – weak, poorly equipped, deluded by their apparent chastening of the French in Andalucía and feeling secure in their positions south of the Ebro – were about to be struck an immense blow at lightning speed, all orchestrated by the master of warfare himself.

The defeat of Blake's Ejército de la Izquierda

As the right wing of the French armies advanced into Spain, *Maréchaux* Victor and Lefebvre, came into contact with Blake's Ejército de la Izquierda on 31 October, just as the 1er de Catalunya, vanguard of the Denmark veterans, began to arrive in the Spanish front line. After advancing from Bilbao to Valmaseda during the early days of November 1808, Lefebvre had discovered Blake in possession of the narrow pass of El Berron and decided to retreat, leaving *Général de Division* Villatte's division, which actually belonged to Victor's I Corps, in observation of the Spaniards. This placed Blake in an awkward position; knowing that Victor was on his right and seeing Villatte on his front, he imagined that the French plan was to isolate and attack his Asturian divisions under the command of *General* Acevedo. In response he concentrated his forces at Valmaseda and launched an attack on Villatte, throwing him back to Bilbao, where he was able to unite with *Général de Division* Sebastiani's division of Lefebvre's IV Corps, but suffering significant loss on the way. Whilst this action was taking place, the Conde de San Román had arrived on the scene with his Denmark veterans, now bearing their new name of the División del Norte, and was ordered by Blake to remain in place at El Berron as a reserve. Lefebvre had to respond, and after concentrating his forces he began to advance upon Blake's Ejército de la Izquierda on 7

November, after a storm of criticism had been unleashed upon both him and Victor by Napoleon for their stuttering progress. Victor, having taken the brunt of the tirade, advanced again, this time towards Guenes. Meanwhile, Lefebvre took possession of Balmaseda on the 8th where he was joined by Victor on the 9th, the same day as Blake arrived at Espinosa de los Monteros, with his troops suffering severely from the exposure and hunger they had been subjected to during several days of campaigning in the appalling autumnal conditions of the Cantabrian foothills. In fact, he had by then lost some 6,000 men to straggling, desertion and enemy action.

Blake was never intending to fight at Espinosa, but when he received news from the Conde de San Román that his Denmark veterans, who now constituted the rear-guard of his army, were in serious trouble, he found himself caught on the horns of a dilemma: should he disperse into the mountains, thus avoiding a battle against the vastly superior French forces, or stand and fight in an effort to save San Román and the honour of his army? He chose the latter, sacrificing relative safety for what would eventually become a difficult retreat.

On 10 November Villatte launched six of his battalions at the men from the Baltic as they stood firm on the high ground above the River Trueba, the position chosen by Blake as the place for his right flank. Resisting stoutly, they held their ground for some two hours in the face of the French onslaught. Victor then brought up strong reinforcements in an attempt to dislodge San Román's stubborn veterans, who themselves had received reinforcements, and by the end of the day the Spaniards, after a stiff contest of even numbers, still held the crest of the ridge. On the following day, *Maréchal* Victor launched a heavy attack upon the extreme left of Blake's position. The raw Spanish troops on that flank could not stand, and as they fled the field the whole of the Spanish line crumbled and retreated. Many of the Spaniards simply removed themselves from the path of the advancing French by taking to the hills, their losses in battle amounting to about 3,000. When Blake regrouped at Reynosa only half of the 23,000 that had taken the field were present, and these were in a state of extreme exhaustion. Most of the casualties in the fighting had been sustained by the Denmark veterans; their commander, San Román, was killed in action, just one of the 1,000 men lost by La Romana's old host, which began the day with 5,300 effectives.[10]

La Romana takes direct command of the Ejército de la Izquierda/Galicia

Once at Reynosa Blake's half-starved men received two days rations, but a period of rest and recuperation proved impossible. The French were following up quickly, reducing Blake's options for a retreat onto the plains of León. The continuing advance of Victor was beginning to sow seeds of

---

10   Arteche, *Guerra de la Independencia*, Vol. III, Ch. IV, pp.270–280.

TRANSPORTATION OF LA ROMANA'S TROOPS TO SPAIN

panic amongst the now thoroughly disorganised and dispirited Spaniards, and once it seemed that all of their escape routes were blocked, many of them abandoned their equipment and stores and made off into the Cantabrian foothills.

On 15 November, Blake was officially relieved from his post and replaced by the Marqués de La Romana after the latter's recent nomination as the commander in chief of what was now to be called the Ejército de Galicia.[11] Blake remained in charge for a while as the *de-facto* chief of what remained of the army, successfully extricating it from the freezing, northerly hills to a place of relative sanctuary close to the city of León, where the marqués was waiting to welcome his new host. The much-depleted ranks of Denmark veterans were about to be reunited with their old saviour.[12]

---

[11] Both the names, 'Ejército de la Izquierda' and 'Ejército de Galicia' appear to have been used to describe the host of Blake/La Romana, the former title having been superseded by the latter at about the time when La Romana assumed command. Later references revert to the original name.

[12] Oman, *A History of the Peninsular War*, Vol. I, p.428.

7

La Romana and Sir John Moore, November 1808 to January 1809

Retreat of the Spanish forces to León and the advance of Sir John Moore into Spain

The order for La Romana's appointment to lead the Galicians was signed by the *Junta Suprema* on 5 November, and he received the news of his new commission a few days later when he halted at Astorga, *en-route* to Madrid after his return from England. After accepting his new appointment, he made his way to Santander where he arrived on 11 November, the day after Blake's defeat at Espinosa. After taking stock of the situation, he issued orders for a retreat upon the city of León and by mid–December 1808 he was at the provincial capital. By then he had become more fully informed about the nature of the defeat at Espinosa, and it is clear from the proclamation he subsequently issued from his new headquarters, where he thought the blame for it all lay:

> The scandalous and disorderly retreat made by the Ejército de la Izquierda from Balmaseda to this city [León], the dispersion of troops without legitimate reason, the atrocities committed along the march and those still being committed by men who have not returned to their banner, stand as proof of the absence of discipline amongst the units of which it is composed. The commanders and officers must never abandon their post, nor the men they command. Whether from the superiority of the enemy or for some unforeseen disaster of war our armies are beaten, they must be reformed by the zeal, intelligence and activity expected of their commanders and officers, before being reorganised and turned to face the enemy …[1]

---

1 Published on 13 December 1808. *Archivo Histórico Militar* (henceforth, *AHM*) *Estado*, 42A, 459–462.

As La Romana began to re-organise his army in the vicinity of León, news began to arrive of the proximity of the British army under Sir John Moore; unbeknown to them at that moment in time, the two men were about to play a role in one of the most significant events of the war on the Iberian Peninsula.

Moore Receives Unwelcome Intelligence

Moore began his march into Spain on 11 October and arrived at Salamanca on 13 November. Two days later he received a letter from Major General Leith, then attached to Blake's headquarters as an observer. The news was not good:

> I regret to inform you that the army of General Blake, in which was lately incorporated the infantry of the Marqués de La Romana's division, has been defeated in several attacks since the 5th instant, and is entirely dispersed …
>
> The different attacks have been at Zor[n]osa, Balmaseda, Arantia, and the total deroute [came] after a defeat at Espinosa de las Montañas [*sic* for Monteros]. About 7,000 re-assembled at Reynosa on the 13th instant, but without any order; from thence they retreated after dark … as a half-starved and straggling mob, without officers, and all mixed in utter confusion…[2]

At this time Moore was languishing at Salamanca, hesitant about what he should do next whilst continuing to receive intelligence reports from British agents, and frantic appeals from the Spanish authorities encouraging him to advance on Madrid as the French drew near. At Spanish headquarters in León, La Romana had already decided to throw in his lot with Moore's army when it came to taking up the fight once more. However, Sir John would soon be reminded of the weakness of the marqués's new host via a further report submitted by Lieutenant Colonel Symes, his attaché to La Romana's headquarters. Nevertheless, the marqués was proposing to Moore that, with their combined forces, they should make a joint attack upon Soult, then on the River Carrion some 75 miles to the east of León. Such a move would leave the allied force a secure retreat towards La Coruña via the passes of Manzanal and Foncebadon, should they suffer a defeat at the hands of their opponent. This cautious approach, by no means a universal trait amongst Spanish generals of the time, illustrates the doubts La Romana had about the allies' chances against Soult. He may have had some confidence in the capabilities of Moore's army, but in a letter to Cornel, *Secretario del Estado y del Despacho Universal de Guerra* (Secretary of State and War Office, henceforth *Secretario del Estado*) dated 2 December, he wrote of his new host:

> With the Ejército de la Izquierda under extenuated circumstances due to the hunger and fatigue suffered during its disorderly retreat, the majority of its men in

---

2   Leith to Moore, 15 November 1808. James Carrick Moore, *A Narrative of the Campaign of the British Army in Spain* (London: Joseph Johnson, 1809), pp 40–42.

a state of nakedness and entirely without shoes; without pay for a month and not even a penny to hand; without an ounce of food and unsure even of a daily ration of bread; without the required number of mules and carts to transport supplies; without generals and staff of headquarters; with few competent commanders and officers; with many absentees from the units recently returned from Denmark; without [field] hospitals and the equipment to form them, the greater part of the units without instruction; without any discipline and a complete relaxation of subordination; with an over-staffed government without organisation, because Asturias has its own and Galicia another, and neither of them with a number of competent Commissaries; I cannot expect [to achieve] the happy results that I seek, and Your Excellency, together with the *Junta Suprema* of the kingdom, need to be aware of it …[3]

Moore was still at Salamanca as the beginning of the third week of December approached. Writing to Castlereagh on the 12th, he spoke of his plans to advance on Valladolid with the intention of threatening French communications between Bayonne and Madrid. Of La Romana, he says he had heard nothing.[4] However, Moore had written to the marqués on 28 November informing him of his whereabouts, and two days later, on the 30th, the marqués had actually replied to Sir John from his headquarters at León,[5] explaining that he was fully occupied with the reorganisation of the remnants of Blake's army after its defeat in Biscay, and that local intelligence had warned him of the presence of a French general at Carrion de los Condes. The letter is cordial and must have been warmly received by Sir John. It was the first exchange of correspondence between the two men who, it may be recalled, had been in (fairly) close proximity to each other in the Baltic region earlier in the year during the time the marqués was beginning to realise that Spain's alliance with France had been broken. Having read each other's introductory letters, Moore entered into regular correspondence with his Spanish ally on 6 December: 'My wish has always been to cooperate with the Spanish Armies for the good of the common cause … my wish is to unite with you; and to undertake with you such operations that we may judge best for the support of Madrid, and the defeat of the enemy'.[6]

Moore left Salamanca on 13 December still with the idea of making a move upon Valladolid. He was anxious to hear from La Romana, to whom he had written on the 6th and 8th, but the marqués, still at León, did not respond until the 11th, informing the British commander that he would send an attaché to meet him at Zamora.[7] In a further letter on the 14th, he again informs Moore of the presence of a French force of some 10,000 men

---

3   La Romana to Cornel, 2 December 1808, *AHN Estado*, 42A, 443–447.
4   Moore to Castlereagh, 12 December 1808. Moore, *A Narrative*, pp.291–295.
5   La Romana to Moore, 30 November 1808, Arteche, *Guerra de la Independencia*, Vol IV, Apendice 6, p.526.
6   Moore to La Romana, 6 December 1808. Moore, *A Narrative*, pp.93–95.
7   La Romana to Moore, 11 December 1808, Arteche, *Guerra de la Independencia*, Vol. IV, Apendice numero 6, p.526.

between Sahagun and Almanza,[8] and on 21 December he wrote suggesting a combined attack on the them via a move on Saldaña, offering the assistance of some 10,000 of 'the best dressed and equipped men' of his army.[9] Ultimately, the British commander in chief decided upon a plan to march his troops northwards from Salamanca to Zamora where he would combine with Baird, his intention being that of making a junction with La Romana even further to the north before turning eastwards and marching upon Burgos.

Moore's Predicament is Relieved

It was at or about this time that a huge slice of luck befell Sir John. A French officer-courier, *en-route* from French headquarters at Chamartín (Madrid) to Soult, then at Saldaña, was ambushed and killed by Spanish peasants. The documents he was carrying found their way to British headquarters, and amongst them was a letter from *Maréchal* Berthier. This proved to be a veritable mine of intelligence from which the British were able to deduce the current and projected strength of Soult's forces. It also revealed the movements of other French army corps in Spain, as well as their objectives, the state and whereabouts of Spanish forces throughout the country and an indication of where French headquarters thought Sir John's force was presently located, namely in full retreat upon Lisbon. In his final paragraph Berthier informs Soult that, 'Madrid is very quiet; the shops are open and life is beginning to return to normal.'[10]

This changed everything. Sir John seemed to have been contemplating a 'fortress Galicia' strategy, which would have offered him the security of a retreat to the coast *in extremis*, but the British general was now full of optimism, thinking that he was about to bring Soult's corps to battle by a combined movement of his own force and that of La Romana. Then, on 16 December, his high hopes were tempered by some unwelcome news. Colonel Symes, still with La Romana's headquarters, wrote to Sir David Baird on 14 December giving a full and frank description of La Romana's force and his opinion of their projected worth on the battlefield. Neither were flattering to Moore's ally, nor encouraging to Moore himself. In essence, Symes had written off La Romana's troops as an effective fighting force…[11]

On the same day as Symes wrote his report the marqués, also at Spanish headquarters in León, wrote to Moore, informing him that he was still attempting to re-fit and re-kit his army. He went on to say that with Soult's corps in front of him he could not move; if he did so the Frenchman would be free to move northwards into Asturias, thus threatening the communications with Galicia. However, he did foresee the time fast approaching when he

---

8   La Romana to Moore, 14 December 1808, Arteche, *Guerra de la Independencia*, Vol. IV, *Apendice numero* 6, pp.526–527.
9   La Romana to Moore, 21 December 1808, Arteche, *Guerra de la Independencia*, Vol. IV, *Apendice numero* 6, p.528–529.
10 Berthier to Soult, Arteche, *Guerra de la Independencia*, Vol. IV, *Apendice numero* 5, pp.524–525.
11 Symes to Baird, 14 December 1808. Moore, *A Narrative*, pp.128–132.

would be able to move towards Tordesillas in concert with Baird, before uniting with Sir John.[12]

By 18 December Sir John was at Castronuevo de los Arcos, some twenty miles north-west of Zamora, whence he wrote to La Romana who, surprisingly, had recently taken the decision to retreat towards Galicia:

> I received, upon my arrival here yesterday afternoon, a letter from Sir David Baird, inclosing [sic] one which he had just received from you, dated 16th, in which you mention your intention immediately to retreat, by Astorga and Villafranca, into the Galicias. I beg to know whether this be still Your Excellency's determination, as it is one which must materially affect my movements. I own that I expected Your Excellency would have left the road through the Galicias to Corunna open for the British army, as it is that by which, if obliged; we can alone retreat …[13]

In response to this a letter from La Romana was delivered to Mayorga on the following day. In it, the marqués explained to Sir John that his idea of retreating into Galicia had been based on Sir David Baird's earlier determination to do the same. Now that things had changed, he said, he no longer intended to retire and was willing to cooperate with British plans.[14] Sir John replied as follows: '… The body of the French under Marshal Soult is still at Saldaña. I shall march in that direction tomorrow, and shall attack them the moment I can. If Your Excellency can make any movement in favour of this attack, or take advantage of any success I may meet with, I take for granted you will do it.'[15] La Romana replied saying that he was willing to cooperate with the British commander but pointed out that he had been able to equip only some 7,000 of his 20,000 men and that the former were at Mansilla.[16]

By 23 December Sir John had united his forces with those of Sir David Baird at Mayorga, which lies at the mid-point between Benavente and Sahagun, and was ready to make his move toward the French. In light of the latest intelligence, he was aware that Soult's force of about 8,000 men was positioned along a line running north-west to south-east, stretching from Almanza on the River Cea to Saldaña on the River Carrion. He would advance the twenty-five miles from Sahagun to Carrion de los Condes, which would allow him to attack northwards towards Soult's left at Saldaña. The French, he knew, would be unable to draw back from him as they would soon find themselves in the mountainous country to their rear, and to escape via a movement to his right, Soult would require the bridge that crossed the River Esla at Mansilla. Moore wrote to La Romana that day:

---

12 La Romana to Moore, 14 December 1808. Arteche, *Guerra de la Independencia*, Vol. IV, Apendice numero 6, pp.526–527.
13 Moore to La Romana, 18 December 1808. Moore, *A Narrative*, pp.141–143.
14 La Romana to Moore, 19 December 1808. Arteche, *Guerra de la Independencia*, Vol. IV, Apendice numero 6, pp.527–528.
15 Moore to La Romana, 22 December 1808, Moore, *A Narrative*, p.158.
16 La Romana to Moore, 23 December 1808. Arteche, *Guerra de la Independencia*, Vol. IV, Apendice numero 6, p.529.

I shall march this night to Carrion where, I have reason to believe, some of the enemy are collected. Tomorrow I shall march on Saldaña. If Your Excellency would march from Mansilla, either direct on Saldaña, or pass the river a little above it, whilst I march from Carrion, I think it would distract the attention of the enemy, and considerably aid my attack…[17]

Napoleon Plans to Destroy the British Army

All seemed set. The British army was about to fight its first battle against the French on Spanish soil. Suddenly, upon receipt of intelligence from sources sympathetic to the British cause, it was revealed to Moore that the French force at Carrion de los Condes had been significantly reinforced. Then a courier arrived at British headquarters with the news that the French corps which had been marching west towards Extremadura had been halted at Talavera de la Reina, south–west of Madrid. More messages were received as the day progressed, the most worrying for Sir John must have been that by which he was informed that the French forces at Madrid had left the city and were advancing northwards. Finally, an urgent message arrived from La Romana:

> A 'confident', whom I have stationed on the Duero, wrote to me on the 18th inst. assuring me that the enemy troops stationed at El Escorial have made a movement towards here. He added that, if the person who advised him did not that day come to meet with him, he himself would travel to Villacastin [fifty miles north–west of Madrid] in order to observe the roads leading to Zamora and Segovia.
>
> I hasten to provide Your Excellency with this intelligence in order that you may take the measures which you judge to be appropriate.[18]

As Andrés Cassinello so succinctly puts it in his biography of the marqués, 'The plan of Napoleon to keep the British on the tail of Soult whilst he cut off their line of retreat, had been discovered.'[19]

Upon hearing the news Moore had no alternative but to turn his men about in mid–step and make a precipitate retreat towards the River Esla, with *Maréchal* Ney already at Tordesillas, just 80 miles from Carrion de los Condes. The celebrated retreat of the British army to La Coruña had commenced. La Romana's letter of 23 December, earlier referred to, had advised Moore of the whereabouts of the Spanish *i.e.* at Mansilla (de las Mulas) on the River Esla, some fifteen miles south–east of León:

> I have the honour to inform you of my arrival here with the troops I intend to employ in the auxiliary movement [we agreed]. I could bring no more than 7,000 infantry, one hundred and twenty cavalry and eight pieces of artillery … I [will]

---

17 Moore to La Romana, 23 December 1808. Moore, *A Narrative*, p.159.
18 La Romana to Moore, 22 December 1808. Arteche, *Guerra de la Independencia*, Vol. IV, *Apendice numero* 6, p.529.
19 Cassinello, *El Capitán General*, p.130.

await your report before making a movement, which I shall not begin until I have received a communiqué informing me of your plans and intentions …[20]

La Romana is informed of Moore's Intention to Retire

From his letter of 23 December, it is clear that La Romana was still expecting Moore to fight an action against the French, and was seemingly unappreciative of the analysis Sir John would have made of the situation once he became aware of Soult's recent reinforcements and the converging movements of other French corps then underway. The British commander replied to the marqués explaining that he then considered his mission accomplished. It was now time to try all within his powers to save his army from annihilation. He wrote:

> I … Shall take immediate measures for retiring on Astorga. There I shall stand; as my retreat thence, if necessary, will be secure … I can maintain myself, and, with Your Excellency's aid, defend the Galicias …I hope this plan will meet with your approbation …
>
> P.S. … I am sensible of the zeal and activity Your Excellency has displayed, in thus hastening to cooperate with me; but … I believe the attempt no longer possible. It will, however, be of use, and will blind the enemy, should you continue with your corps a few days at Mansilla.[21]

Once Moore had finalised the details of his retreat he wrote to La Romana once again, providing him with an outline of his plans and asking him to do all that was in his power to delay the French in their pursuit of his army; in essence he was asking him to defend or destroy the bridge at Mansilla.[22]

Between Mansilla de las Mulas and Benavente there were just three crossing points on the River Esla. From north to south, these were: the bridge at Mansilla, the ferry crossing at Valencia de Don Juan and the bridge at Castrogonzalo, just east of Benavente. Once he was on the west bank of the Esla with those three crossings destroyed, Moore could feel more secure about his retreat. Confident that Baird could be trusted to burn or sink the boats which were employed as ferries at Valencia de Don Juan, and that his own column would destroy the bridge at Castrogonzalo, he was left to trust in La Romana for the destruction of the bridge at Mansilla. As such his heart must have sank when he received the following communication from Colonel Symes:

> The marqués's idea seems to be that of retiring on Astorga, but not precipitately: to put León in the best possible state of defence and to leave there 2,000 men and some guns… Mansilla is not capable of defence; and breaking the bridge, the

---

20 La Romana to Moore, 23 December 1808. Arteche, *Guerra de la Independencia*, Vol. IV, *Apendice numero* 6, p.529.
21 Moore to La Romana, 23 December 1808. Moore, *A Narrative*, pp.164–165.
22 Moore to La Romana, 24 December 1808. Moore, *A Narrative*, pp.166–167.

marqués thinks, will not be any material obstacle to the enemy. In the present state of the weather, I think it would impede his progress.[23]

Moore Discovers La Romana's army at Astorga

When the British commander arrived at Astorga on 29 December he was joined by Sir David Baird's column which, after crossing the Esla, had gone by Villamañan, Santa María del Páramo and Hospital de Órbigo, where they partly dismantled the beautiful old bridge which crosses the River Órbigo, before continuing their march. Meantime, some fifteen miles along his own route from La Bañeza, Moore was much disappointed to find the walled town of Astorga already occupied by La Romana's army, and to be informed that the Spaniards had not destroyed the bridge at Mansilla as requested.

The Allies Separate

It was at Astorga where Moore decided to detach Brigadier General Craufurd to lead two brigades of light infantry on a flank march along the road to Orense via Foncebadón, with the aim of reaching the Galician port of Vigo on the Atlantic coast. Most of the British troops were to leave Astorga by 30 December and La Romana, requested by Moore to keep his troops clear of the road to La Coruña, had by then marched his men off in the wake of Craufurd along the more southerly route into Galicia.

During their march the Spaniards were to suffer severely at the hands of the French cavalry, which came up against their rear-guard on two occasions taking prisoner no fewer than 5,000 of the marqués's host, which, if anything, was in its worst condition of neglect since its defeat at Espinosa. Poorly clothed, unshod and ravaged by a strain of typhus, it was no surprise that they had been unable to resist Soult's determined thrust towards León and beyond. By the time they reached the small town of Puente de Domingo Flórez on the River Sil, half of the men who had marched out of Astorga had been lost. Here, in the mountainous country of El Bierzo and close to the frontier with Galicia the marqués, conscious of the fact that his force by then constituted a *de-facto* rear-guard for Craufurd's fleeing light infantry, took up a defensive position at the bridge which crosses the Sil. It may be supposed that few of the Baltic veterans were still with their colours by this time, and this supposition is supported by the following example: in a return of the 1er de Catalunya, taken on 10 February 1809, the strength of the unit was given as 248. When it left Denmark some six months earlier it had a strength of some 1,129.

On a brighter note, since his return to Spain the marqués had been seeking some form of official recognition for the efforts of his men, both for the spirit shown in the Baltic and for their subsequent behaviour against the French in

---

23 Symes to Moore, 15 December 1808. Moore, *A Narrative*, pp.171–172.

Biscay, such as that displayed at Espinosa. On 3 January 1809, in response to La Romana's solicitations, Antonio Cornel addressed the following remarks to him:

> The King, Don Fernando VII, desires that, in his Royal Name, the *Junta Suprema Gubernativa del Reino* give public testimony of the appreciation and consideration deserving of the troops of the North, who have demonstrated their loyalty, patriotism and zeal in overcoming so many risks during their escape to Spain in order to defend the cause of King and Nation. [As further proof of his recognition, the King] has ordered that all officers belonging to the Corps who returned in the company of the Marqués de La Romana, will be awarded a rank one step above that which they hold, whenever such a vacancy exists. Equally, His Majesty orders that the soldiers, corporals and sergeants of the same Corps receive one extra *escudo* per month in pay.[24]

---

[24] Cornel to La Romana, 3 January 1809, *AHN, Estado* 42A, 505.

8

La Romana in the Wilderness, January 1809 to January 1811

By the time Moore's army was fighting its battle for survival at La Coruña, La Romana's exhausted host, for what it was, was struggling to exist in the desolate mountains of Galicia close to the border with Portugal. It would seem that the French had decided that it was not worth chasing him down, preferring instead to let the cruel winter of north–west Spain take its inevitably heavy toll of the surviving Spaniards.

In early January 1809, the marqués was given notice that he would soon be called away to Asturias, having been nominated *Capitán General* of the principality, but, before he set off, he would place *Mariscal de Campo* Mahy in command of the army. The force he was about to leave behind in Galicia was much reduced in comparison with its strength whilst under the command of Blake. It now consisted of barely 6,000 men and, small as it was, there were still many in its ranks without arms or uniforms, and subsistence during the winter months was proving difficult. Fully cognisant of its limitations, La Romana's strategy was simply to maintain a defiant presence in the face of the superior forces of *Maréchaux* Ney and Soult; always threatening, but never venturing an action against his adversaries.

In early March, at the commencement of the 1809 campaign, Soult began his movement from Galicia into Portugal, but at a location close to the town of Gudiña he was to find his route blocked by a force of some 1,200 of La Romana's army, which included the Baltic veterans belonging to the regiments of Zamora and Barcelona. The action resulted in a rout of the Spaniards with the loss of some 700 in killed, prisoners and wounded, which represented a further and significant diminishment in the number of survivors from Denmark still with their colours.

The failure of the Spanish was the cause of much bitterness amongst their Portuguese allies, then active in the northern frontier territory that separates the two countries. *Tenente-General* Silveira, the Portuguese commander who had expected the Spanish to unite with him in defence of his country, placed all of the blame for his subsequent troubles firmly at the door of La Romana for not having informed him of his intention to retreat. In response La Romana claimed that he had been forced to change his plans to rendezvous with Silveira, and instead retreat in an easterly direction towards Puebla de Sanabria, in order to keep out of the path of the oncoming French who had an overwhelming superiority in cavalry.[1]

Leaving a force of some 2,000 at Sanabria the marqués dispersed his remaining units towards the towns of El Bierzo such as Ponferrada, Villafranca, Toreno, Palacios del Sil, Vega de Espinareda and Lillo. For most of the month of March 1809, the Ejército de Galicia did nothing much other than march and counter-march between the northern and southern extremes of El Bierzo. By this mode of activity La Romana became known locally, and somewhat disparagingly, as '*el Marqués de la Romería*' (the Rambling Marqués). However, one notable and morale-boosting success was achieved. Local intelligence had informed him of the presence of an isolated French battalion at Villafranca, and on 17 or 18 March Mendizábal, at the head of the Vanguardia of the army, attacked the enemy who at the time was firmly ensconced within the walls of the impressive castle situated on the southern fringes of the town. The French garrison of some 1,000 surrendered on the 20th. It was a singular achievement.[2] In fact, Mendizábal decided to attack the town only on the appearance of Mahy, who arrived in El Bierzo to join his comrade dragging along a heavy cannon and ammunition, which his men had exhumed from the remote spot in the Sierra Negra where they had buried it some two months earlier whilst fleeing from the French. As the Spaniards approached the town, the French retreated to the castle and were prepared to put up a fight until the cannon was trundled into view and aimed at the gates of the place.

La Romana takes up his duties as *Capitán General de Asturias*

It was not until April 1 1809 that La Romana actually left Galicia for Asturias, his escort comprising one of the Baltic regiments, Princesa, with José O'Donnell at its head. In attempting to trace the fortunes of the Denmark veterans after their return to Spain we have so far spoken only of the infantry regiments, as these were thrust into the action at Espinosa almost immediately after they had disembarked at Santander. As we have seen, most of the Baltic cavalry went off to Andalucia to be re-mounted, but after the defeat at Espinosa the handful which remained in Cantabria and Biscay was forced to retreat westwards, along the northern coast of Spain, into Asturias.

Whilst the desperate fighting in Biscay was at its height, the principality of Asturias was under the control of a body which liked to refer to itself as the *Junta Suprema (de Asturias)* and think of itself as a completely autonomous institution having more or less full executive powers within the region. In December 1808 its members began to insist that the cost of maintaining the men of Blake's defeated host still present in the principality, including about 1,000 sick and wounded in the hospitals, should fall upon the *Intendentes* (Treasuries/Corporations) of La Coruña and Santander, as ordered by the

---

1 Cassinello, *El Capitán General*, pp.172–173.
2 Cassinello, *El Capitán General*, p.189.

national *Junta Suprema* almost certainly because it was those two ports which were initially expected to receive the Baltic escapees on their return to Spain. It was during this period that La Romana had been elevated to the position of *Capitán General de Asturias*.

The *Junta* was also insisting upon exclusive command of 'its own' army, and these demands began to infringe upon the position of the marqués, who insisted he had full command of all troops in the principality. Much trouble was to follow amongst the various parties involved in the dispute, and in the end La Romana took the decision to dissolve the (Asturian) *Suprema* on 2 May 1809, citing the proclamation of 1 January issued by the national governing body, the *Junta Suprema*, which dictated that, 'All *Juntas* which held the title of '*Suprema*' during the time of the *Gobierno Soberano Nacional*, [*i.e* the monarchy before the French usurpation] must now take the title of, *Junta Superior Provincial de Observación y Defensa*.'

La Romana's proclamation of 2 May included the following words:

> For the motives indicated and others which I choose to withhold, I have determined that all of the *vocales* [members] making up the said '*Junta Superior*' [note: he uses '*Superior*', not '*Suprema*'] will cease in their function from now on, and that all tribunals or commissions created by them be abolished…[3]

Whilst attempting to bring the Asturians to heel La Romana did not lose sight of events in Galicia. In his biography of La Romana, Cassinello Pérez cites two letters which the marqués sent to his commanders of division: *Mariscal de Campo* Mendizábal of the Vanguardia, *Mariscal de Campo* Mahy of the 1er División and *Teniente-General* Gil Taboada of the 2o División. Both written in January 1809 before he left for Asturias, they contained instructions to his generals on how the coming campaign should be fought. Unfortunately, Mahy, in the absence of his commander in chief, decided upon a more adventurous attitude than that advised, all of which led to some embarrassment, and he was soon rebuked for it on 24 April 1809 via another letter from the marqués, then at Oviedo. Mahy could have no complaints because, in his earlier letters, La Romana had illustrated to his subordinate the tactics he must necessarily adopt due to the continuing superiority of the enemy in Galicia.[4]

> My friend Mahy: from the dispatch that you sent to me with Vorster I can see that you have been obliged to return to your old cantonments. Do me the favour of remaining there until we have everything that we need to enable us to do something, and believe me that, although little, I do have some experience of warfare having studied and thought much about it. To those impulses to attack without paying attention to the means by which it can be done and believing in the probability that it will result in victory, you must not listen, nor should you

---

3   Romana, T. XXX 46(1) as cited by Cassinello in *El Capitán General*, p.209. Note, from the format of the reference identifier it would seem that the article referred to is held in the La Romana family archive, to which Cassinello had access whilst writing his life of the marqués.
4   Romana, T. VIII 26(13) as cited by Cassinello in *El Capitán General*, pp.160–161.

give them merit. We will achieve more than a little if, by employing whenever opportunity presents itself our small and ill-prepared forces, we manage to contain the enemy at La Coruña. In their present condition, should they obtain the smallest advantage over us, they will be revived, and by using all the means that their desperate situation will allow they could alter the current situation, which is by no means unfavourable to us …[5]

The Effect in Galicia of Wellesley's Victory at Oporto

On 12 May 1809 Wellesley, then operating in Portugal after his return to the Iberian Peninsula, decided to attack Soult at Oporto. Once the Anglo-Portuguese army had established itself upstream of the French on the north bank of the River Duero, the French marshal was forced to make a precipitate retreat towards the Spanish frontier, using various mountain tracks as the safest means of escape and leaving most of his baggage and artillery behind. Once back in Galicia, Soult's forces were thinly spread and increasingly harassed by a popular uprising which took its cue from the presence of La Romana's forces, weak and poorly equipped though they were. However, Kellerman had retaken Villafranca and strengthened the French presence at Lugo during late April, thus securing their vulnerable line of communication between Castilla and Spain's Celtic province.

With stronger forces now available in north-west Spain, the French decided to make a three-pronged incursion into Asturias under the overall command of Ney, with Kellerman leading one of the two remaining spearheads, Bonnet the other. The Spanish should have been able to frustrate their enemies but they failed to defend the difficult passes of Pajares and Letariagos, and as the French approached the provincial capital, Oviedo, La Romana was forced to flee to Gijon whence he was able to make good his escape to Galicia by sea. This failure, coupled with the marqués's earlier 'relegation' of the *Junta* in Asturias and his refusal to communicate regularly with the *Junta Suprema* in Seville, were soon to prove his downfall. Meanwhile, the struggle in Galicia continued.

In June Soult, having to some degree recovered from the beating he suffered at the hands of Wellesley in Portugal, was back in Galicia seeking the cooperation of Ney in a plan to destroy La Romana's army. By the end of May, the two Frenchmen had resolved their differences on tactics and agreed that Ney, setting off from Lugo, should march down the Atlantic coast upon Vigo via Santiago whilst Soult, some 70 miles inland on the eastern flank of the pincer movement, moved south towards the Portuguese frontier via Monforte and Orense. Once at the latter place Soult would await the arrival of his colleague who would approach from the direction of Vigo, thus closing the southern end of the pocket in which they hoped to trap the Spaniards. These movements would force La Romana to choose between fight or flight.[6]

---

5   *AHM, Colección Duque de Bailén, L. 12. Carpeta XLV.*
6   Cassinello, *El Capitán General*, p.226.

The plan of the French marshals did not succeed due to an unexpected and wholly creditable defence of the bridge at San Payo, some ten miles north-west of Orense, by a force consisting mainly of armed peasants and civilians led by the Conde de Noroña, recently despatched to Galicia by the *Junta Suprema* as part of a secret plan to oust La Romana from his position as *Capitán General de Asturias*. Before, during and after the action, Noroña had been hoping that La Romana would assist him, either by coming directly to his aid or by manoeuvring his force such that Ney might suspend his approach towards Santiago. On his part, Ney was hoping for something similar from Soult, but the latter responded that his movement had already displaced La Romana's force, thus causing the marqués to cross the frontier into Portugal to seek the support of *Tenente-General* Silveira of the Portuguese army. Having accomplished all that he thought was expected of him and claiming that he had received instructions for a new and urgent mission, Soult led his troops out of Galicia via Puebla de Sanabria on 25 June 1809, entirely unmolested by the marqués. Ney, having admitted defeat at San Payo as he approached his intended rendezvous with Soult retreated and immediately began his own withdrawal from Galicia, arriving at Astorga on the 30th thus leaving the Celtic province free from occupation. Within a short time, French forces would also abandon Asturias. Clearly, after Wellesley's victory at Oporto, Napoleon's armies in Galicia and western Asturias were in danger of being cut off should the British general continue his movement to the north. This, combined with the ever-present threat in the minds of the French of a possible British landing on the north coast of Spain, might have spelt disaster for them had they remained where they were.

As a final word on the combat at San Payo we should make mention of a familiar name amongst La Romana's Baltic veterans: Don Ambrosio de la Quadra was the man in command of the Vanguardia of Noroña's force, and it was he who occupied the pass of Caldelas, situated some five miles upstream of the action, as the battle unfolded, thus restricting the movements of the French and contributing to their defeat.

La Romana Deprived of Command

After the disappearance of Soult and Ney from north-west Spain, La Romana may have felt well justified by his actions in the region, but on 8 June the *Junta Suprema* wrote to him criticising his lack of communication over the previous two months and for his failure to halt the earlier French advance into Asturias. *Secretario del Estado* Cornel ended his communication in no uncertain terms by demanding of La Romana a full explanation of his behaviour. Thus, the reason for the sudden appearance of the Conde de Noroña in Galicia would have become apparent to the marqués, if he did not suspect it already.

The next two months or so were to witness a protracted power struggle between La Romana and Noroña for control over affairs in Galicia and Asturias. In July 1809 the marqués nominated *Mariscal de Campo* Mahy as the *Comandante General de Asturias*, signalling that after bringing the regiments of Navarra and Princesa, the latter a Baltic regiment, up to full strength, he should combine these units to form a single division. Such actions did not please Noroña and the squabbles continued, mainly with respect to competing claims upon the funds, weapons, munitions and equipment then arriving in Asturias from England, as well as the scant resources the *Junta Suprema* was able to supply. All came to a head on 13 August 1809 when La Romana, then at Villafranca in El Bierzo, received a letter from Cornel dated 19 July 1809 at Seville, instructing him to separate the governments of Asturias and Galicia and nominate *Teniente-General* Arce as the overall authority for the *Costa de Cantabria y Asturias*. The *Secretario del Estado* went on to say that the marqués should leave in Galicia only a small part of his army to act as a garrison and send the rest to the town of Carbajales de Alba with the intention that it would operate in conjunction with Beresford, presumably somewhere on the Portuguese frontier. That order was later withdrawn on the 27 July to be replaced by instructions that the troops in Galicia and Asturias should unite against the enemy. The marqués's command was still secure for the present, but the writing was now clearly on the wall for all to see.[7]

La Romana, frustrated by the meddling of the *Junta Suprema* in far off Seville, vented his spleen in a letter to Cornel dated 21 August, and on the 24th, as a response to the latter's communiqué of 19 July, the marqués distributed to his subordinates a paper detailing an order he had received from Don Martín de Garay dated 6 July 1809, instructing him to devolve the command of his army to: 'somebody other than *Mariscal de Campo* Conde de Noroña because, having been nominated as *Segundo Comandante General* of the kingdom of Galicia, he [Noroña] must take up permanent residence in that kingdom.'[8]

La Romana's circular of the 24th, written whilst he was at his headquarters in Astorga, concludes with a paragraph which begins, 'In complying with the preceding Royal Order, I have conferred the command of the Army upon *Mariscal de Campo* Don Gabriel de Mendizábal, and that of the kingdom [Galicia] upon the Conde de Noroña.'[9]

In recompense, or in an act of diplomacy designed to let him down gently, de Garay's order went on to inform the marqués that the reason for his removal from the command of the Ejército de la Izquierda was that his valued services were required by the *Junta Suprema* in Seville. On 25 August, La Romana said farewell to his troops in an emotional address which began:

> Soldiers. In Denmark, we came to hear the anguished voice of Fernando and we obeyed it to its echoes. The motherland called for our help and a generous nation [Britain, whose ships,] ploughing tempestuous seas, carried us to a union with our brave compatriots …

---

7   Cassinello, *El Capitán General*, pp.237–238.
8   Excerpt from a Royal Order written by Martin de Garay, *Secretario de la Junta Suprema*, on 6 July 1809, as cited by Andrés Cassinello in his biography of La Romana: *El Capitán General* pp.243–244.
9   Cassinello, *El Capitán General* p.244.

The motherland has not taken full account of your services; but the actions at Villafranca, Vigo, Campo de Lugo, Santiago and San Payo, in which your valour has shone, has silenced all criticism of your refusal to fight those battles whose outcome could only have been disastrous …

Yes, brave Spaniards! When I think of this day, I lose the composure I have kept whilst at your front.

I am no longer your General; His Majesty separates me from you so that I may occupy a place in the *Junta Central*. If it were not for his irresistible will, nobody would tear me from your side nor cause me to renounce the right I have to participate in your future victories. Under the new Chief and Generals that now command you, receive, soldiers, the final words of your General; and from this day remember the paternal love and gratitude of your compatriot and companion in arms.

El Marqués de La Romana.[10]

On 19 November 1809, whilst La Romana was absent from the military scene, the Spanish Ejército del Centro, under the command of Areizaga, suffered a crushing defeat at the hands of Soult near Ocaña, which lies to the south of Madrid close to Aranjuez, the Spanish commander losing almost half his strength of some 46,000. On 25 November Del Parque, at the head of the Ejército de la Izquierda and two brigades belonging to the Ejército de Extremadura, was just as comprehensively beaten by Kellerman at Alba de Tormes, a short distance south of Salamanca. Del Parque lost some 3,000 of the 30,000 men present on the day of the battle, but his losses increased rapidly over the coming weeks through desertion and sickness.

On 31 January 1810 the French, with King Joseph at the head of his army, took possession of Seville, the members of the *Junta Suprema* having fled the city some weeks earlier for Cádiz. During those three months of turmoil the marqués held the post of deputy in the *Junta Suprema*, but it would appear that he did not play an active role in any of the business conducted by the government.[11]

Reinstatement of La Romana

On 24 January 1810, the Marqués de La Romana was reinstated as commander in chief of the Ejército de la Izquierda by proclamation of Don Francisco Saavedra, President of the *Junta Suprema*, which suggests that the label, Ejército de Galicia, had been officially discarded.

When he arrived at the city of Badajoz to take up his post, he found only a skeleton of the force led into battle at Alba de Tormes by the Duque del Parque; two reduced divisions were all that remained. In this situation he made contact with Wellesley, now ennobled as Lord Wellington and at that time close by in Portugal with the whole of his army. His proposal to the duke

---

10   *AHM, Colección Duque de Bailén, Carpeta I2. L. IX.*
11   Cassinello, *El Capitán General*, pp.278–285.

was that he should ally his 'brigade' with Wellington's host, thus enabling the joint force to move upon Salamanca. Wellington declined his offer.[12]

Throughout the spring of 1810 La Romana maintained his forces in the proximity of Badajoz, close to the frontier with Portugal, and placed his provisional vanguard within the walls of the city, thus providing it with a resident garrison. His 1er División was at Campo Mayor, the 2o División at Albuquerque and the 3er División at Olivenza. As the campaigning season approached, the Spanish troops began to receive uniforms and arms from their British allies, and a programme of instruction from their commander in chief. By this time *Maréchal* André Masséna, Duc de Rivoli, Prince d'Essling, was leading his army into Extremadura charged with the mission of evicting Wellington's host from Portugal. In support of what was to become the third French invasion of the country, *Général de Division* Bonet re-entered the province of Asturias and *Général de Division* Clausel was ordered to capture Astorga, which fell on 22 April 1810, thus securing Masséna's northern flank.[13]

Masséna arrived at Salamanca on 29 May 1810 where he was to meet with *Maréchaux* Ney and Soult in order that they coordinate their movements in support of what Napoleon saw as the primary mission: Masséna's expulsion of the British from the Iberian Peninsula. That evening Ney, with his forces in place, commenced his siege of Ciudad Rodrigo. Wellington, wishing to conserve his army to defend against the anticipated assault upon Portugal, felt unable to go to the aid of the Spanish troops who were forming a screen in front of the place to the east of its walls. Neither could he offer any help to its governor, Pérez de Herrasti, who was responsible for directing the garrison within the fortifications. It was clear that serious efforts would be required to frustrate Masséna's ambitions, and for a brief moment La Romana's hopes for involvement in the defence of Ciudad Rodrigo were raised, when Wellington moved his headquarters from Portugal to Alberca in Spain. It was there where the two men met, but Wellington was already resolved in his decision. Aware of the strength of French forces committed to the enterprise of taking Lisbon, he could not commit any of his divisions to the fighting in Spain. The Spanish would have to defend the city alone, and they were to put up a creditable defence; Herrasti's men withstanding Ney's siege for some six weeks before surrendering on 10 July 1810.[14]

After the fall of Ciudad Rodrigo La Romana moved his army south of the River Tagus, and by the beginning of August he had established his headquarters at the town of Zafra which lies some 50 miles to the south-east of Badajoz. It was there where he concentrated the divisions of La Carrera and Ballesteros. In the meantime, *Mariscal de Campo* Mendizábal was given overall command of the Spanish force that was sent out in search of the French. When he came upon the enemy, he found them already arrayed in order of battle at Cantalgallo, but instead of awaiting the arrival of the rest of the Spanish divisions Mendizábal, displaying all the impetuosity possessed

---

12   Cassinello, *El Capitán General*, p.289.
13   Cassinello, *El Capitán General*, pp.289–302.
14   Cassinello, *El Capitán General*, pp.303–306.

by too many of the Spanish high command, launched his men into the attack with the usual result; he was severely beaten. In his report to the new *Secretario del Estado*, Bardaji, La Romana explained that his orders had been not to bring on an action, as the intention was simply to observe the enemy until, with all units reunited, a concerted attack could be made; but, he said, 'Ardour and impatience for victory amongst the troops, combined with an anxiety for glory amongst the generals, took the place of the prudence and circumspection that must be maintained.'[15]

Closer Cooperation with British Forces

On 18 July 1810, Lieutenant General Rowland Hill sent a warning to La Romana, informing him that Reynier had crossed the Tagus; but by the end of the month the French commander had been called towards Masséna, causing him to remove his force from Extremadura and enter Portugal. This provided the marqués with an opportunity finally to concentrate his forces without fear of being assailed by superior numbers of French. Once his army was united, he fixed his gaze upon Mortier's division to the south, situated on the road leading to Seville. If the marqués was in need of any encouragement with his thoughts of finally dealing a blow to the French, it came on 8 August 1810 in rather entertaining form from Bardaji in the following letter:

> As a consequence of the departure of Reynier from his station in Andalucía – and I am not one of those familiar [with the business of] instigating a military operation whilst sitting at his desk – but if I hear that we are with our arms crossed while the enemy presents us with an opportunity to operate against his forces, then we must renounce all hope of prospering. As I pointed out to your grace in my last letter, those points which the enemy has to cover in Andalucía are widely separated, and as a consequence he cannot detach appreciable forces in order to oppose an attack upon him elsewhere. I repeat, I do not consider myself capable of dictating laws which require better knowledge of the forces involved, and what they may achieve, but if you remain in the position you currently occupy and the French create mischief against the Anglo–Portuguese, they will afterwards turn upon you with their undoubted superiority and annihilate you. Whilst they have their attention fully focussed upon Portugal there will be an opportunity to deal them an unexpected blow [*un porrazo de sopetón*] in Andalucía; and seeing themselves threatened from Granada, Jaen and la Mancha, we could place them in a position of great embarrassment, having in our favour the season and the assistance offered us by the towns and villages, [whose people are] exhausted and demoralised with the weight of circumstances they have to bear. Blake must act soon, and then we here can make a movement to distract the attention [of the French, so I am] expecting that you will offer a threat from elsewhere, and that you will give us notice before you act. Finally, it is necessary to give [the French]

---

15   *Archivo Histórico Naciónal (AHN) Madrid. Diversos Colecciónes (Depósito de la Guerra)* as cited by Cassinello, *El Capitán General* p.332.

some sign that we are still alive, and that the provinces convince them of our spirit to resist.[16]

Seemingly unruffled by Bardaji's intervention La Romana reassembled his forces, and on 15 September 1810, as he moved into the valley of the Guadalquivir, he came upon a strong enemy force at Ronquillo, which had been sent by Soult to intercept his march under the command of *Maréchal* Mortier. On this occasion, with the marqués in full control, a retreat was ordered. Slow in their movements, the French were able to come up with the Spanish rear-guard at Fuente de Cantos, south of Zafra, on the 20th. Total disaster was avoided only by the timely intervention of the Portuguese cavalry under the command of a British officer, Major Madden.

Operating so close to the frontier with Portugal it is unsurprising that Wellington came to know of the state and capability of La Romana's forces, and as the Spanish formations began to merge with the British on the periphery of the lines of Torres Vedras and the lower reaches of the Tagus, in the aftermath of Bussaco, he felt more obliged to appeal for funds and equipment from London in order to clothe, feed and arm La Romana's men. Even as late as January 1811 he sent a dispatch to his brother, the Marquis Wellesley, British Ambassador to Spain, informing him that the Spanish were wanting for much if they were to become an efficient force capable of operating in an effective fashion with their allies, the British and Portuguese:

> The army of the poor Marqués de La Romana has not a shilling, except for what I give him; he has no magazines and nothing that will permit him to keep his forces united, nor to allow them to operate like a military unit … all of this constitutes a theme for serious consideration. Either Great Britain has an interest in maintaining the war in the Peninsula, or not. If it is interested, there is no doubt about the necessity to make an effort to put into action against the enemy all of that great force that the Peninsula can bring to bear.[17]

Wellington continued to ask for permission to assist La Romana's army, but he also made it clear to the Spanish government that their troops would have to collaborate with his plans or his help would be withdrawn.[18]

It would appear that Wellington did eventually identify a role for the marqués and his troops, and on 6 October La Romana wrote to him assuring the duke that he had received his marching orders, and that his advanced guard was pressing the French at Villafranca de los Barros and at Almendralejo, which lies to the south of Merida and some 40 miles east of the Guadiana as it runs south from Badajoz. He then went on to inform Wellington that he had instructed Don Carlos de España to make a move upon Valverde del Fresno to threaten Masséna's supply lines. On the following day he issued orders to O'Donnell, instructing him to move from

---

16 Romana, T. XXII 41 as cited by Cassinello, *El Capitán General* p.330.
17 Wellington to Marquis Wellesley, Gurwood, *The Dispatches of Field Marshal, The Duke of Wellington* (London: Parker Furnival and Parker, 1844, Eight Volumes Edition), Vol. IV, p.565.
18 Cassinello, *El Capitán General*, pp.331–338.

Albuquerque to Estremoz in Portugal, but there was some delay in setting the Baltic veteran on his way, so on 18 October the marqués wrote to Charles Stuart, British diplomat and then joint *Chargé d'Affaires* in Madrid, from his headquarters at Montijo, which lies between Badajoz and Merida, explaining the reason why: 'Sir, I am very sorry to inform you that I have been forced to remain here for longer than I would have liked. For three days the rains have left me isolated, making all roads impassable … I believe I will be able to begin my move this evening.'[19]

By the end of October 1810 La Romana had entered Portuguese territory to integrate the divisions of O'Donnell and La Carrera with the Anglo-Portuguese forces defending the lines of Torres Vedras. All seemed to be going well for the great Spanish patriot when, in the following month of November, his spirits were laid low by tidings totally unexpected. He wrote the following to his secretary, *Brigadier* Baylin:

> My friend Baylin: we have not had much time to ruminate upon the news of the arrival [in Spain] of our Fernando, now brother-in-law of the infamous Napoleon …[20] If it is so, then I do not want it, and neither does the nation want it; we have to become free of all French influence so that that cursed and execrable nation involves itself to the minimum degree in our affairs…[21]

The Sudden Death of the Marqués de La Romana

In January 1811 Soult, under pressure from Napoleon, was persuaded to mount an invasion of the Spanish province of Extremadura which shares a border with southern Portugal. The objective of this movement was to alleviate the situation of Masséna, who had been awaiting reinforcements throughout the winter months. During that time his army had suffered severe depredations in its situation before the lines of Torres Vedras, due mainly to the severe climate and the hunger engendered by the effects of Wellington's scorched earth retreat of the previous autumn. In effect, the French were attempting to subsist in a huge area of Portuguese territory left almost bereft of population and resources. Whilst Wellington left 'General Winter' to degrade his enemy, La Romana, from his headquarters at Cartajo, continued in his attempts to orchestrate the movements of those of his forces still operating on the Spanish side of the frontier. It was in this capacity, whilst attempting to persuade Mendizábal to follow his orders and retreat from Olivenza as Soult drew near, that Spain suffered a sudden and unexpected loss. On 22 January 1811, after composing a final letter to Mendizábal, the marqués suffered what appears to have been a fatal heart attack.[22]

---

19   Cassinello, *El Capitán General*, p.353.
20   Unless there were rumours of a marriage between Fernando VII and a sister of Napoleon, it is difficult to understand La Romana's statement.
21   Cassinello, *El Capitán General*, p.358.
22   Cassinello, *El Capitán General*, p.363.

With the death of La Romana, it is perhaps time to call a halt to our attempts to trace the fortunes of his Baltic veterans as the war continued in Spain. To be fair, it must be supposed that most of the men disembarked on Spain's northern coast in October 1808 would have become casualties or simply deserted by the beginning of 1811, by which time many of the Spanish regular armies had been beaten by the French and pushed towards the mountainous regions which make up much of the country's periphery. In the next chapter we will investigate further the fortunes of the Spanish troops who were left behind in Denmark after the evacuation of their compatriots, and as a consequence became prisoners of the French.

9

Formation of the Régiment Joseph–Napoleon

We saw in Chapter 5 how a significant part of La Romana's army was left stranded on the island of Zealand in August 1808 as Keats's convoy sailed for Gothenburg. The great majority of those left behind belonged to the infantry regiments of Asturias and Guadalajara, and the reason for their failure to escape was that they were being held under close arrest by the French, whilst the daring rescue operation by the Royal Navy to embark their comrades was being successfully concluded on the east coast of Langeland. The cavalry regiment of the Algarve was also prevented from leaving Denmark; captured at the point of making their embarkation from Jutland to Funen by a cavalry force sent by Kindelán to frustrate their hopes of flight to Spain.

We last we heard of these Spanish detainees was at the time of their arrival in France, having been marched across Germany on their way into captivity. Our aim now is to follow their fate via the stories of two of their number, Rafael de Llanza of Guadalajara and Manuel López of Asturias, as the war in Europe continued. The reader should bear in mind that the previous chapter closed with the death of La Romana in January 1811, which means that in order to pick up the thread of the Spanish prisoners of war from the point where we last heard of them, we shall have to take a step back in time to October 1808, before continuing with our story to the end of the war in 1814/15.

Dispersal of the Baltic Prisoners Across France

As a result of a report submitted on 17 October 1808 by Napoleon's Minister of War, *Général de Division* Clarke, it was decided that all of the Spanish prisoners transported from Denmark to France were to be widely dispersed across the face of the country, and by January 1809 they had arrived at their allocated detention centres. The minister had come to the conclusion that the security risks associated with the continued concentration of the Spanish troops whilst held in captivity, were too great. The number of detainees was quite significant, representing about one third of the original strength of La Romana's army of 15,000, and Table 6 provides the details of their dispersal.

Table 6 Location of Spanish Prisoners in France at the end of January 1809

Depot/Town	Officers	NCOs and Other Ranks
Mezieres		425
Luxembourg		550
Thionville		500
Phalsbourg		456
Le Petite-Pierre	23	
Lichtenberg	23	
Besancon, Fort Griffon	24	553
Fort Barraux	24	
Fort l'Ecluse	24	
Chateau d'Amiens	23	
Chateau de Peronne	23	
Lille		444
Fort de Scarpe, Douai		397
Dijon	20	4
Perigueux	1	1,265
Total	**185**	**4,574**
Employed elsewhere		7
In hospital		543
Grand Total	**185**	**5,131**

Source: Boppe, *Les Espagnols*, p.83.

Napoleon Considers Recruiting the Baltic Veterans to his Cause

Towards the end of 1808, Napoleon decided to take direct command of his armies in Spain having previously delegated the subjugation of his southern neighbour to his various commanders of army corps. Unfortunately, things south of the Pyrenees had not gone as smoothly as he had hoped they would whilst he was settling accounts elsewhere in Europe, the Spanish having pushed the French invaders back from the high-water mark of their occupation to the north-east corner of the country, the slice of territory bounded by the River Ebro to the south, the Pyrenees to the north and the Mediterranean coast to the east. The Emperor of France was now about to unleash overwhelming forces against his southern neighbour in order fully to subdue her. As a means of increasing the number of men available for the coming offensive and, no doubt, of destabilising the political situation in Spain, he fixed upon the idea of creating a Spanish force willing to fight in his cause. The seed corn for this force, he reasoned, was already available, scattered amongst the depots in France at which the prisoners from La Romana's army were being held in captivity. He wrote to his brother Joseph, then King of Spain, on 5 December 1808:

> With regard to the Spaniards, you have soldiers who behave well. Within La Romana's corps of the Army of the North there are some individuals who deserve our gratitude, including one general [Kindelán] and several colonels. Bring this general, at present in France, to Spain, and place him at the head of a Spanish

FORMATION OF THE RÉGIMENT JOSEPH-NAPOLEON

regiment. I think this regiment should be known as the 'Royal-Napoléon d'Espagne' with the aim in mind that this title will make the men understand their duty…[1]

From his letter, it is clear that the new Spanish regiment was to be just one of several which Napoleon was keen to create by recruiting deserters and prisoners of war from a number of countries formerly or currently at war with France. In another letter written to his Minister of War, Clarke, on 7 January 1809, he says:

I also believe that there is a good number of Spanish soldiers who remain faithful [to me]. It would be necessary to meet with the Duque de Frias in order to agree upon how we could form a Spanish regiment at my cost. The general who has given such good service in the north [Kindelán] could provide you with a list of officers who merit our confidence and from these he could suggest some possible appointments.[2]

Kindelán and his Son José are Presented to Napoleon

On 24 January 1809 Frias, as King Joseph's Spanish Ambassador in Paris, presented *Mariscal de Campo* Juan Kindelán and his son and *aide-de-camp*, José, to Napoleon. The emperor seems to have been sufficiently satisfied with the impression he received of the general, and on that basis, he appears to have banished any remaining doubts he may have harboured concerning the formation of a Spanish regiment. Later that day he wrote to Clarke:

Minister of War,
I approve the creation of a regiment of Spanish infantry. I approve the appointment of *General* Kindelán as its colonel. Assemble the regiment at Nancy; give it the same structure as a French regiment; give it the name of Royal-Napoléon with the aim that the individuals who enter into service with it will be fully aware of the kind of commitment they are making.

Equally, I authorise the recruitment of Prussian and Spanish prisoners of war by the Portuguese…[3]

It is clear from a letter he wrote three days later on 27 January 1809, that he was still minded to send the regiment to fight in Spain. As a potential source of fresh recruits for the unit, he instructed his brother to send to France all the Spanish prisoners taken during the recent fighting in Spain. Once there, he reasoned, some of them might become willing to join the new regiment, which could then be sent back across the border to fight on the side of the

---

1　Napoleon to Joseph, Bonaparte, *Correspondance*, no. 14531, t, XVIII, pp.114–116.
2　Napoleon to Clarke, Bonaparte, *Correspondance*, no. 14659, t, XVIII, p.210.
3　Napoleon to Clarke, Bonaparte, *Correspondance*, no. 14735, t, XVIII, p.280. Note that the 'Portuguese' referred to by Napoleon would have been those who had joined the French cause at some stage during the war.

French. There was no need, he thought, to send a guard with those who Joseph thought could be trusted, but he was convinced that 'It is better to form the regiments in France and then send them [back] to you; it should not prevent the formation of the units I have suggested to you'.[4]

Meanwhile Clarke had been busy. He had made an approach to Kindelán, asking him to provide precise information regarding the possibility and the means by which a Spanish regiment could be formed. In this task Kindelán excelled himself, submitting to Clarke on 18 January 1809 a comprehensive report on his recommendations, which included an assessment of the morale of the Spanish soldiers upon whom Napoleon was about to call, for a second time, to take up 'the honour of serving [France].'[5]

By 13 February, Kindelán's report had been analysed and some of his recommendations accepted, but it would seem that the original plan to include a newly-formed regiment of Spanish cavalry was eventually dropped. Napoleon later issued a decree as part of his response to Clarke's submission, it consisted of seven articles defining the formation of the proposed Spanish force, all of which refer only to 'a regiment of Spanish infantry under the title of Joseph-Napoleon'. Kindelán was to become the colonel of the regiment on a provisional basis, and one of the first tasks assigned to him was that of selecting the officers who would be commissioned to serve with it. On 19 February he wrote to Clarke:

> In the first place, the choice of officers who might serve with the regiment has to be made from those belonging to Guadalajara and Asturias; I am not very familiar with them, so it will not be an easy task ... I beg Your Excellency to issue suitable orders requesting that Messrs Marti, *teniente-coronel* of [the Regimiento] de España, and Alcedo, a *sub-teniente* of Asturias, both now to be found at Bordeaux, go immediately to Paris with Messrs. Rodriguez Arellano, *mayor* of Asturias, and [Rafael de] Llanza, a *capitán* of Guadalajara; both currently in the depots holding Spanish officers who served in the north...[6]

Some days later Kindelán submitted his opinions regarding the recruitment of NCOs and other ranks, and on 21 February, he wrote to Clarke.

> I believe that in order to ensure that the levy is to be a success, and at the same time inspire confidence in the soldiers now held in the depots, it would be best to nominate two superior officers from amongst those who served with the Spanish division in the north and are already present in France.[7]

Things continued to move at an impressive pace. On 7 March 1809 Napoleon decided that the regiment would be organised at Avignon, and on 17 April

---

4 Napoleon to Joseph, Bonaparte, *Correspondance*, no. 14749, t, XVIII, pp.289–290.
5 *Archives Nacionales (France)* (henceforth, *ANF*) AF, IV, 1100, as cited by Boppe in *Les Espagnols*, p.86.
6 Kindelán to Clarke, as cited by Boppe in *Les Espagnols*, pp.95–96, *Archives Administratives de la Guerre (AAG)*.
7 Kindelán to Clarke, as cited by Boppe in *Les Espagnols*, p.96, *AAG*.

FORMATION OF THE RÉGIMENT JOSEPH–NAPOLEON

Kindelán submitted his proposals for the nominations of its officers to Clarke, who endorsed them and passed them to Napoleon on 16 May, as follows:

> Article 6 of the decree of 13 February states that, upon receipt of the necessary detailed proposals from *Maréchal de Camp* Kindelán, the choice of officers will be assigned to me, and that the list of officers so selected will be sent to the Minister of War in Spain to be certified by the government there.
>
> *Maréchal* Kindelán has now completed his task, and I approved his proposed selections on 2 May …[8]

Kindelán's nominations were given final approval by Napoleon on 17 May 1809, and in a letter of the same date Clarke informed Kindelán that he had made suggestions for the posts of *major*, *adjutant–major* and *intendant–militaire* (quartermaster) as follows: Tschudy (then with the Portuguese Legion) [*major*], Captains Delaloge and Carle [*adjutant–majors*] and Robert [*intendant–militaire*]. All were French.

The regiment was to have six cadres, each of which would be formed and organised at Avignon. However, it would seem that the recruitment of Spanish prisoners of war demanded a significant effort on the part of those hoping to convince them to take up the colours. The soon to be, *Sergent–Major* López, whose description of the insurrection on Zealand we have already seen, provided an account of what happened at the Besancon depot when his fellow prisoners were offered the chance to serve in the new regiment.

> The Archbishop of Besancon came up to the citadel on two occasions and harangued the Spanish, using the abdication at Bayonne to demonstrate to them that they could not, without placing themselves in a state of rebellion, refuse to take up service. The prisoners gave credence to the assertions and reasoning of the prelate, and those with the requisite abilities, together with individuals who did not yet have the right to leave, took up the offer to serve in the Régiment Joseph–Napoleon. Indeed, some of them enlisted with the Portuguese Legion.[9]

Joseph–Napoleon is deemed ready to take the field

On 11 October 1809 Clarke sent a report to Napoleon with regard to the new regiment; it contained the following statement, 'On 25 September, the Régiment Joseph–Napoleon had a strength of 57 officers and 1,016 NCOs and other ranks.'[10] We note from the numbers stated by Clarke that by no means all of the Baltic prisoners, who numbered some 5,000 in total, had yet enlisted.

---

8 Extract from Clarke's submission of Kindelán's report to Napoleon on 16 May 1809, as cited by Boppe in *Les Espagnols*, p.98.
9 Extract from a report by López submitted to Clarke circa October 1809, as cited by Boppe in *Les Espagnols*, footnote 2, p.101.
10 Extract from a report by Clarke to Napoleon, dated 11 October 1809, *ANF*: AF, IV, 1117, as cited by Boppe in *Les Espagnols*, p.101.

The regiment was fully organised by 21 February 1810; but the original idea of Napoleon was to create a complete army corps consisting of Spanish defectors and send it to fight in Spain, that this did not come to pass was due to his growing scepticism about the loyalty of the Spaniards. In the end he made up his mind to abandon the idea of sending to Spain any new units whose ranks were filled with expatriates, despite his brother's pleading that Joseph–Napoleon should be placed at his disposal. Perhaps the driving force behind the emperor's change of mind was a report which Kindelán had recently submitted to Clarke, stating that the regiment, 'was of bad spirit,' and that, 'its officers had demanded that it should be moved away from the Spanish frontier.'[11]

The Emperor seems to have taken Kindelán's analysis to heart, and on 25 April 1810 Napoleon, perhaps with a view to disbanding the unit, decided that it should be dispersed. Its five constituent battalions were to be separated and sent to distant destinations, and by 3 May Clarke was able to confirm the following relocations:

- 1er bataillon: from Aix to Grenoble and then on to Saint–Jean–de–Maurienne, where it would act as a labour battalion maintaining the roads
- 2e bataillon: from Avignon to Lyon, Dijon, Lille and then to Flessing to work on the fortifications of that place. This order was later superseded and the battalion re-directed to Antwerp.
- 3e bataillon: from Avignon to Lyon to act as a labour battalion.
- 4e bataillon: not being fully equipped by this time Napoleon ordered that as soon as it was ready it would be sent to San Remo whence, on the suggestion of Clarke, it would be moved to Monaco. Bonaparte overruled his minister and had it sent to Alessandria in the north of Italy instead.
- 5e bataillon: This unit was dissolved and its men sent to join the other battalions at their respective postings.

By 25 September 1810 the 1er and 3e bataillons of Joseph–Napoleon had been moved once more.

- 1er bataillon: to Turin, Borgo–Forte, Palma Nova & Mantua (November 1810).
- 3e bataillon: to Maestricht (December 1810).[12]

Napoleon Begins to Plan for the Invasion of Russia

By the end of 1810, Napoleon was convinced that war with Russia was inevitable and began to make plans for it. He was going to need every man and every unit he could find in order to build the huge expeditionary force required to mount an invasion of the vast Russian territories before Moscow.

---
11   Boppe, *Les Espagnols*, p.104.
12   *ANF*: AF, IV, 1108, as cited by Boppe in *Les Espagnols*, pp.108–110.

FORMATION OF THE RÉGIMENT JOSEPH–NAPOLEON

The Régiment Joseph–Napoleon was to figure in his plans. On 16 April 1811 he wrote to *Maréchal* Davout, Prince d'Eckmuhl, then at Hamburg as commander in chief of his Corps d'Observation de l'Elbe.

> My cousin, I am going to send you two magnificent Spanish battalions, the whole consists of a general and 2,000 men.[13] They are good soldiers serving as willing volunteers and they have been under arms for two years. I think they will fight as well as the Portuguese.[14] There are a few [potential] deserters amongst them and care must be taken not to place them in advanced positions, nor in strongholds of great importance. The probability is high that they will be approached by ill-intentioned agitators and it would be advisable to keep these battalions under secret surveillance. Your agents must keep an eye on them; they will discover many who are spies for the English.[15]

Clarke, always efficient in his services to the emperor, was soon in touch with Kindelán asking him for his thoughts on the suitability of employing the Spaniards in the forthcoming campaign. On 22 April 1811 the Minister of War sent a new report to Napoleon.

> I saw *Général* Kindelán yesterday; he is now out of the sick bed to which he has been confined due to severe rheumatism, and will very shortly be leaving for Nimegen to review the two battalions of the Régiment Joseph–Napoleon presently there. He intends to separate all aged officers from the regiment, as well as those of dubious commitment, and send them to the depot. He will apply the same procedure to the soldiers. His intention is to spend a few days at Aix-la-Chapelle whilst the two battalions are on their way to Germany. He is hoping to improve his health so that he can take up his post at the end of May or earlier, if necessary …[16]

The battalions selected to join the Armée d'Allemagne were the 2e and 3e, by then stationed at Antwerp and Maestricht respectively. The 1er and 4e bataillons were still in Italy.

Whilst Napoleon was planning his Russian campaign and allotting resources to the various army corps destined to take part in it, Clarke was once again deeply involved in the details. Towards the end of July 1811, he asked for a general report on the morale of Joseph–Napoleon from *Major* de Tschudy. This was duly submitted on 6 September 1811:

---

13 It will be as well here to note that Napoleon addressed all of his marshals as, 'Cousin'.
14 Napoleon was referring to the Portuguese Legion commanded by Tschudy until he was given a majority with Joseph–Napoleon.
15 Napoleon to Davout, Bonaparte, *Correspondance*, no. 17611, t. XXII, p.79.
16 *ANF*: AF, IV, 1157 and 1158, as cited by Boppe in *Les Espagnols*, p.106. Note: At this time, the French were toying with the idea of creating a second Spanish regiment and Clarke had been ordered to make some tentative plans in that direction. The winter campaign of 1808/09 had provided the French with a huge number of Spanish prisoners in the wake of the heavy defeats suffered by their forces, and by 1 December 1810 there were 3,404 Spanish officers in captivity along with 29,214 NCOs and other ranks. By April 1812 the annual cost to the French treasury of keeping these prisoners was stated at 3,111,050 Fr. and Napoleon was desperately looking for a means to offset this cost.

> On the whole, the spirit of the corps is good; there is no reason why it should be otherwise. There is no doubt about the political opinion of the colonel in charge, as he refused to support the [actions of] the Marqués de La Romana [in Denmark]. All of the officers, though they would have supported their general-in-chief had they had the opportunity to do so, are now persuaded that their actions would have been ill advised with regard to their national and personal interests. They are now convinced of the futility of the efforts being made by the English to maintain themselves in the Peninsula; they can see clearly that anarchy has reigned wherever they have been, whereas those provinces under the rule of His Majesty have begun to enjoy the tranquillity that has resulted by virtue of their [new] sovereign ...[17]

So it went on:

> The officers have displayed a measure of zeal from the beginning of the organization process of the corps, as demonstrated by their sharing with the soldiers the feelings that they profess. The soldiers, who are all volunteers, are happy with their lot. Like all Spaniards, they are extremely docile and devoted to their officers. As such, all of the general officers who have known this corps have underlined its excellent discipline. It is a judgment that it fully deserves ...
> ...the inspectors' reports on regimental affairs mention the regularity and the strict economy of the administration of the unit...
> ...the appearance of the regiment is magnificent and their instruction is of an advanced nature when considering the short period of time dedicated to it and the distances between the [the depots] of its constituent battalions.
> ...*Général* Kindelán displays every day much talent and activity ...[18]

A glowing report! However, a number of observations were included in a postscript to the main text:

> It can be seen that, with the exception of five or six bad characters and men of doubtful loyalty, one can, in general, count upon the spirit that animates the officers. However, their passion for the cause they have embraced could always be increased by offering them some advancement via the formation of a second Spanish regiment. The corps could be employed to advantage everywhere, except in Spain, where the soldiers would no doubt desert; not to take up arms against us, but to return to their homes which they believe would offer them shelter from those who might pursue them...[19]

On 13 October 1811 the 2e and 3e bataillons left Nimegen for Utrecht under the command of Kindelán who wrote to Clarke, 'We arrived on the 15th and were cantoned in villages some three leagues from the town.'[20]

17　*AAG*, as cited by Boppe in *Les Espagnols*, p.118.
18　*AAG*, as cited by Boppe in *Les Espagnols*, p.119.
19　*AAG*, as cited by Boppe in *Les Espagnols*, p.119.
20　*AAG*, as cited by Boppe in *Les Espagnols*, pp.120–121.

FORMATION OF THE RÉGIMENT JOSEPH-NAPOLEON

Napoleon was present in person at Utrecht, and Kindelán was with his regiment when the emperor carried out a review of his troops. In his letter he goes on to describe the occasion to Clarke:

> After [observing] some manoeuvres the Emperor was directed towards the battalions of Joseph-Napoleon, which were formed in the second line. And as he approached, he was received with acclamations of '*Viva el Emperador.*' He reviewed the two battalions ... putting many questions to the NCOs and soldiers ... That day was, for all members of the regiment, the happiest of their lives; it redoubled the love for the Emperor that each man carried in his heart...[21]

We last heard of Rafael de Llanza was when Kindelán asked that he be allowed to travel to Paris. We may now take up his story once more because it was on that day, 15 October 1811, whilst his regiment was being reviewed by Napoleon, that he was made commander of his unit. He describes the moment of his promotion thus:

> Thirty battalions were assembled, in the midst of which were to be found the two Spanish battalions. On this day ... the Emperor made me *Chef de Bataillon* for being the most senior by age, and I immediately received the order to march for the Baltic coast via the city of Rostock...[22]

On 30 October, just a few days after inspecting his army, Napoleon ordered the striking of the camp at Utrecht, instructing *Maréchal* Berthier to, 'Give the order to the Spanish regiment to move to Minden, where they will come under the orders of the Prince d'Eckmuhl and form part of the Corps d'Observation de l'Elbe.'[23] On the same day he wrote to Davout to inform him of his new acquisition, 'My cousin, I have ordered that two superb Spanish battalions, with a combined strength of 1,600, leave the camp at Utrecht and proceed to Minden. You will place them with Friant's division; I expect he will be happy; they were formed one year ago.'[24] Is it possible to detect just a hint of sarcasm in the emperor's words here? Was he still to be convinced of the apparent loyalty of the Spanish troops?

During the following month the old animosities with the Swedes resurfaced, providing Napoleon with a convenient pretext to occupy Swedish Pomerania. As part of that operation the Spaniards were moved to Stralsund, the scene of their first action as a Napoleonic unit under La Romana some two years earlier; they were about to take the field once more.

Seemingly unconvinced about the merits of employing the Spanish troops, Davout wrote to Friant on 10 November 1811, and the tone of his correspondence demonstrates once more that the French had little trust in the Baltic veterans:

---

21 *AAG*, as cited by Boppe in *Les Espagnols*, pp.121–122.
22 Bobadilla, *Un Español*, p.41.
23 Napoleon to the Prince de Neuchatel, Bonaparte, *Correspondance*, no. 18216, t. XXII, p.63.
24 Napoleon to Davout, Bonaparte, *Correspondance*, no. 18220, t. XXII, p.633.

A Spanish regiment is to be attached to your division. It is *en-route* for Rostock where it is expected between the 20th and 25th of this month. I would like you to place yourself at Rostock so that you may keep an eye upon it.

Take notice that there are emissaries who will seek to disturb the troops, and can succeed if you do not keep the regiment under close observation. Work in concert with the officers of the unit in order that you may become aware of the slightest disturbance that might occur *vis-à-vis* the troops, and if an emissary or civilian dares to suggest to you any rash advice then, on the basis of a report by your officers, you will ensure that justice is applied promptly …[25]

Kindelán Asks to be Relieved of his Post

On 12 December 1811 the then *Général de Brigade* Kindelán, arrived at Rostock (Germany) with the 2e and 3e bataillons of his regiment. Whilst there he wrote to Clarke explaining that he had met with Davout in Hamburg, before asking the minister if he could be relieved of his command due to the state of his health. After a short delay Clark agreed to send him 'home' to France, he would play no part in the invasion of Russia.

It would seem that, in the short term at least, little was done to provide the regiment with a commander in chief to replace Kindelán, and in the absence of a clear authority at its head things soon began to slip. *Général de Division* Friant then decided to take a closer look at the Spanish contingent of his division, asking *Général de Brigade* Grandeau to make an inspection of the unit and submit a report on his findings. On receipt of the document, Friant shared his thoughts with Davout:

> I am at present considering a review of the Spanish regiment made by *Général* Grandeau, which covers everything from its armaments and uniforms to its heavy equipment.
>
> The general will provide me very shortly with a list of everything that the corps is in need of in order to bring it to the standard of the rest of the regiments in my division, if that is possible.
>
> May I ask you to send me the major whom *Général* Kindelán has already requested, in order that he may take up the administration and command of the regiment.
>
> I cannot disguise from you the fact that I have little confidence in the *chef de bataillon* left to me by Kindelán, with the intention that he take command of the corps. After listening to his opinion of the individual concerned, I would presume him to be a Spaniard in every form of the word; above all, he possesses a mind that would be easily seduced by trouble makers.
>
> Yesterday a soldier of the 15th was murdered, stabbed to death by a Spanish soldier. I have moved heaven and earth to discover the perpetrator, who I intend

---

25 Davout to Friant, Charles de Mazade, *Correspondance du Davout* (Paris: Plon and Nourrit, 1885), no. 998, tome III, p.281.

to have shot straight away. It is forbidden for all the NCOs and soldiers to carry a knife.[26]

On 18 January 1812, *Major* de Tschudy was promoted to the rank of *colonel* in response to Friant's demand that a senior officer be appointed, and he was placed in overall command of the regiment thereafter. Once in charge, de Tschudy wrote to the minister of war highlighting the needs of his new command, especially those relating to artillery. In this respect he asked for the shortage of equipment to be made up and for the transfer into the regiment of 'two experienced French artillery officers.'[27]

It was on that date that Napoleon ordered *Maréchal* Davout to march upon Pomerania, and one month later the whole of the Corps d'Observation de l'Elbe was united under its commander in chief ready to cross the Oder, a feat it achieved some two days later at Stettin (modern-day Szczecin).[28]

On 3 March 1812 Berthier, Prince de Neuchatel, informed Napoleon that *Général de Division* Friant was expected to arrive at Stettin on the 9th or 10th of the month.

Having confirmed that the 2e and 3e bataillons of Joseph–Napoleon were on the banks of the Oder by mid-March 1812, it is now time to examine the movements of the 1er and 4e bataillons, last mentioned whilst at their garrison towns in Italy at the end of 1810. During the first months of 1811 the two battalions were at Palma–Nova and Alessandria in Italy, and were about to be included amongst the new formations demanded by Napoleon in preparation for the war against Russia. With this in mind, on 24 April 1811, Clarke informed the emperor that he had issued orders on the 18th for the 1er bataillon to move from Palma–Nova to Vicenza, and for the 4e bataillon to move from Alessandria to Bolzano.[29]

The subsequent stages of their march would take both units to Mantua sometime between the 10 and 15 May. *Major* Doreille was to take overall command of the two battalions once united, and on 16 December 1811, Napoleon gave instructions to Prince Eugene, his stepson, to incorporate them into the 14e Division under *Général de Division* Broussier.[30]

Final preparations for the Russian campaign of 1812

On 1 April 1812 Napoleon renamed his Corps d'Observation de l'Elbe to that of I Corps de la Grande Armée, under Davout. It comprised the 1er, 2e, 3e, 4e, 5e and 7e Divisions, and the 2e and 3e bataillons of Joseph–Napoleon were assigned to the 2e Division under the command of *Général de Division* Friant. In a similar manner the old Corps d'Observation d'Italie became

---

26 *AAG*, as cited by Boppe in *Les Espagnols*, p.127.
27 *AAG*, as cited by Boppe in *Les Espagnols*, p.128.
28 Napoleon to the Prince de Neuchatel, Bonaparte, *Correspondance*, no. 18511, t. XXIII, pp.283–285.
29 Boppe in *Les Espagnols*, pp.129–131.
30 Napoleon to Eugene, Bonaparte, *Correspondance*, no. 18340, t. XXIII, pp.86–89.

the new IV Corps, under Prince Eugene. It comprised the 13e, 14e and 15e Divisions, and the 1er and 4e bataillons of Joseph–Napoleon were assigned to the 14e Division under the command of *Général de Division* Broussier. We may note that the commanders of the four Spanish battalions at this time were:

- 1er bataillon: *Chef de Bataillon* José Kindelán.
- 2e bataillon: *Chef de Bataillon* Ramon Ducer.
- 3e bataillon: *Chef de Bataillon* Rafael de Llanza.
- 4e bataillon: *Chef de Bataillon* Alejandro O'Donnell.

On 9 February 1812 Berthier was able to provide Napoleon with detailed plans for the movement of the Grande Armée into Russia. IV Corps was to begin its move from Northern Italy towards Glogau on the 23 February, arriving at Ratisbon by 14 March. However, a change to these plans was later transmitted to Broussier instructing him to divert from his original route towards Ratisbon once he arrived at Innsbruck and make for Augsburg instead, before moving on to Nuremberg where he arrived on 15 March 1812. Glogau had been chosen as the point of concentration for the whole of IV Corps, and once Broussier was at Nuremberg he was instructed to begin the next leg of his march on 20th, scheduled to arrive at Dresden on 4 April. From there the final stage of the march to Glogau began, and he arrived at that place between 16 and 18 April 1812. All four units of Joseph–Napoleon were then in place, ready for the great advance of the Grande Armée into Russia which would commence on 24 June.[31]

We will shortly return to Manuel López and examine his account of the experiences suffered by his regiment during the disastrous 1812 campaign. The greater part of his story is now held in the French archives, thanks, in the main, to the actions of *Colonel* de Tschudy, who at some time after the war took possession if it and verified its content. It goes under the title of, *Précis historique des actions ou se sont trouves les 2e et 3e bataillons du regiment Joseph–Napoleon avec le 2e division du 1er corps de la Grande Armée dont ils on fait partie pendant la derniere campagne.* By 1840 the document was with Soult who handed it over to the French National Archives. We should note here that López had been promoted to *sous-officier* in 1809, shortly after he joined Joseph–Napoleon, and that he was commissioned to the rank of *sous-lieutenant* in 1812.

---

31 Boppe, *Les Espagnols*, pp.133–138.

10

Notes on the Russian Campaign by Manuel López and Rafael de Llanza

López's account of the Russian campaign begins with a description of how the Régiment Joseph-Napoleon was structured; noting that the ranks of regimental major, adjutant major and quartermaster were all held by French appointees. There was also a French NCO in charge of the financial accounts of each company, but the remaining officer roles were filled by men recruited almost exclusively the regiments of Asturias and Guadalajara who were left behind when La Romana's army was evacuated from Denmark in August 1808. There was one exception: Alejandro O'Donnell, a son of José O'Donnell, La Romana's *aide-de-camp* in Denmark, who arrived in France directly from Spain to take up the post of *chef de bataillon* with the 4e bataillon of the new unit. Most of the NCOs and soldiers of the new regiment had also served with the two aforementioned regiments in Denmark; the exceptions being those recruited from the many prisoners taken during the fighting that occurred in Spain after the French surge of October and November 1808. In fact, some of the latter may well have been Baltic escapees who were eventually (re)captured during the battles that took place in Biscay in late 1808, having been thrust into action almost immediately after their return from Denmark.

Interestingly, López, who was with the 2e bataillon, gives Don Rodrigo Medrano as the commander of the 3e bataillon of the regiment but, as we have seen, Rafael de Llanza was given command of that unit on 15 October 1811 whilst it was at Utrecht. The head of the regiment, *Colonel* de Tschudy, vouches for Llanza's position as chief of the 2e bataillon in the following statement, and goes on to endorse his leadership qualities in the second:

> The *chef de bataillon*, Medrano, did not lead the 3e bataillon in Russia. Aged and exhausted from previous service, he remained with the [regimental] depot [then at Maestricht (later moved to Namur)] and was replaced by *Capitaine* Llanza

following a proposal made by *Général* Kindelán at the time of Napoleon's review of the regiment at Utrecht.[1]

Raphael Llanza, captain of the Grenadiers, possessed a great zeal for his position, combined with a great sense of honour, bravery and finesse, he would make a good *chef de bataillon*. He was very stylish, of strong character and had been recommended as interim commander [of the 3e bataillon] by *Général* Kindelán. This officer, continued Tschudy, commanded the 3e bataillon of the regiment during the whole of the Russian campaign. Wounded at Krasnow [Krasny] he was taken prisoner on 18 November 1812.[2]

The 2e and 3e Bataillons enter Russia

López's account of the 1812 campaign begins shortly after the 2e and 3e bataillons of Joseph–Napoleon had taken part in the operation to expel the Swedes from Stralsund in January 1812 (the city having been re-occupied by the Swedes after being expelled by the French in 1807– with the help of La Romana's army):

> Towards the end of January 1812, the Swedish garrisons of Stralsund and Rügen were made prisoners of war and sent to France. Friant's division was then moved to Danzig via Anklam and Stettin…
>
> The 2e and 3e bataillons of Joseph–Napoleon left Danzig with Friant's division, destined to take part in the coming hostilities with Russia. All six divisions of I Corps were reviewed by Napoleon on 18 June 1812 near Gumbinnen [modern-day Gusev in Russia] and on the following day the 2e Division began its move to a position on the left bank of the Niemen between Tilsit and Kovno [modern-day Kaunas].
>
> The 1er and 4e bataillons, which left Alexandria under the command of *Major* Doreille and belonged, I believe, to the 13e de ligne, [actually14e de ligne] arrived at the banks of the river together with their respective *chef de bataillon*, [José] Kindelán and [Alejandro] O'Donnell, and at the same time as the Armée d'Italie, which was with its commander in chief, Prince Eugene. On the following day, 24 June 1812, the army crossed the Niemen.[3]

It would seem that IV Corps actually arrived on the Niemen on 29 June at the village of Pilony, and on the following day Broussier's 14e Division (which contained 1er and 4e bataillons of Joseph–Napoleon) crossed the river.[4] In fact, the columns of the Grande Armée were so immense and cumbersome that it took a full five days to get them from the west bank of the Niemen to the east.[5]

---

1 Extract from de Tschudy's account, as reproduced by Boppe in *Les Espagnols*, p.141, footnote 2.
2 Tschudy's account in Boppe, *Les Espagnols*, p.141, footnote 2.
3 López's précis as cited by Boppe in *Les Espagnols*, pp.143–144.
4 Eugene Labaum, *Relation Circonstanciée de la Campagne de Russie en 1812* (Paris: CLF Panckoucke, 1815, 4th Edition), Livre I, p.50.
5 Andrew Roberts, *Napoleon the Great* (London: Penguin, 2015), p.580.

NOTES ON THE RUSSIAN CAMPAIGN

Llanza had the following to say about the attacks on Stralsund and Rügen, and from some of his comments we can begin to discern his anti-French sentiments:

> On 26 January 1812 [Friant] received the order to invade Swedish Pomerania, [an act of aggression] which took place without any declaration of war … Perfidy and deception, the favourite weapons of the French, did the job. [It was] under the specious pretext of having to cross that territory in order to occupy parts of Prussia, that we took Stralsund and the island of Rügen. Immediately, and with the most revolting insolence, the two Swedish regiments and all of the city authorities were made prisoners …
>
> On 29 March 1812, I left Neuwarp for Danzig with my battalion; crossing the Oder at Stettin and continuing along the Baltic coast to our destination, which we reached on 13 April…
>
> The army continued its march … through East Prussia, passing the city of Gumbieren [Gumbinnen?] … and arriving upon the heights which dominate the River Niemen on 24 June.[6]

Llanza next provides us with an impression of the scenes he witnessed as the army rolled across the bridges of the Niemen at Kovno:

> Dawn offered us an imposing sight. All of the French armies had been united at this place… the numbers reached some 300,000 men, 100,000 horses, 1,500 pieces of artillery and an incalculably large supply column…
>
> There were three bridges across the Niemen, one for the infantry, one for the cavalry, and a third for the artillery and baggage … There was neither man nor beast to be seen [on the far bank]; all had fled into the woods to avoid the clash of such an imposing multitude, furious in its desire to reach the other side of the river to join in with the horrors of the sacking and the torching; in one word, the extermination of human kind.[7]

When the French reached Vilnius, capital of Lithuania, they were detained for two days, the Russians having destroyed the bridge across the Neris. It was during this enforced halt that a propaganda leaflet was published by the order of Napoleon:

> The French army has taken up arms against the tyrannical Russians, oppressors of Poland, with the aim to regain for the Poles their rights and their liberty. The inhabitants of Lithuania must consider the French army as its liberators and as the force that will break the chains with which the barbarous Russians have for so long enslaved them.[8]

Llanza goes on to ponder just how grateful the Poles and Lithuanians must have felt for the sacking of their settlements, the theft of their livestock and

---

6 Bobadilla, *Un Español*, pp.42–43.
7 Bobadilla, *Un Español*, p.48.
8 Bobadilla, *Un Español*, p.48.

the lifting of their crops. Then, after some 25 days of what he describes as the 'most excessive fatigue,' he muses upon the early signs of diminution in the strength of the army, 'The dysentery had created gaps in our ranks; the soldier who had the misfortune to be unable to keep up was left in the shade of a tree where illness and hunger put an end to his existence. [In some cases] the peasants would apply the *coup-de-grace*.'[9]

The Action at Vitebsk (Witepsk) 27 July 1812

López now takes up the story:

> The 2e Division of I Corps was detached to join the advanced guard under the command of the King of Naples [Murat]. It arrived before Vilna [modern-day Vilnius] on 29 June, taking possession of the town without a fight, and departed towards Polotsk on 1 July 1812 where we arrived on the 23rd at about 10:00 p.m., half dead with hunger and worn out with fatigue, so rapid were our movements in pursuit of some thousands of Cossacks who the Russians, in their retreat, had left at the rear of their army to keep us under observation…
>
> On 27 July, the 2e and 3e bataillons of Joseph-Napoleon moved to a point close to Vitebsk and took up a position in the French second line during the action which took place there, in the course of which the 1er and 4e bataillons of the regiment played a more significant part…
>
> Having crossed the Dwina [Dvina] on foot – at the double – upstream of the town, the whole of Friant's division then set up camp some seven miles beyond Vitebsk, where it remained until 9 August when it began to move again with the advanced guard towards the Dnieper, close to Orcha, [Orsha] and then on to Smolensk.[10]

Llanza says of the fighting at Vitebsk:

> We took the city of Vitebsk when we arrived there on 24 of July. At last, after forty days in pursuit of the Russians, marching night and day with men and horses dying of fatigue, we came up with those '*señores*' some ten leagues from the city. On the 24th, 25th and 26th there were bloody combats, the result of which was the retreat of the Russians upon the town…
>
> [In] that splendid position [with the river to their front, they] made us believe that they were going to risk a general action … but when dawn broke on the 30th we were to find that they had retired.[11]

---

9   Bobadilla, *Un Español*, p.49.
10 López's précis as cited by Boppe in *Les Espagnols*, p.144.
11 Bobadilla, *Un Español*, pp.49–50.

The Battle of Smolensk 17 August 1812

Firstly, López:

> On 17 August, the 2e and 3e bataillons of Joseph-Napoleon took part in the successful battle for possession of Smolensk. We formed the left of the 2e Division and linked up with the right of the 1er Division of I Corps. During this action Friant's division came under fire from the artillery of the place at the same time as the Russians were being forced from its trenches and ramparts by Grandeau's light infantry.
>
> On the 18th the Division left Smolensk with I Corps, and that night, having made their march at the double, they came to the aid of Gudin's division, already seriously engaged in a wood traversed by a road, in which they were fighting hand-to-hand with the enemy, no orderly movement being possible. The arrival of Friant's division led to a ceasefire which the Russians took advantage of by abandoning the position, leaving it littered with corpses…
>
> On 19 August Friant's division accompanied I Corp on its march to the battlefield of the River Moskowa,[12] where we arrived on the night of 5 September 1812…

Llanza gives the following account of the fighting at Smolensk:

> On the 14 August the French army arrived at the Dnieper, the Russians having already crossed the river and abandoned [the far bank]. This allowed the French to cross without difficulty and once on the far bank they continued their march towards Smolensk, their vanguard arriving on the 17th when it took part in a significant action, which cost each side a lot of blood. I did not take part in the fighting which I witnessed at a short distance. Night had fallen by then, though the struggle had begun at daylight. The battle came to an end at half past eleven, and I am quite persuaded that it was due to a shortage of men on both sides …
> The French lost some 11,000 men, the Russians no less; the obstinacy being equal on both parts.[13]

Battle of Borodino (Moskowa) 5–7 September 1812

Before examining the accounts of Borodino and its aftermath left to us by the two Spaniards, we should recall that López was with the 2e bataillon of Joseph-Napoleon, Llanza was with the 3e, which may explain any discrepancies between their accounts of the various engagements in which their regiment was involved. Interestingly, in this excerpt from his story we are given an indication of how Llanza judged the attitude of the French towards their Spanish allies:

---

12   We should note that the battle we now refer to as 'the Battle of Borodino' was originally named after the river on which it was fought, the Moskowa, that is 'the Battle of Moskowa', as Napoleon first referred to it.
13   Bobadilla, *Un Español*, p.53.

López, 5 September:

A strongly fortified but temporary redoubt defended the left wing of the Russian front line, and *Colonel* de Tschudy was ordered by *Général de Division* Friant to establish his two battalions between the fortification and a burning village just a short distance to its left. This was done in order to provide cover for the [rest of the] division.[14]

No sooner had the two battalions formed square when the 111e Régiment, then deployed just beyond the village at a short distance from the enemy's front line, was charged and broken by the Russian cavalry which, in chasing the fleeing infantrymen, was attracted towards our square by the sound of the fire coming from our light infantry. In the bad light the horsemen were prevented from seeing us and received the fire from two faces [of our formation] at point blank range.

Then we heard voices calling out, 'Don't shoot! Don't shoot! We are French,' but we continued to fire as we observed the cavalrymen retiring at the gallop towards the flames [of the burning village], leaving many dead on the field …[15]

Tschudy's report on the action of 5 September described above follows closely that of López, but provides a little more clarity on the casualty figures, 'The cavalry retired in disorder leaving ten dead in front of our square, amongst them the commander of the unit. There must have been a great many wounded – both men and horses. We didn't lose a single man from our battalions.'[16]

Llanza 5 September:

On 5 September, I found myself with the vanguard when we caught up with the Russian army [to find it] formed in order of battle and seemingly resolved to fight a general action. To their front there was a line of redoubts and one of these, which covered their left, stood in a position a little in advance of their front line. The Emperor gave the order to attack it.

The resistance was obstinate. Nevertheless, by eleven o'clock that night it had been taken, the cost to the French being 8,000 men and the losses amongst the Russians being no less. Whilst that bloody clash went on, my own battalion advanced in square formation and joined in the combat. At nine thirty it was attacked by a strong force of Russian cavalry, the result of which was usually the breaking and destruction of the infantry,[17] but such was our luck that a single volley resulted in the retreat of the horsemen who no doubt overestimated our strength due to the darkness of the night. What a perfect opportunity it was to have gone over to the Russians, carrying our banners as we went!

Both Spanish battalions were in advance of the French army, and I have no doubt that we were placed in a position of such obvious risk with the hope that we

---

14 López is describing the first phase of the Battle of Borodino.
15 López's précis as cited by Boppe in *Les Espagnols*, pp.145–147.
16 Tschudy's account as cited by Boppe, *Les Espagnols*, p.147, footnote 1.
17 In most of the works on the Peninsular War writers and observers are fairly unanimous in their opinion that, in Napoleonic times, infantry squares were almost invariably impenetrable to cavalry charges.

would be exterminated. If we had had the faintest idea that we would have been welcomed by the Russians we would have gone over to them ... and perhaps we could have given them some interesting service that night ...[18]

López, 6 and 7 September:

On 6 September the whole of the army was in position, and at seven on the morning of the 7th the two battalions of Joseph-Napoleon provided support for the artillery of *Général de Brigade* Balthus as it bombarded the extreme left of the enemy's front line. Later, at one in the afternoon, they were moved to the left of Friedrich's division with the intention of taking the enemy in reverse, but were forced to return to the division when *Général de Division* Friant was seriously wounded and stretchered to a field ambulance.

Llanza 7 September:

It was on the night of 7 September that *Général de Division* Friant was severely wounded and later removed from the scene of action by field ambulance, his place at the head of the 2e Division taken by *Général de Brigade* Dufour. The battle commenced with the fire of the heavy artillery from both sides, this was soon augmented by that of the guns of smaller calibre and continued for most of the day, firing mainly shrapnel. The dust and smoke did not allow me to observe much of what was going on, which was mainly an artillery duel.

[When the infantry advanced] the redoubts were furiously attacked and diabolically defended, leaving the ditches strewn with the men and horses which had found their end within them. The first redoubt was taken at ten o'clock, the second at twelve. By two in the afternoon the Russians had declared victory, but then the artillery of the Imperial Guard forced their cavalry to retreat. As it did so it was immediately attacked by the infantry, and by half-past four the battle had been won by the French, even though the Russian right maintained its position despite the threat of it being surrounded; a fate which in the end did not befall them due to the lateness of the hour, but which would have eventually occurred had not the Russian army made its retreat towards Moscow via the city of Mojaisk ...

At sunset on this fatal day the French stood victorious. The Russians, with admirable order, had retreated. Silence had replaced the horrendous uproar of a multitude of artillery and one could now hear only the sorrowful moans of thousands of men whose mortal wounds had not yet extinguished their existence, leaving them to suffer the horror of a slow death. Then came the night, which added to the sadness of the situation as it grew colder, causing the survivors to build fires. In a few hours these were surrounded by the wounded, both Russian and French, who had dragged themselves towards the flames hoping to ease the pain of their injuries by the warmth they gave out.

What a sad spectacle! And more, if one considers that so many thousands had to be abandoned upon that field of horror when the following day arrived; scant reward for their valour; for the victory won by some and for the brilliant and

---

18   Bobadilla, *Un Español*, p.53.

valiant defence sustained by others. This was the recompense and payment which the infamous tyrant gave to his warriors.[19]

After the action of 7 September Tschudy recorded, 'During this affair, the regiment lost two killed and thirty-four wounded, including two officers: *Lieutenant* la Vega and *Sous-Lieutenant* Montnel [both wounded].'[20] Interestingly, he failed to note Friant amongst the casualties.

Above, we are given further glimpses of the difference in attitudes between López and Llanza. The former had already affirmed his admiration for Napoleon, and by extension perhaps the purported aims of the French Revolution itself, even if the emperor, once in power, began to exhibit a taste for many of the things the early revolutionaries abhorred. In contrast Llanza, in the passage immediately above and in earlier instances, tends to express his mistrust of the French and a dislike of their attitude towards the people of the countries with which they were at war. We should note that López was brought up in Spain under humble circumstances, as opposed to Llanza, who had a more distinguished family background. López was to remain in France after the war, embracing fully its culture and its values.

De Tschudy's report on the battle of Borodino is in close agreement with that given by López, and in a list labelled, 'a', in his submission, the colonel provides us with the details of the officer casualties amongst his regiment, as follows:[21]

Killed:
Ducer, *Chef de Bataillon* (2e bataillon)
Carel y Mureio, *Lieutenant*. (listed as Carely in the regimental return given below)

Wounded:
De Tschudy, *Colonel*
Llanza, *Chef de Bataillon* (3e bataillon).
Roberti, *Capitaine*.
Retamar, *Capitaine*.
Gutcerez (Guttierrez?) *Capitaine*.
Ordoñez, *Capitaine*.
Torregrossa, *Capitaine*.
Cardeña, *Lieutenant*
Corvalan, *Lieutenant*
Biedma, *Lieutenant*.

For some reason the names mentioned earlier, La Vega and Montnel are not included.

López continues with a description of the Spanish involvement in the battle as the Russians re-grouped some eight miles to the east at the town of Mojaisk on 8 September:

---

19   Bobadilla, *Un Español*, pp.56–57.
20   Tschudy's account in Boppe, *Les Espagnols*, p.147, footnote 3.
21   Tschudy's account in Boppe, *Les Espagnols*, pp.149–150, footnotes 1 and 2.

NOTES ON THE RUSSIAN CAMPAIGN

The Battle of Mojaisk

Lopez 8 September:

> On the 8th [September] Friant's division, by then commanded by *Général de Brigade* Dufour, once again joined the advanced guard, which was forced to repulse several cavalry charges as it debouched from a wood situated on some flat ground in front of Mojaisk. It was there where it [would later] establish its bivouac…

Lopez 9 September:

> Then, on the morning of the 9th, we came under fire from the heights of Mojaisk, the first of the shots falling amongst our squares [the formation in which we had passed the night] … We eventually took possession of the settlement after repelling several cavalry charges, one of which was made with great determination. Later, with the King of Naples at the head of our column, we advanced for almost five *lieues*.[22]

Lopez 10 September:

> On the afternoon of the 10th the colonel of the regiment, Baron de Tschudy, was ordered to march at the head of the advanced guard, which by then comprised our two battalions and the 33 de ligne … We were instructed to cross a thicket which covered some rising ground ahead of us, from which we emerged onto a plain in front of the hamlet of Zelkowo [Selkovo] driving out the enemy as he was in the act of establishing his bivouac … The Russians retreated and we took up the pursuit, but without cavalry cover … after a long chase we were to suffer severely when we found ourselves exposed to a heavy and concentric fire coming from a large number of masked artillery pieces and musketry from an extended line of sharpshooters. Our column could not deploy and had to sustain several cavalry charges. When the first charge was delivered, we were unable to deploy properly due to a lack of space and could form only an imperfect triangle. With hardly any space between us we were soon reduced to a compact mass and suffered severe losses. The Spanish battalions losing 14 officers and 340 other ranks in killed and wounded.[23]

After the fighting at Borodino Llanza found himself with the advanced guard of the French army once again as it followed up the Russians in their withdrawal to the town of Mozhaisk, where they halted determined to make another stand against their pursuers. His diary continues.

> At eleven in the morning on the 8 September, we were on the move … The Russians awaited us at the entrance to the city of Mojaisk [where] there was a great artillery bombardment which continued until nightfall. [Despite its ferocity] the

---

22 Five *lieues* was about 20 kilometres or 12.5 miles.
23 López's précis as cited by Boppe in *Les Espagnols*, pp.148–149, covering 6 to 10 September 1812.

171

enemy retained possession of the town, but with our men at close quarters. I had never been so tired or in such a frenetic state of mind, envious of the luck of those who had ceased to exist and were now free of such an arduous life…

On the 9th the Russians awoke us with more canon fire … The Cossacks and the Kalmucks forced us to form square and close columns on several occasions so as to avoid their brutal, crudely-fashioned lances…

The arrival of our reinforcements then obliged the Russians to continue their retreat…

On the 10th, I found myself in command of the vanguard of the vanguard, and as the sun set I climbed to the peak of a small hillock from where I could see that the Russians had halted, seemingly to bivouac. I ordered my men to halt also. Within a few moments the King of Naples arrived … and ordered us to make a bayonet charge against the enemy … The first opposition we encountered was a mass of thirty squadrons of cavalry, most of them Cossacks and Tartars. These put up no resistance … we were then confronted with a line of infantry and a battery of field artillery. With the first shots my horse was killed by a ball. I mounted another and a piece of shrapnel took away part of my saddle, a second hit my mount in the ribs and a moment later a third caught it beneath the ear and caused it to fall, forcing me to go on on foot … I was then ordered to retire … and did so as soon as I could…

We halted as the action continued. By then all discipline had been lost … I had just given the order to fire to the left when I was struck by a ball which entered through my right cheek and came out through my mouth, smashing my jaw and cutting through an artery. My good friend, Don José Hernández, a captain in my battalion, took hold of me and brought me out of the combat…. On the following day I was sent to Mojaisk. The city had been put to the torch, just like all the rest.[24]

López takes up the narrative after the battle had ended:

From 10 until 14 September, the day upon which we entered Moscow, there were only light skirmishes to contend with. We marched 5 to 6 *lieues* per day to the outposts, and at night we slept in square formation with two lines standing and one line sitting … On the 14th the whole of the advanced guard traversed the city of Moscow, setting up our bivouac beyond its north–eastern suburbs. On the 17th the guard moved again, pursuing the enemy in various directions before finally moving towards Kaluga. Every day, and in all directions, the advanced guard was involved in tenacious struggles, and on 4 October, after having fought until twilight, we began to reorganise.[25]

Llanza, badly wounded, had chosen to follow the French advance to Moscow in a coach belonging to 'the colonel', by which we must suppose he meant *Colonel* de Tschudy:

Sitting inside the coach I suffered as I followed the division, mixed amongst the [transports of the] artillery…

---

24 Bobadilla, *Un Español*, pp.62–63.
25 López's précis as cited by Boppe in *Les Espagnols*, pp.150–151.

NOTES ON THE RUSSIAN CAMPAIGN

At half past three on 14 September 1812 the vanguard of the army arrived at a range of hills which dominated the great city of Moscow. The Russians had abandoned the position during the morning, retiring upon the city of Kaluga ... The army made its entry ... the Emperor, along with his personal guard and some other troops, set up his quarters in the Kremlin...

This immense city was set alight and consumed by flames during the 15, 16, 17 and 18 September ... Whoever the arsonists were, it was difficult to discover ... It seemed to me that Moscow was torched by both Russians and French...

After the battle of Mojaisk the French army was short of provisions ... three days before we took Moscow we were already eating horse flesh, but with the possession of the great city we became the owners of immense quantities of provisions. If order had been maintained the whole army could have subsisted upon them for many months. However, destiny or divine providence had determined upon the destruction of everything. For little did the great resources of that huge city serve, and for even less did the millions worth of gold and silver that was taken come to serve. In the end everything came to remain upon the soil from which it was stolen. Amongst all the booty I managed to pick up a magnificent coach, one of three which my celebrated colonel acquired with the intention of taking them back to France for his daughter...[26]

Llanza was eventually taken to a hospital in Moscow for the treatment of his wounds, but rather than stay in the city whilst his injuries healed he preferred to take his chances at the front. He was prepared to die during the coming weeks rather than stay in Moscow, and for the next 14 days he remained with the army as it sought out the enemy, not knowing for certain the route by which they were making their retreat:

On 29 September we finally caught up with the Russians. There was a great cannonade and they ceded the ground to us at an appreciable cost. On the 30th we advanced no more than a league, the enemy not wanting to yield. I had no doubt that more than 10,000 rounds of canon were fired on that day.[27]

So it continued, until 4 October when the Russians decided that they would retreat no more:

The Russians having come to a halt there began a bloody combat [which continued] until nightfall put a stop to it. Both sides had stood their ground...

On the following day the fighting ceased ... the King of Naples then arrived at the front to speak with the generals, and the news he brought caused many to believe that an armistice had been called and that peace would arrive at any moment.[28]

---

26   Bobadilla, *Un Español*, pp.66–67.
27   Bobadilla, *Un Español*, p.75.
28   Bobadilla, *Un Español*, p.75.

The Battle of Vinkovo (Tarutino) 18 October 1812

All remained quiet with both sides expecting an informal ceasefire to be called for until, on 18 October, Kutuzov's blow fell upon the unsuspecting French. The ferocity of the Russian attack upon the vanguard was irresistible, throwing it back towards the town of Vinkovo or Tarutino; Llanza refers to it as 'Wozoroff'.

After fleeing in disorder from the Russian cavalry over a distance of some five leagues, Llanza, as he crested a low hill, saw what he described as 'an ants trail of people' (*un hormiguero de gente*) covering a huge expanse of territory. What he was witnessing was the beginning of the great retreat from Moscow, Napoleon's precipitate flight for survival. The huge column, said Llanza, was heading towards Vinkovo, but before the French were clear of the great city the emperor ordered that the Kremlin be destroyed by detonating the mines which had been prepared in anticipation of just such a situation:

> At midday we discovered an immense collection of carriages of all descriptions spread across a wide plain. They had all left Moscow and were following in the wake of the army. I had no doubt that there were about ten or eleven thousand vehicles in all, amongst them perhaps two thousand beautiful coaches and many thousands of covered wagons, all loaded with the provisions of war. There was not a single soldier who did not carry in his rucksack a quantity of gold and silver.[29]

Battle of Maloyaroslavets 24 October 1812

We begin with López's account of the fighting:

> On 19 October our division, the second, re-joined I Corps on the route from Moscow to Malojaroslawetz. On the 24th we arrived at that place where IV Corps displayed prodigies of valour. To get to the town we had to traverse a wooded country containing many clearances, where masses of Cossacks would suddenly appear and fall upon the flanks of our column of transports whenever their escort appeared weak. On several occasions they succeeded in capturing pieces [of artillery] and came close to posing an immediate threat to the emperor and the King of Naples.
>
> After the affair at Malojaroslawetz we were directed to Mojaisk, Wiasma, [Vyazma] and Smolensk, making our retreat to the latter place with the rest of I Corps. It was there where we halted for two or three days… *Maréchal* Ney then took command of the rear-guard, having been granted the reinforcement of Friant's division which contained the 2e and 3e bataillons of our regiment.
>
> The rear-guard left Smolensk on 16 November some twenty-four hours after the rest of the army, and marched without trouble until the 18th, when it came to Krasnoe [Krasny] …[30]

---

29 Bobadilla, *Un Español*, p.80.
30 López's précis as cited by Boppe in *Les Espagnols*, pp.152–154.

Llanza is more expansive in his description of the fighting at Maloyaroslavets:

> On 24 October the vanguard of the army … arrived at Maloyaroslavets … It was there where we discovered the vanguard of the Russian army, which had arrived an hour and a half before us to take possession of the place. A most obstinate and bloody fight soon began which went on until ten o'clock that night. The losses were great on both sides … the Russians assured me that it cost them 15,000 men, even though they had the advantage of an excellent position which they lost before taking up another a league away.
>
> At nine on the morning of the 25th, the emperor arrived with all of the army and formed it in order of battle…
>
> By nine on the morning of the following day the army was still ranged in order of battle, but had not been able to force the Russians to engage. In this critical situation the emperor ordered it to continue its memorable retreat, re-tracing the route it had taken during its advance. All along the way the land had been converted into the most awful desert; it was not even possible to recognise the places where the villages had stood. The houses, being constructed of timber, had been completely consumed by the fires that were set.
>
> At nine, the immense convoy of carriages measuring some two leagues in length and four or five files in width, began to roll off …[31]

Llanza's unit joined the enormous column as it headed south from Moscow towards Kaluga. He was still in considerable pain from the wound to his jaw as he sat, slumped in the seats of the carriage taken as booty by de Tschudy:

> During the first days of the retreat there was order, but it wasn't long before the Russians came up with our rear-guard and appeared on our flanks… On the 2 and 3 of November the corps of the army, which was shielding the retreat, was attacked and almost exterminated. By this time the horses were beginning to die of hunger and as they fell they were butchered, their meat consumed by the men. It is difficult to describe the speed with which the anatomy of the animals was removed to reveal a perfectly clean skeleton.[32]

Despite the desperate situation in which he found himself, Llanza's wound was beginning to give him less trouble. A problem with his legs had come and gone, which was just as well, because the group with which he was marching was forced to dismember de Tschudy's misappropriated carriage and use it for fuel with which to cook the horsemeat that was their only ration. It was at about this time that the weather worsened as the temperature began to fall. The snow, he said:

> Arrived to complete the scene of horror, and each day more than 3,000 were dying of hunger, cold and fatigue, their corpses littering the road…The men, losing all sense of humanity, did nothing to help as their friends sat on the ground or sought out a resting place, never to rise again. The only act of kindness practiced was to

---

31　Bobadilla, *Un Español*, pp.87–88.
32　Bobadilla, *Un Español*, p.90.

strip them naked before they died, with the intention of taking their money or their clothing if it was in good condition. Many of those who put up a struggle in their last few moments I saw being helped to die by being punched or clubbed with muskets. Like this it was easier for their assailants to remove their boots or shoes, which were the items most sought after… The most horrendous thing to consider was that today's killers became tomorrow's victims, as hunger took hold and strength diminished…[33]

The army continued its march towards Smolensk, its hopes raised by rumours that the depots located there were well stocked with flour and other provisions, 'We arrived at last. The army was in the most deplorable situation … The cold was insufferable and the scarcities not remedied, but the stores held only flour, and hardly enough to provide each soldier with a handful.'[34]

Ney, who was commanding the French rear-guard at that time, was ordered by Napoleon to hold Smolensk until 16 November. Upon arriving at that place on the 14th, with the Russians in hot pursuit, he united with Llanza's Spaniards who had been ordered to remain where they were so as to augment his force. At two o'clock in the morning of the 16th, the rear-guard slipped out of Smolensk to continue its retreat as the mines set to destroy the fortress began to detonate. Llanza claims that a hospital containing some 8,000 sick and wounded was blown up before they could be removed. At midday on the 18th the Spaniards arrived at Krasny; a ghostly image shrouded in a dense fog:

> Ney, unable to see the enemy because of the mist, ordered my corps to attack with the bayonet. To the noise of the drums and trumpets the 1,000 survivors from the 17,000 who began the campaign advanced towards the enemy.[35]
>
> I was struck by a piece of grapeshot; its force threw me a distance of some ten paces, leaving me stretched in the snow. Luckily, my satchel absorbed most of the oblique impact upon my right hip … I lost consciousness. When I came to myself, I felt to find the wound I was sure I had sustained…
>
> The field was deserted; the combat had ended with the death of the attackers. Groans and horror were all that I could hear and see. Stumbling to right and left I could not find a gully which would have sheltered me from the hurricane of grapeshot that had not yet ceased.[36]

Eventually Llanza arrived at a small town where he joined a number of soldiers of all arms belonging to the Grande Armée. He was the only senior officer present; Ney, he says, had abandoned the field after witnessing the destruction of his corps. Hardly knowing what he was doing, Llanza organised the 4,000 survivors he was with and marched at the head of his column towards the waiting Russians.

---

33 Bobadilla, *Un Español*, p.91.
34 Bobadilla, *Un Español*, p.91.
35 The figure of 17,000 probably applies to the original strength of Friant's division.
36 Bobadilla, *Un Español*, pp.93–94.

NOTES ON THE RUSSIAN CAMPAIGN

In this situation he realised that his long-awaited opportunity to go over to the Russians had finally arrived, so he sent a junior officer to offer his capitulation to the enemy, and after some delay a Russian colonel arrived:

> The colonel spoke to me in French, telling me that his father, Prince Gallitzin,[37] a general in the Russian army, would offer all of my troops good treatment if they surrendered without bloodshed. I replied, 'Señor, I am a luckless Spaniard …' He cut me short, exclaiming 'Spaniard! My emperor does not make prisoners of Spaniards. Your country and mine are in alliance. The Russian armies offer protection to all Spaniards whom chance places in our hands.'
>
> I then said to him, 'Sir, I have nothing more to discuss. I, together with my officers and soldiers, accept the protection of your emperor [and of] your father and general. With regard to this multitude of Frenchmen, you may do with them whatever you please.'[38]

Llanza then continues with his story, which takes the reader through the winter of 1812/1813 as he enjoyed some of his long-lost comforts whilst in the company of Russian society. We shall not dwell upon the interesting details he has to offer about that period. Instead, we will shortly leap forward to the end of July 1813, by which time a British squadron had docked at the Russian naval base of Cronstadt in the Baltic. Its mission was to embark those Spaniards who had been taken prisoner during the campaign of 1812. However, before we turn our attention to Cronstadt, we will allow López to take us through the final days of the retreat from Moscow.

Battle of Krasny 15 November 1812

At Krasny the 2e and 3e bataillons of Joseph-Napoleon were engaged in heavy fighting and sustained significant casualties. In his report on the action De Tschudy lists the total casualties for the two battalions as '76 men; as many killed as wounded, with 8 officers and 54 soldiers taken prisoner.'[39] The colonel then lists the officers lost as follows:[40]

Killed:
Canut, *Lieutenant*

Prisoner of War:
Herrera, *Chef de Bataillon* (2e) promoted on 25 September 1812 as replacement for Ducer
Llanza, *Chef de Bataillon* (3e)
Abreu, *Aide-Mayor*

---

37 Prince Golitsyn.
38 Bobadilla, *Un Español*, pp.95–96.
39 It is not clear if the 62 prisoners are to be included in the overall figure of 76; if so, then the number of killed would be seven, with seven wounded.
40 Tschudy's account in Boppe, *Les Espagnols*, p.155, footnote 1.

Gonzales, *Capitaine*
Zambrana, *Lieutenant*
Chansarel, *Sous-Lieutenant*

Missing:
Oliver, *Lieutenant* (Oliver is given as 'Present' in return of the regiment taken on 5 March 1813)

A comprehensive casualty list of the officers serving in the 2e and 3e bataillons of Joseph–Napoleon during the whole of the campaign in Russia, was eventually compiled by de Tschudy as part of his regimental return for 5 March 1813. His figures are presented in Table 7.

Table 7 Regimental return (officers only) of the 2e and 3e battalions of Joseph–Napoleon, taken on 5 March 1813

Name	Unit	Rank	POW/KIA/W/NK (not known)
De Tschudy (Joseph)	QG	Colonel	Present
Jordanis (Jean–Ant)	QG	Intendant	Present
Abreu (Francois)	QG	*Adjudant-Major*	POW on 18/11/12
Pujades (Laurent)	QG	*Adjudant-Major*	POW on 18/11/12
Sales M.	QG	*Adjudant-Major*	KIA on 21/12/12
Ducer M.	2e bn	*Chef de Bataillon*	KIA, 10/9/12
Herrera (Thomas)	2e bn	*Chef de Bataillon* [13/10/12]	POW on 18/11/12
Gallardo (Mariano)	2e bn	*Capitaine*	Present
Gonzales M.	2e bn	*Capitaine*	POW on 18/11/12
Guttierrez (Luis)	2e bn	*Capitaine*	POW on 18/11/12
Martínez (Francois)	2e bn	*Capitaine*	Present
Maseres M.	2nd bn	*Capitaine*	Transferred to 1st bn
Ordoñez (Emmanuel)	2e bn	*Capitaine*	Present
Torregrosa (Emmanuel)	2e bn	*Capitaine*	POW date unknown
Biedma (Nicholas)	2e bn	*Lieutenant*	W on 10/9/12. POW on 18/12/12
Canut (Pascal)	2e bn	*Lieutenant*	KIA on 18/11/12
Chansarel (Jacques)	2e bn	*Lieutenant*	POW on 18/11/12
Labaig M.	2e bn	*Lieutenant*	W & POW on 18/11/12 whilst with the artillery
Salinas M.	2e bn	*Lieutenant*	KIA on 21/12/12
Sequerra (Joseph)	2e bn	*Lieutenant*	POW on 18/11/12
Tierra (Domingo)	2e bn	*Lieutenant*	Transferred. Left bn whilst in Russia
Vasquez (Basilio)	2e bn	*Lieutenant*	KIA on 4/10/12
Zayas (Francois)	2e bn	*Lieutenant*	POW on 18/11/12
Dhainaut (Constant)	2e bn	*Sous-Lieutenant*	Present
López (Manuel)	2e bn	*Sous-Lieutenant*	Present
Menendez (Joseph)	2e bn	*Sous-Lieutenant*	Present
Llanza (Rafael)	3e bn	*Chef de Bataillon*	POW on 18/11/12
Arcos (Joseph)	3e bn	*Capitaine*	Present but incapable
Buergo (Michel)	3e bn	*Capitaine*	Present
Hernández (Joseph)	3e bn	*Capitaine*	Present but incapable
Retamar (Mathias)	3e bn	*Capitaine*	POW on 18/11/12
Roberti M.	3e bn	*Capitaine*	W on 10/9/12

NOTES ON THE RUSSIAN CAMPAIGN

Name	Unit	Rank	POW/KIA/W/NK (not known)
Vasquez (Mariano)	3e bn	*Capitaine*	Present
Vega (Fernando)	3e bn	*Capitaine*	POW on 10/12/12
Algarra (Policarpe)	3e bn	*Lieutenant*	POW on 18/11/12
Cardeña (Gabriel)	3e bn	*Lieutenant*	POW on 18/11/12
Carely M.	3e bn	*Lieutenant*	KIA on 10/9/12
Corvalan (Joseph)	3e bn	*Lieutenant*	Present
Sanchez (Jean)	3e bn	*Lieutenant*	KIA on 10/12/12
(La) Vega (Fernando)	3e bn	*Lieutenant*	POW on 10/12/12
Zambrana (Leandre)	3e bn	*Lieutenant*	POW on 18/11/12
Aldao (Antoine)	3e bn	*Sous-Lieutenant*	POW on 24/7/12
Aldao (Thomas)	3e bn	*Sous-Lieutenant*	Present
Cuesta (Pierre)	3e bn	*Sous-Lieutenant*	KIA on 18/12/12
Mirambel (Jaime)	3e bn	*Sous-Lieutenant*	Present
Montnel M.	3e bn	*Sous-Lieutenant*	POW on 18/11/12 whilst with the artillery.
Oliver M.	3e bn	*Sous-Lieutenant*	Present
Renaud (Francois)	3e bn	*Sous-Lieutenant*	Present
Ribas (Eugene)	3e bn	*Sous-Lieutenant*	Present

Source: Boppe, *Les Espagnols*, Appendix I, pp.216–221.

López continues after the events at Krasny: 'We made our retreat with III Corps … to Orcha, continually having to fight off our enemies as well as the effects of hunger and fatigue. It was there where we re-joined the army at about two in the morning after having met up with Broussier's division, an occasion which filled us with joy.'[41]

López was with the 2e and 3e bataillons of his regiment, Broussier's division contained the 1er and 4e; hence the joy at meeting up with their fellow Spaniards. In fact, the happiness of the encounter increased when the Spaniards discovered the presence of the Portuguese Legion nearby, a detail confirmed by Theotonio Banha, an officer with the Legion: 'On 19 November 1812, we met with the remnants of the Spanish regiment, Joseph-Napoleon, a corps which at the outset of the campaign had an effective strength of 3,000 men. It was now reduced to no more than four officers and 100 men.'[42]

The Crossing of the Beresina 6 December 1812

López again:

> On our arrival at Orcha we re-joined I Corps and crossed the Beresina in company with it on 6 December 1812. Four days later we were at Vilnius, and it was from that place that I turned back alone for a distance of nineteen versters to

---

41 Boppe, *Les Espagnols*, pp.155–156, footnote 2.
42 Theotonio Banha, *Apontamentos para a Historia de Legiao Portugueza ao Servicio de Napoleao I* (Lisboa: Imprensa Nacional, 1863) pp.77–78.

retrieve a banner that one of our sergeant-majors had left at our last bivouac.[43] I returned with it and reached Vilnius once more at about two o'clock on the following morning. I was to carry that standard to the banks of the Rhine.

At four in the morning we departed for Kovno, moving on to Gumbinnen and from there to Thorn [Torun, Poland], the point of rendezvous for I Corps … From that place our retreat continued to Coblentz, which we did not enter until March 1813 after countermarching from Frankfurt to Erfurt before retracing our steps to Frankfurt *en-route* to our final destination.

By then the debris of the 2e and 3e bataillons comprised just 14 officers together with 50 NCOs and other ranks.[44] We were to remain at Coblentz until May 1813, and it was there where a single battalion was formed in place of the four of which the regiment had originally been composed. [In order to bring it up to full strength] the officers, NCOs and soldiers returning from Russia, together with the officers, NCOs and soldiers from the depot [at Maestricht] and a number of prisoners of war [recently] sworn in, were all required.

The remnants of the 1e and 4e bataillons, then at Glogau [160 in all], combined with a detachment from the 2e and 3e bataillons at Stettin, would form part of the light infantry as soon as they could be moved… The command of the new 1er bataillon was given to M. Dimpre, who had previously belonged to the 5e léger. The unit was to see action in Saxony and Silesia as part of the 2e Division of VI Corps, together with the 37e léger, the 27e de ligne and the 4e régiment de canonniers de la marine … It also fought at Lutzen and Bautzen in May 1813 and later, during the month of October 1813, at Meissen, Leipzig and Hanau …

Sometime after the formation of the [new] 1er bataillon, a [new] 2e bataillon was formed at Namur and sent to Magdebourg under the command of Villalba…[45]

We now return to Llanza's story, having left it at the point where he surrendered to the Russians on 18 November 1812. Treated as a soldier of an allied country, he was able to recover from his state of exhaustion and the wounds he had suffered during Napoleon's Russian campaign. Being an officer, he was also able to mix with polite society and formed a number of friendships before eventually returning to his homeland:

At the end of July 1813, we were advised that a number of British frigates had arrived at the isle of Cronstadt with the intention of taking us to Spain. On 1 August, I received an order to leave [St. Petersburg] with my first battalion and make for the island.

At this point Llanza digresses a little to provide readers with a *tour-de-force* of his journey to Cronstadt and his meetings with various members of Russian high society, before continuing his narrative:

I said goodbye to my amiable and good princess [Gallitzin] and embarked on 5 August for passage to the famous Department of Cronstadt…

---

43 *Verster*: an old Russian and German measure of distance equating to about 1,100 metres.
44 Lopez's figures are in line with those of Banha, if not an exact match.
45 López's précis as cited by Boppe in *Les Espagnols*, pp.156–163.

> On the 11th, I embarked on the English frigate, *Retreat, No. 494*.[46] Four days later, on the 15th, we made sail in light winds…[47]

Llanza continues with his story, going on to describe his voyage across the Baltic and *Retreat*'s navigation of the narrow straits formed by the Danish islands located at the entrance to that northerly body of water, such as Funen and Zealand, all places he was familiar with having served there alongside La Romana some five years earlier. At one point he feared for his life during the storms that raged as the ships of his convoy rounded the tip of the Jutland Peninsula; an uncomfortable sailor it would seem. On 22 September he caught sight of England for the first time, as the Norfolk coast came into view, the convoy later passing the Downs on the 24th to reach Portsmouth on the following day where his ship dropped anchor. The next leg of his voyage took him past the Channel Isles on the 27th as the *Retreat* headed south towards the Bay of Biscay.

It was not until 1 October 1813 that he finally caught sight of his beloved Spain, the mountain peaks of its northern coast visible, he claimed, at a distance of some 30-35 miles. Unsure of where he was as his ship neared the Spanish littoral, the English captain asked Llanza if he recognised the coastline. The Spaniard, admitting his ignorance, suggested that he fire a few canon shots to draw the attention of local shipping, and in response they were greeted by the arrival of a launch, the crew of which informed them they were off the coast of Asturias. As the Spanish sailors clambered aboard the *Retreat* they were assailed by their fellow countrymen, keen to know all they could tell them about the events in Spain of recent times. Eventually the English captain handed control of his ship to the Spanish skipper, who sailed her to Santander after setting off from 'San Vicente de Luarca',[48] and entered the bay of the great port city some two days later. By this time Llanza was acting as interpreter for the commands that were called out to the English crew by the Spanish pilot.

At nine o'clock on the morning of 3 October 1813, almost five years to the day since his Baltic comrades returned home to exactly the same spot, the *Retreat* dropped anchor in the bay of Santander. At two in the afternoon Llanza was rowed ashore, 'at last setting foot in the land for which I had suffered so many miseries, well worth it for finally finding myself at home, having lost all hope of ever seeing it again.'[49]

The final words from the survivors of Joseph–Napoleon who served during the Russian Campaign of 1812 we shall leave to Manuel López.

---

46 What Llanza took for a frigate was almost certainly a transport, perhaps an armed merchant vessel.
47 Bobadilla, *Un Español*, pp.124–125.
48 Probably San Vicente de la Barquera or Luarca, two ports located on that stretch of the Asturian coast.
49 Bobadilla, *Un Español*, p.128.

The Battle of Leipzig October 16 1813

Although it would be true to say that the 'new' Régiment Joseph-Napoleon fought at Leipzig, we can see from what went before that very few of the men serving with it at that time could have been veterans of La Romana's Baltic campaign. There were still a few of those gnarled old soldiers present in the ranks, of course, and Manuel López was one of them, but the vast majority would have become casualties of one sort or another, or simply deserted from the ranks.

In *Miscellanea Napoleonica* by Baron A. Lumbroso there is a passage taken from the memoirs of *Major* Gallardo de Mendoza. It describes events at the battle of Leipzig where Mendoza fought as a captain in the 3e compagnie, 1er bataillon of the re-formed Régiment Joseph-Napoleon, in which Manuel López was by then serving as an adjutant-major. Our intrepid chronicler was to receive a third severe wound during the fighting, this to add to the two he sustained in Russia and afterwards. Mendoza says:

> [T]he cannonade commenced at eight on the morning of 16 October 1813, it was very heavy; an awful day! We were resting at Leipzig, formed in squares by battalion and surrounded by innumerable enemies. Russians, Austrians and Prussians attacked us in mass...
>
> We were out-numbered about four-to-one, weak and disheartened, but together with the 37e léger and the 4e régiment de canonniers de la marine, we were able to resist all assaults made by the Prussians during the afternoon...
>
> Towards the evening we advanced at the charge and chased the enemy from a height. They retreated, but as we arrived at the crest, we could see several lines of the enemy ahead; they were supported by artillery and we were forced to retreat. Our brigade [commanded by *Général de Brigade* Jamin] then withdrew to a point close to Leipzig.
>
> At nightfall we set up camp. Our *adjutant-major*, López, was wounded and I had been struck on the leg by a spent ball...[50]

This was the point at which Manuel López's war ended. After recovering from his wound, he would go on to make a glittering career for himself in the service of France, as we shall shortly see. However, before we do so, we will first study the fate of the Spanish veterans of Napoleon's army in the immediate aftermath of his (first) abdication.

Spanish Officers Nominated as *Chevaliers de la Legion d'Honneur*

On 28 June 1813, the following officers belonging the Régiment Joseph-Napoleon were nominated as *Chevaliers de la Legion d'Honneur*: *Colonel* de Tschudy; *Capitaines* Vasquez, Hernandez and Tierra; *Capitaine Adjudant-Major* Cardona; *Lieutenants* Corvalan and López; *Sous-Lieutenant* Laborda.

---

50 *Mémoires du Major Gallardo de Mendoza*, translated and published by Roger Peyre in *Miscellanea Napoleonica*, Series 3 to 4 (Rome: Modes and Mendel, 1898), pp.343-450.

It should be noted that López had been promoted to *capitaine* shortly before he became a *chevalier*;[51] so it would seem that López's citation was submitted whilst holding a lower rank than that held when his nomination came through.

The First Abdication of Napoleon

After the Battle of Leipzig, on 24 December 1813, the 1er bataillon Joseph–Napoleon was dissolved, as was the depot battalion then at Namur. All foreign soldiers in the service of France were at that time designated as 'pioneers' and it would seem that this was simply a means of giving all such men a 'tag' by which they could be referred to as a singular grouping.[52] During this period the (new) 2e bataillon of the regiment was still at Magdebourg, where it remained until May 1814 when it was moved to Strasbourg. It had been formed in April 1813, and apart from the few senior officers at its head, most, if not all, of the recruits would have been selected from Spanish prisoners of war taken by the French during hostilities in Spain between late 1808 and early 1813. As such, very few of them would have been survivors from La Romana's expeditionary force to Denmark. However, we do not preclude the possibility that some of La Romana's men may have been amongst its ranks. These would have taken part in the battle of Espinosa and other subsequent actions, up to the point at which they were captured. As such, they may well have been processed by Kindelán and recruited into Joseph–Napoleon before and during Napoleon's Russian campaign.

However, we should perhaps note here that, by the summer of 1809, the Spanish had learned at great cost that to fight pitched battles against the French on the rolling plains of the hinterland was suicidal. Apart from their stunning victory at Bailén in the summer of 1808, most confrontations of this ilk ended in disaster for the Spanish. Yet they were not battles of complete annihilation. Instead, the Spanish formations involved often melted away at the end of the contest and regrouped in the safety of one or other of the many mountain ranges which dot the country, especially its periphery. However, there was usually still something of a price to pay in terms of casualties, and the French would often glean a sizable harvest of prisoners from their early battles, a number of whom would have been offered the chance of serving with the French in countries other than Spain, with formations such as Joseph–Napoleon.

During the years subsequent to 1809 the Spanish changed their tactics. By then their forces, regular and otherwise, had in many cases gravitated to 'safe zones' in the more rugged and inaccessible terrain which forms the periphery of the country. Large scale, exclusively French–Spanish confrontations rarely took place anymore as the Spanish forces began to adopt the tactics of asymmetric or guerrilla warfare, all of which meant that the flow of prisoners

---

51 *AAG*, as cited by Boppe in *Les Espagnols*, p.162, footnote 1.
52 Boppe, *Les Espagnols* pp.164–165.

of war across the Pyrenees would have slowed to a trickle, thus reducing the number of potential recruits for the Régiment Joseph-Napoleon.

In his story, Manuel López explains how things progressed with respect to the many thousands of foreign troops who found themselves stranded both in France and abroad after Napoleon's first abdication, all of them survivors of the emperor's various campaigns:

> When Napoleon abdicated on 11 April 1814, all French units on foreign soil were withdrawn to French territory; amongst them were the Spanish soldiers previously at Glogau, Stettin and Magdebourg. A decree was then issued by the provisional government of France, which related to an earlier Imperial Decree of 25 November 1813. It was that first decree which had classified all prisoners of war held by the French, as well as all foreign soldiers in the service of France, as 'pioneers'. The new decree called for the repatriation of all such men, and it was something that was not universally welcomed by those amongst the latter grouping to whom it applied. Those men felt they had given good and honourable service to France, and as such were not being fairly treated. However, Fernando VII of Spain insisted that he would not allow the return of any general officers who had served in the cause of France; that is, all ranks from captain to general. Lieutenants, sub-lieutenants, NCOs and private soldiers would be allowed to return, but only on the condition that they renounced their rank…[53]

The following letter, written in support of the Spanish soldiers of the Grande Armée by the general in command of the 12e Division Militaire, Rivaud de la Raffiniere, was sent to *Général de Division* Dupont, the French Minister of War, in May 1814:

> From: Rivaud de la Raffiniere, La Rochelle, 7 May 1814
> To: *Général* Dupont
>
> Monseigneur,
> In accordance with the dispositions of Your Excellency's letter of 17 April, I have licensed the regiment of Spanish pioneers presently at Niort, and I have ordered that all soldiers belonging to that unit will be returned to their own country. They commenced their march [to Spain] fifteen days ago.
> Many of the officers, NCOs and pioneers … have expressed a desire to continue their service in France as Your Excellency's letter, quoted above, authorizes them to do. They are brave soldiers, the majority of them wounded and many of them holders of the *Ordre de la Legion d'Honneur*. They make an urgent request to be allowed to remain in France, and with Your Excellency's interests in mind I appeal to you to find employment for them in any regiments which, according to your judgement, would be suitable. All of the men have served with the French army in Russia, and many are amputees who deserve the consideration of the government. They cannot be returned to Spain, where their service with the French during the period of [our] war with that country is seen as a crime, and as a consequence

---

53 López's précis as cited by Boppe in *Les Espagnols*, p.166.

they are being held at Niort where I have established their depot. It is there where they will await the decision of Your Excellency.[54]

Manuel López explains:

The licensing of NCOs and soldiers returning to France at the end of 1813 was put into effect at Niort and Saint Maixent at the end of August 1814. With regard to the officers, these were sent to Pau, where they arrived at the end of September, and were treated as refugees.

The licensing of the soldiers of Joseph-Napoleon still in Germany, and therefore not affected by the decree … was carried out depending upon when and where they re-entered French territory. It was usually the case that NCOs and soldiers were allowed to return to Spain or to remain in France.[55]

The (new) 2e batallion was one of the units still in Germany at the end of the war, and it began its march from Magdeburg to Strasbourg by order of *Général de Division* Lemarois on 16 May 1814. Once in France it was kept on the move, with nobody seeming to know what to do with it until it came to rest at Belfort. There, after much desertion from the ranks, the state of things was quantified by another of the Baltic survivors, Ordoñez, in a letter to Dupont dated 26 June he says:

From: Ordoñez, *Chef de Bataillon*, 2e bataillon.
To: *Général* Dupont, *Ministre de la Guerre*.

In the face of this desertion, the commandant … of Belfort ordered the battalion to be disarmed… at two o'clock one morning; and two hours later it was forced to resume its march to Lyon.

When it arrived at Besancon on 30 June its strength was no greater than that of fifteen officers and one hundred and seventy-two men. *Général de Brigade* Bourmont … recalling the two Spanish battalions he had under his command in Russia, showed some consideration for this unhappy debris of Joseph-Napoleon, who were not accustomed to such treatment … In addition, he provided them with a recommendation to the military authorities they would encounter on their way … When the battalion arrived at Lyon it was directed to Perpignan, where it arrived on 30 July. The NCOs and soldiers then made their way to Spain and the officers were sent to the depot for Spanish refugees at Montauban.[56]

Things rumbled on for a while until 1815 when Napoleon abdicated for the second time, after which the men of the regiment were re-designated as 'licencees' and the officers as 'refugees', López informs us that:

The Spanish officers who had been designated refugees in order that they were not sent back to Spain, refused to accept such an imposed status. They never ceased

---

54   Boppe, *Les Espagnols*, pp.166–167.
55   López's précis as cited by Boppe in *Les Espagnols*, p.166.
56   Extract from Ordoñez's letter as reproduced by Boppein *Les Espagnols*, p.166, footnote 4.

to point out that those who took part in La Romana's Denmark expedition had been sent to France by the government of Carlos IV to fight in the service of that nation, thus providing them with a legal claim to be true soldiers of France. Their position was reinforced when it was pointed out that their certificates of service had all been signed in the name of the Emperor of France at that time.

In 1817 the French government conceded, recognising the status of the foreign soldiers in France and treating them as '*demi-soldes*' – soldiers retained on half pay. A short time later many of the officers took advantage of a decree by Louis XVIII via which they could become naturalised citizens of France.[57]

Manuel López was one of those who did so, and it is at this point where we part company with our chronicler and attempt to build a final picture of what may have become of the 3,600 or so Spaniards who began the 1812 campaign as soldiers of Joseph–Napoleon. However, before moving on it may be of interest to take a brief look at how the fortunes of '*el soldado raso de 1802*' (the private soldier of 1802) fared during the rest of his life in his adopted country of France. We begin by recalling that López, a native of Galicia serving with the Regimiento de Asturias, had been promoted to the rank of *sargento* in 1804, the rank he held until being made a prisoner of war by the French. On commencing service with Joseph–Napoleon towards the end of 1808 he was assigned to the rank of *sergent–major*, before obtaining a commission and rising through the officer ranks: *sous–lieutenant* October 1812; *lieutenant* April 1813; *capitaine* July 1813. In April 1814 he became a licencee, as explained earlier, before being made a *capitaine* in the 6e Régiment Etranger. Once he became a naturalised citizen of France he was nominated *capitaine* in the Corps Royal d'Etat-Major on 12 December 1818, rising to *aide–de–camp* to *Généraux* Ordonneau, d'Henin, Bigarré and Colbert, before becoming *chef d'escadron* in December 1831. Retiring in July 1845 he was nominated *Commissaire du Gouvernement de la 13e Division Militaire* in January 1849. He died on 14 March 1862. A stellar career for the humble boy from Melide in remote Galicia.

The Spanish Soldiers who Became Prisoners of the Russians

There is one more loose–end to tie up before we close the story of La Romana's men who fought in Napoleon's 1812 campaign: we need to discover what happened to those who fell into the hands of the Russians during the fighting. The number of men from the Régiment Joseph–Napoleon who were taken prisoner is nowhere clearly stated, but we can make an estimate of the figure from some of the data supplied by Paul Boppe in his magnificent history of the regiment.

In Manuel López's account of the campaign, quoted at length by Boppe, he states that by March of 1813 the 2e and 3e bataillons of his regiment were at Erfurt, having extricated themselves from Russian territory after their retreat

---

57   López's précis as cited by Boppe in *Les Espagnols*, pp.169–170.

from Moscow. The combined strength of the two battalions at that time he gives as '14 officers and 50 NCOs and soldiers.' He goes on to state that there was also a small detachment from those two battalions then present with the 1er and 4e bataillons, which were at Glogau.[58]

Boppe quotes a report by the French Minister of War dated 6 February 1813, confirming that there were 160 men of the Régiment Joseph–Napoleon at Glogau (he also states that there was a detachment from the 2e and 3e bataillons still at Stettin, but as we are given no indication of the numbers involved, we will not take them into account).[59] Taken together, the statements by López and Boppe suggest that those survivors of the Russian campaign who had managed to reach their rallying points at Erfurt and Glogau by 6 February 1813, numbered just 224.

López informs us that during the Russian campaign, all four battalions of the regiment came together at Orcha on 20 November 1812.[60] As chance would have it the Portuguese Legion was also at Orcha on the same day and, as we have seen, the Portuguese officer Theotonio Banha claimed that the Spaniards numbered, 'no more than 4 officers and 110 men.'

From our calculations above it would seem that, either Banha was mistaken in his estimate of the number of survivors present at Orcha, or there were many Spanish stragglers still to come in by the time he arrived at the place. His figure of 3,200 for the original strength of the regiment is quite accurate when compared with the battalion returns for 12 January 1812 provided by Boppe in footnotes on pages 127 and 133 of his work, which are as follows:

1er bataillon:	1,055
2e bataillon:	1,088
3e bataillon:	752
4e bataillon:	820
Total:	**3,635**

In March 1813, during the aftermath of the Russian campaign, the French high command set to work in an attempt to rebuild the regiment, making use of the survivors from the original 2e and 3e bataillons then at Coblentz, the men taken from the regimental depot and some Spanish prisoners of war recently sworn–in to serve with the French. After much reorganisation, two new battalions were formed and these participated in the fighting that was to continue up until the end of 1813, as we have already seen.

Returning to our calculations, we may now attempt to ascertain a figure for the total casualties sustained by the Régiment Joseph–Napoleon in Russia. Even if we accept Banha's figure of 3,200 for the strength of the regiment at the start of the campaign in June 1812 and subtract from it the numbers of survivors present at Coblentz and Glogau in February 1813 (224) we arrive at a figure of 2,976. If accurate, that is the combined number for

---

58   López's précis as cited by Boppe in *Les Espagnols*, pp.156–157.
59   Boppe, *Les Espagnols*, p.159, footnote 1.
60   López's précis as cited by Boppe in *Les Espagnols*, p.155 and footnote 4.

those killed, wounded or taken prisoner (wounded or otherwise) in Russia, and amounts to almost 93 percent of the initial strength of the regiment. In other words, just seven percent of the Spaniards who took part in the Grande Armée's Russian campaign managed to escape to France after the retreat from Moscow. For the Grande Armée as a whole the figure varies between three-and-a-half and five percent according to whichever source one chooses to rely upon, so the figures just quoted would seem accurate.

It would be helpful to know the number of men who became prisoners and what percentage of the total losses it represents. In Appendix I of his book, Boppe includes a table (See Table 7, above) indicating the return for the officer ranks of the 2e and 3e bataillons of Joseph–Napoleon on 5 March 1813. The figures were certified by de Tschudy, and it might be enlightening to consider a simple statistical analysis of the data contained therein. Here are the percentages it suggests for the various categories of losses and 'non-losses':

Table 8 Analysis of Officer Casualties

Killed in action.	8 (16 percent).
Wounded.	1 (2 percent).
Wounded and prisoner of war.	2 (4 percent).
Prisoner of war.	18 (37 percent).
Present (unscathed).	18 (37 percent).
Transferred.	2 (4 percent).
Total officer casualties.	**29 from an initial strength of 49.**
Percentage casualties amongst officers.	**59 percent.**
Percentage unscathed or transferred.	**41 percent.**

It would be unwise, perhaps, to suggest that these percentages would apply to the rank and file of the regiment. From the overall numbers at Coblentz and Glogau in March 1813 it is clear that nowhere near 41 percent of NCOs and soldiers managed to return 'unscathed'. The percentages of killed, wounded and prisoners amongst the 'other ranks', must have been significantly higher than those amongst the officers. So how many men belonging to Joseph–Napoleon became prisoners of war in Russia and were subsequently repatriated to Spain in 1813? Napier provides us with a clue. In volume one of his work he includes a description of the battle of Espinosa, which, as we have seen, took place between French and Spanish forces in the province of Biscay in November 1808; amongst the latter were those of La Romana's infantry who had escaped from Denmark. Here is an edited extract from Napier's passage:

> On 10 [November] the Duc de Belluno [*Maréchal* Victor] came up, and at two o'clock in the afternoon, the head of a French column, driving back La Romana's infantry, seized the wood…
>
> Meanwhile the contest on the right was maintained with vigour and the Spaniards, supported by six guns in their centre, even appeared to be gaining ground when the night closed in and put an end to the action, leaving the French in possession of the wood. … The [Spanish] generals San Román and Riquelme were mortally wounded … next morning, Victor … renewed the attack…

NOTES ON THE RUSSIAN CAMPAIGN

... the whole Spanish army gave way in terrible confusion ... Those whom the sword missed went to their own provinces ...

It has been said that, Spartan-like, La Romana's army died to a man in their ranks; yet in 1812, Captain Hill of the Royal Navy, being at Cronstadt to receive Spaniards taken by the Russians during Napoleon's retreat, found that the greater proportion were men who had escaped with La Romana from the Danish Isles in 1808; captives at Espinosa, they had served Napoleon for four years, passed the ordeal of the Moscow retreat and were still above four thousand strong![61]

We need to treat Napier's words with a little circumspection. In his history of the Peninsular War, he is rarely complimentary about the Spanish contribution to the defeat of Napoleon's forces in Iberia. Regarding the passage quoted above, what Napier is implying is that a large number, possibly thousands, of La Romana's men who fought at Espinosa became prisoners of the French, and that these had been enrolled *en-masse* into the Grande Armée by 1812. He bases his assertion on the suggestion that there were some 4,000 Spanish prisoners of war at Cronstadt in 1812 (in fact, he should have given the year as 1813) awaiting repatriation, and assumes that such numbers, in the main, could only have come from the prisoners taken from amongst the Baltic escapees during the fighting in Spain in late 1808.[62] He is seemingly unaware of the fact that something like that number of Spanish soldiers were captured by the French in the Baltic in 1808; that many of them participated in the invasion of Russia whilst serving with Joseph-Napoleon, and that many of these would have become prisoners of the Russians.

There should be little doubt that some of La Romana's men (the 'escapees' from Denmark) would have been amongst the prisoners taken at Espinosa, and some of these no doubt did join the French and may well have ended up in the Régiment Joseph-Napoleon, but they did not make up the full 4,000 men that Napier claims were embarked by Captain Hill at Cronstadt in October/November 1813, or anything like it. In fact, Napier's figure is greater than the 3,635 given in the regimental return of January 1812; but could there have been 4,000 Spaniards at Cronstadt in 1813? The figure becomes credible if one is willing to accept the idea that more Spanish volunteers could have entered Russia during the campaign, which is a distinct possibility. In his biography of Napoleon, Andrew Roberts informs us that, during the 35-day occupation of Moscow, Napoleon received 15,000 reinforcements and that during his retreat from the capital he was hoping to rendezvous with a fresh division of reinforcements.[63] Perhaps some of these men were destined for Joseph-Napoleon. There is also the possibility that there was a number of Portuguese amongst the Spaniards awaiting repatriation from Russia.

Bobadilla provides us with much detail relating to the Spanish troops who became prisoners of the Russians during 1812 which, in numerical

---

61 W.F.P. Napier, *A History of the War in the Peninsula*. (London: Constable, 1992), Vol. VI, pp.395–397.
62 O'Donnell, in his statement to the *Comisión de Jefes*, claimed that, 'In total 215 officers and 4,950 men became prisoners of war [in Denmark].'
63 Roberts, *Napoleon the Great*, pp.615–619.

terms, suggests that the survival rate amongst the Spaniards in Russia was very high. The fact that Spain was an ally of the Tsar at the time his army was gathering Spanish prisoners, allowed him to bestow upon them the colours of a new regiment, the Imperial Regiment of Alexander (Regimiento Imperial [de] Alejandro). The new unit officially came into existence at St Petersburg on 20 May 1813 under the command of Alejandro O'Donnell, with an initial strength of some 2,500 men, but it would seem that, besides these, there were still some groups of Spanish and Portuguese soldiers scattered across the face of western Russia. The main groupings, apart from those at St. Petersburg, were as follows: some 265 men at Memel under the command of *Adjutant–Major* Cardona (Joseph–Napoleon), who were shipped separately to England to await their eventual transport to Spain, which seems to have commenced in late September 1813 when the convoy carrying the bulk of the Spanish troops from St Petersburg – those embarked at Cronstadt – called at Portsmouth during its passage to Spain. A second group of some 200 soldiers, which had somehow found its way to Gothenburg, appears also to have been swept up by the convoy from Cronstadt as is passed the Swedish coast. This indicates that a total of some 2,965 veterans of Napoleon's 1812 campaign were transported to Spain in late 1813, courtesy of the Royal Navy. Adding these to the 224 men who managed to escape to France with the rest of the fugitives of the Grande Armée (see above) gives a grand total of 3,189. If we keep to the figure of 3,200 for the initial strength of the Régiment Joseph–Napoleon as cited by Theotonio Banha, and ignore any possible reinforcement of the unit whilst in Russia, then the survival rate for the regiment comes to a remarkable 99 percent. If we use the official figure of 3,635 as the initial regimental strength on the eve of the invasion of Russia then the survival rate falls to 89 percent.[64] However, it may be the case that there was a significant number of men from the Portuguese Legion amongst the Spaniards in the Regimiento Imperial [de] Alejandro (essentially the Régiment Joseph–Napoleon by another name) if so then the survival rate for the Spaniards just quoted would have to be reduced accordingly. In the final analysis it would seem that very few Spaniards lost their life in Russia and that the vast majority were eventually repatriated to Spain in 1813.

---

64 Bobadilla, *Un Español*, Appendix D, pp.143–146.

Bibliography

Archival Sources

The National Archives, Kew.
    ADM 80/145, Book of Orders and Letters of Captain (afterwards Admiral) Keats.
    ADM 1/7, Letters from Commander-in-Chief, Baltic, Nos 170-312.
    ADM, 1/6, Letters from Commander-in-Chief, Baltic, Nos. 1-169.
    ADM 51/1823, Log of HMS *Brunswick*.
    ADM 51/1944, Log of HMS *Calypso*.
    ADM 51/1857, Log of HMS *Devastation*.
    ADM 51/2336, Log of HMS *Edgar*.
    ADM 51/1948, Log of HMS *Hound*.
    ADM 51/1896, Log of HMS *Jasper*.
    ADM 51/1828, Log of HMS *Mosquito*.
    ADM 51/1757 & 1946, Log of HMS *Nassau*.
    ADM 51/2764, Log of HMS *Racoon*.
    ADM 51/1938, Log of HMS *Semiramis*.
    ADM 51/1845, Log of HMS *Sparrowhawke*.
Archivo General Militar de Madrid, Colección Duque de Bailén.
    Legajo2, Carpeta 4, Asunto 7272.2, Memoria de Estanislao Sanchez Salvador.
    Legajo2, Carpeta 4, Asunto 7272.2, Memoria de Fernando Mijares.
    Legajo2, Carpeta 4, Asunto 7272.2, Memoria de Joachin Astrandi.
    Legajo2, Carpeta 4, Asunto 7272.2, Memoria de José Agustín de Llano.
    Legajo2, Carpeta 4, Asunto 7272.2, Memoria de José O'Donnell.
    Legajo2, Carpeta 4, Asunto 7272.2, Memoria de Rafael Lobo.
    Legajo2, Carpeta 4, Asunto 7272.2, Memoria de Santiago Miquel.
    Legajo2, Carpeta 4, Asunto 7272.2, Memoria del Barón de Armendáriz.

Published Sources

Aspinall, A. (ed.), *The Later Correspondence of George III, Vol. V* (London: Cambridge University Press, 1970).

Banha, Theotonio, *Apontamentos para a Historia de Legiao Portugueza ao Servicio de Napoleao I* (Lisboa: Imprensa Nacional, 1863).

Bobadilla, Ignacio Fernández de (ed.), *Un Español en el Ejército de Napoleon. Diario de Rafael de Llanza y de Valls* (Madrid: Almena Ediciónes, 2008).

Bonaparte, Napoleon, *Correspondance de Napoleon Ier* (Paris: Plon et Dumaine, 1858-1870).

Boppe, Paul., *Les Espagnols A La Grande Armée* (Paris/Nancy: Berger-Levrault et Cie, Editeurs, 1899).

Bulow, General Friedrich, *Pallas: eine Zeitschr. für Staats-u. Kriegs-Kunst* (Tubingen: J. G. Cotta, 1808).

Cassinello Pérez, Andrés, *El Capitán-General Marqués de La Romana* (Madrid: Ediciónes Doce Calles, 2012).

Daugaard, Christine, *Biskop Duagaard* (Copenhagen: Unknown, 1896).
Fraser, Alexander Clinton. (ed.), *Narrative of a Secret Mission to the Danish Islands in 1808* (London: Longman, Green, Longman, Roberts and Green, 1863).
Gallardo de Mendoza, Mariano, *Mémoires du Major Gallardo de Mendoza*, translated and published by Roger Peyre in *Miscellanea Napoleonica*, Series 3 to 4 (Rome: Modes and Mendel, 1898).
Gómez de Arteche, José, *Guerra de la Independencia: Historia Militar de España* (Madrid: Imprenta de Credito Comercial, 1868–1881).
Grainger, John. D., *The British Navy in the Baltic* (Woodbridge: Boydell & Brewer, 2014).
Gurwood, John, *The Dispatches of Field Marshal, The Duke of Wellington* (London: Parker Furnival and Parker, 1845).
Knight, Roger, *Britain Against Napoleon* (London: Penguin, 2013).
Kornerup, Jacob, *Roskilde, Ancient Town of Denmark on the Island of Zealand*, [*Roskilde i Gamle Dage*] (First edition: Copenhagen: Unknown, 1892. Recent edition: London: British Library Historical Print Editions, 2011).
Labaum, Eugene, *Relation Circonstanciée de la Campagne de Russie en 1812* (Paris: C.L.F. Panckoucke, 1814).
Londonderry, Marquess of (ed.), *Correspondence, Despatches and Other Papers of Viscount Castlereagh* (London: William Shoberl, 1851).
López, Manuel, *Précis historique des actions ou se sont trouves les 2e et 3e bataillons du regiment Joseph–Napoleon avec le 2e division du 1er corps de la Grande Armée dont ils on fait partie pendant la derniere campagne* (France: Unknown, pre–1840).
Mazade, Charles de (ed.), *Correspondance du Maréchal Davout* (Paris: E. Plon, Nourrit et Cie., 1885).
Moore, James Carrick, *A Narrative of the Campaign of the British Army in Spain* (London: Joseph Johnson, 1809).
Napier, W.F.P., *A History of the war in the Peninsula* (London: Constable, 1992).
Oman, Charles, *A History of the Peninsular War* (London: Greenhill Books, 1995).
Quadra, Ambrosio de la, 'Memorias de los Acontecimientos en el Ejército de Dinamarca, desde los Primeros Rumores de la Abicación de la Corona de España y Congreso de Bayona, hasta la Salida de las Tropas Españoles de aquel Reyno'. *Revista de Historia Militar*, no.72, 1er semestre 1992, pp.228-258 and no.73, 2o semestre 1992, pp,216-246.
Roberts, Andrew, *Napoleon the Great* (London: Penguin, 2015).
Schierne, Frederik, *Spanierne i Danmark* (Denmark: Unknown, 1835).
Sparrow, Elizabeth, *Secret Service. British Agents in France 1792 – 1815* (Woodbridge: Boydell Press, 1999).
Thiers, Adolphe, *Histoire du Consulat et de l'Empire, t. VIII, livre XXVIII* (Paris: Paulin, 1845).

Online Sources

Fabregues, Antonio, *Gazeta de Sevilla*, edition of 15 November, 1808, pp.390–392. <https://archive.org/details/A0632681544155/page/n209> (accessed 15 March 2019).
Anon, *Gazeta de Madrid*, No. 140, 1 November 1808, *Coruña 22 Octubre*, page 1406, accessed by performing a Google search using the string: <Gazeta de Madrid, No. 140> and clicking on the resulting link to <Gazeta de Madrid – Núm. 140, 1o de noviembre de 1808> (accessed 16 March 2021).